In the Name of Allah, the Most Gracious, the Most Merciful.

Those who believed and whose hearts find rest in the remembrance of Allah verily, in the remembrance of Allah hearts find rest. Chapter 13. Ar-Ra`d Verse 28 (Darussalam, 2000)

ALLAH

Praises of Allah, Signs of Allah and Names of Allah mentioned in the Quran

MRS KHAN

Publisher: Independently published, to order more copies please go to https://www.amazon.com

Revised Edition: December, 2021

ALL RIGHTS RESERVED. No Quranic Verses of this book may be reproduced or utilized in any form or by any means, electronic or mechanical, including photocopying and recording or by any information storage and retrieval system, without the permission of the Darussalam Publications Inc. Please see reference section for more details.

Darussalam Publications Inc gave Mrs. Khan the permission on 6/4/2021 *"We allow you use verses from The Noble Quran (any edition) as needed to use in your book or on social media for dawah purposes."* Dawah means to invite people to the teaching of Islam.

Every effort is made to minimize the cost of the book as it is written for dawah purposes. Any proceeds will be donated to the charity or for dawah purposes.

Table of Contents

Introduction	*1*
Three Sections	*4*
Section I	*5*
Praises of Allah mentioned in the Quran	6
Section II	*20*
Signs of Allah mentioned in the Quran	21
Section III	*48*
Names of Allah mentioned in the Quran- *Nine Subsections*	49
Subsection 1	*52*
Ar-Rahman The Most Gracious	53
Ar-Rahim The Most Merciful	60
Ar-Rauf The Most Kind	81
Al-Barr The Gracious Benefactor	83
Al-Kareem The Most Generous	84
Al-Wahhab The Bestower	84
Ar-Razzaq The Ever Providing	85
Subsection 2	*88*
Al-Afuww The Pardoner	89
Al-Ghafur The All-Forgiving	91
Al-Ghaffar The Ever Forgiving	107
At-Tawwab The Accepter of Repentance	108
Al-Latif The Subtle kind	110
Al-Wudud The Most Loving	111
Al-Halim The Most Forbearing	111
Ash-Shakur Most Ready to Appreciate	113
Al-Mujib The Responsive	114
Subsection 3	*115*
Al-Malik The King	116
Maalik-ul-Mulk The Owner of All Sovereignty	117
Al-Hameed The All-Praiseworthy	117
Al-Majeed The All-Glorious	120
Al-Kabir The Most Great	120
Al-Azim The Most Great	122
Al-Muqit The Nourisher	123
Al-Mutaali The Most Exalted	123
Al-Muhyi The Giver of Life	123
Al-Waaris The Inheritor of All	123
Dhu-l-Jalali Wa-l-Ikram The Lord of Majesty & Honour	124
Subsection 4	*125*
Al-Wahid The One	126
Al-Ahad The Sole One	129
Al-Samaad The Self-Sufficient	129
Al-Haqq The Truth	129

Al-Qahhar	The Irresistible	131
Al-Hayy	The Ever Living	132
Al-Qayyum	The Self Subsisting, The Self Existing	133
Al-Ghani	The All Rich	133
An Nur	The Light	136

Subsection 5 — 137

Al-Alim	The All-Knowing	138
Al-Khabir	The All-Aware	163
Al-Hakim	The Most Wise	169
Al-Basir	The All-Seeing	184
As-Sami	The All-Hearing	191

Subsection 6 — 198

Al-Khaliq	The Creator	199
Al-Bari	The Maker	200
Al-Musawwir	The Bestower of Forms	201
Al-Badi	The Originator	201

Subsection 7 — 202

Al-Awwal	The First One	203
Al-Akhir	The Last	203
Al-Zahir	The Manifest	203
Al-Batin	The Hidden	203

Subsection 8 — 204

Al-Quddus	The Most Holy	205
Al-Salam	The Source of Peace	205
Al-Mu'min	The Giver of Security	205
Al-Muhaymin	The Protector, The Watcher over His creatures	206
Al-Hafiz	The Guardian	206
Al-Fattah	The Opener, Judge	206
Al-Wasi	The All-Sufficient, The Boundless	207
Al-Hadi	The One Who Guides	209
Al-Waliyy	The Protecting Friend	210

Subsection 9 — 214

Al-A'la	The Most High	215
Al-Aziz	The All-Mighty	216
Al-Qawi	The Most Strong	232
Al-Qadir	The All-Capable	234
Al-Matin	The Firm, The Most Strong	235
Ar-Raqib	The Watchful	236
Al-Hasib	The Reckoner	236
Al-Jaami	The Gatherer	237
Ash-Shahid	The Witness	237
Al-Wakil	The Trustee, The Best Disposer of affairs	240
Al-Hakam	The Judge	242
Al-Jabbar	The Compeller	243
Al-Mutakabir	The Supremely Great	243
Al-Muqtadir	The Powerful Determiner	243

References — 244

Introduction

In the name of Allah, the Most Gracious, the Most Merciful.

Wherever we look, in the expanses of the earth and heavens, or inwards in our body and heart, we see the working of an Intelligent, and all Perfect Creator. The Torah, the Bible, and the Quran call this entity God. Native Americans call it the spirit of the universe. In Arabic "God" is translated as Allah, so Muslims refer to the Creator and Lord of the universe as Allah.

The human being is the epitome of everything that has been created. In us, our Creator has infused from His Spirit giving us consciousness and intellect, the power to think, reason, and most of all, to make choices. God sent us here to live on Earth, our essence or soul wrapped in the material body. Our body cannot fathom the sacred or divine being of God. Our soul however yearns to love and serve Him. Therefore, God scattered uncountable signs that lead to Him, and also chose the most truthful human beings to convey His message to us. It is up to us to either accept His servitude and be thankful to the One Who gave us every blessing we have; or using our free will we may reject and disobey Him and serve our base bodily desires.

Freedom of choice has to be balanced by accountability; and accountability requires duties, rules, and guidelines. For this purpose, God sent the Prophets, to guide us through the challenging yet captivating life of this world. He taught us how we can know and bond with Him, despite not being able to see Him with physical eyes.

From the prophets that came throughout human history, each one of them only gave one simple message; 'Your Lord is One, He is unlike creation; He has no partners and family; thus, be thankful to Him, through worship and obedience in His commands." The Quran says that, like Prophet Abraham, and Moses, Jesus was also a chosen Prophet of Allah. However, due to his miraculous birth, he was wrongly placed as a son of God by people later on. Also, as time passed, previous books, the Torah and Bible got polluted.

This same message was reiterated by the last and the final Prophet Muhammad (peace and blessing of God be upon him). His message the Quran is the final word of God that has not and cannot be changed in any way. God Himself vowed to Protect it from any change. Therefore, in order to understand Who our Creator is and why He sent us here on Earth, we have to study the Quran.

Quran was revealed by Allah (God) to His final prophet Muhammad (Peace be upon him). In Arabic language the Quran means "the recitation." It is a collection of 114 sermons or chapters dedicated to informing the curious human mind about Who Allah (God) is, what His values are that He wants us to build our personality upon, what are the beliefs in the unseen we must have, and what lessons we must take from former prophets.

The Quran is a direct conversation between Allah and mankind. It introduces us to the names of Allah mentioned in the Quran that emphasize Allah's greatest attributes. Understanding these characteristics will provide a greater connection with our Lord as we are unable to see Him or directly speak to Him.

Chapter 42. Ash-Shura Verse 51
*"It is not given to any human being that **Allah** should speak to him unless by Revelation, or from behind a veil, or He sends a messenger to reveal what He wills by His leave. Verily. He is Most High, Most Wise." (Darussalam, 2000)*

Chapter 6. Al-An`am Verse 103
No vision can grasp Him, but He grasps all visions. He is Al-Latif (the Most subtle), Well-Acquainted with all things. (Darussalam, 1999)

This book is a humble collection of the direct verses from the Quran which are divided in three sections; namely:

Praises of Allah,
Signs of Allah and
The Names of Allah.

These verses have been collected in this book to bring to our attention the attributes of Allah. To learn the answer to the question "Who is Allah?" The easiest and effective way is to read this book and reflect on it.

Chapter 96. Al-Alaq Verses 1~5
*1. Read! In the name of your **Lord** Who has created.*
2. He has created man from a clot.
*3. Read! And your **Lord** is the Most Generous.*

4. Who has taught by the pen.
5. He has taught man that which He knew not. (Darussalam, 2000)

We pray Allah will guide us to the right answer.

Chapter Al-Qasas Verse 56
*"Verily! You (O Muhammad) guide not whom you like, but **Allah** guides whom He wills. And He knows best those who are the guided." (Darussalam, 2000)*

These verses are from different chapters and should not be confused to be one chapter. To avoid confusion verses are divided by giving them separate heading with the name of the chapter and number of the verse.

Three Sections

Three Sections

Section I
- *Praises of Allah*

Section II
- *Signs of Allah*

Section III
- *Names of Allah*

Section I

Praises of Allah mentioned in the Quran

Praises of Allah mentioned in the Quran

In the name of Allah, the Most Gracious, the Most Merciful.

Chapter An-Nur   Chapter 24 Verse 35

Allah is the Light of the heavens and the earth. The parable of His Light is as a niche and within it a lamp: the lamp is in a glass, the glass as it were a brilliant star, lit from a blessed tree, an olive, neither of the east nor of the west, whose oil would almost flow forth, though no fire touched it. Light upon Light! **Allah** guides to His Light whom He wills. And **Allah** sets forth parables for mankind, and **Allah** is All-Knower of everything. (Darussalam, 2000)

Chapter Al-Ikhlas   Chapter 112 Verses 1~4

1. Say: He is **Allah**, One.
2. **Allah**-us-Samad (**Allah**, the Self-Sufficient).
3. He begets not, nor, was He begotten.
4. And there is none co-equal or comparable unto Him. (Darussalam, 2000)

Chapter Al-Baqarah   Chapter 2 Verse 255

Allah! La ilaha illa Huwa (none has the right to be worshipped but He), Al-Hayyul-Qayyum (the Ever Living, the One Who Sustains and Protects all that exists). Neither slumber nor sleep overtakes Him. To Him belongs whatever is in the heavens and whatever is on the earth. Who is he that can intercede with Him except with His permission? He knows what happens to them in this world, and what will happen to them in the Hereafter. And they will never compass anything of His knowledge except that which He wills. His Kursi (Chair) extends over the heavens and the earth, and He feels no fatigue in guarding and preserving them. And He is the Most High, the Most Great. (Darussalam, 1999)

Chapter Al-Hashr   Chapter 59 Verse 1

Whatsoever is in the heavens and whatsoever is on the earth glorifies **Allah**. And He is the All-Mighty, the All-Wise. (Darussalam, 2000)

Chapter Al-Hashr — Chapter 59 Verses 22~24

22. He is **Allah**, besides whom La ilaha illa Huwa (none has the right to be worshipped but He), the All-Knower of the unseen and the seen. He is the Most Gracious, the Most Merciful.

23. He is **Allah**, besides whom La ilaha illa Huwa (none has the right to be worshipped but He), the King, the Holy, the One Free from all defects, the Giver of Security, the Watcher over His creatures, the All-Mighty, the Compeller, the Supreme. Glory be to **Allah**! above all that they associate as partners with Him.

24. He is **Allah**, the Creator, the Inventor of all things, the Bestower of forms. To Him belong the Best Names. All that is in the heavens and the earth glorify Him. And He is the All-Mighty, the All-Wise. (Darussalam, 2000)

Chapter Al-Hadid — Chapter 57 Verses 1~3

1. Whatsoever is in the heavens and the earth glorifies **Allah** and He is the All-Mighty, All-Wise.

2. His is the kingdom of the heavens and the earth. It is He Who gives life and causes death; and He is Able to do all things.

3. He is the First and the Last, the Most High and the Most Near. And He is the All-Knower of everything. (Darussalam, 2000)

Chapter Al-Jumuah — Chapter 62 Verse 1

Whatsoever is in the heavens and whatsoever is on the earth glorifies **Allah**, the King, the Holy, the All-Mighty, the All-Wise. (Darussalam, 2000)

Chapter Ya-Sin — Chapter 36 Verses 81~83

81. Is not He Who created the heavens and the earth, Able to create the like of them? Yes, indeed! He is the All-Knowing Supreme Creator.

82. Verily, His command, when He intends a thing, is only that He says to it, "Be!"- and it is!

83. So glorified be He and exalted above all that they associate with Him, and in Whose hands is the dominion of all things, and to Him you shall be returned. (Darussalam, 2000)

Chapter Al-Buruj — Chapter 85 Verse 9

To Whom belongs the dominion of the heavens and the earth! And **Allah** is Witness over everything. (Darussalam, 2000)

Chapter Al-Buruj — Chapter 85 Verses 13~16

13. Verily, He it is Who begins and repeats.

14. And He is Oft- Forgiving, full of love.

15. Owner of the Throne, the Glorious,
16. Doer of Whatsoever He intends. (Darussalam, 2000)

Chapter Al-Fatiha   Chapter 1 Verses 1~4
1. In the Name of Allah, the Most Gracious, the Most Merciful.
2. All the praises and thanks be to **Allah**, the **Lord** of the 'Alamin (worlds).
3. The Most Gracious, the Most Merciful.
4. The Only Owner of the Day of Recompense. (Darussalam, 1999)

Chapter Al-Baqarah   Chapter 2 Verses 115-~117
115. And to **Allah** belong the east and the west, so wherever you turn there is the Face of **Allah**. Surely, **Allah** is All-Sufficient for His creatures' needs, All-Knowing.
116. And they say: "**Allah** has begotten a son." Glory be to Him. Nay, to Him belongs all that is in the heavens and on earth, and all surrender with obedience to Him.
117. The Originator of the heavens and the earth. When He decrees a matter, He only says to it: Be!"- and it is. (Darussalam, 1999)

Chapter Al-Baqarah   Chapter 2 Verse 163
And your Ilah (God) is one Ilah (God), La ilaha illa Huwa (none has the right to be worshipped but He), the Most Gracious, the Most Merciful. (Darussalam, 1999)

Chapter Al-Imran   Chapter 3 Verse 2
Allah! La ilaha illa Huwa (none has the right to be worshipped but He), Al-Hayyul-Qayyum (the Ever living, the One Who Sustains and Protects all that exists). (Darussalam, 1999)

Chapter Al-Imran   Chapter 3 Verse 6
He it is Who shapes you in the wombs as He wills. La ilaha illa Huwa (none has the right to be worshipped but He), the All-Mighty, the All-Wise. (Darussalam, 1999)

Chapter Al-Imran   Chapter 3 Verse 62
Verily, this is the true narrative, and La ilaha illallah (none has the right to be worshipped but **Allah**). And indeed, **Allah** is the All-Mighty, the All-Wise. (Darussalam, 1999)

Chapter Al-Imran   Chapter 3 Verse 150
Nay, **Allah** is your Maula (Protector), and He is the Best of helpers. (Darussalam, 1999)

Chapter Al-Imran   Chapter 3 Verse 189
And to **Allah** belongs the dominions of the heavens and the earth, and **Allah** has power over all things. (Darussalam, 1999)

Chapter An-Nisa   Chapter 4 Verse 106
And seek the forgiveness of **Allah**, certainly, **Allah** is Ever Oft-Forgiving, Most Merciful. (Darussalam, 1999)

Chapter Al-An`am   Chapter 6 Verse 13
And to Him belongs whatsoever exists in the night and the day, and He is the All-Hearing, the All-Knowing. (Darussalam, 1999)

Chapter Al-An`am   Chapter 6 Verse 18
And He is the Irresistible (Supreme), above His slaves, and He is the All-Wise, Well Acquainted with all things. (Darussalam, 1999)

Chapter Al-An`am   Chapter 6 Verse 59
And with Him are the keys of the Ghaib (unseen), none knows them but He. And He knows whatever there is in the land and in the sea; not a leaf falls, but He knows it. There is not a grain in the darkness of the earth nor anything fresh or dry, but is written in a Clear Record. (Darussalam, 1999)

Chapter Al-An`am   Chapter 6 Verses 101 ~ 103
101. He is the Originator of the heavens and the earth. How can He have a son when He has no wife? He created all things and He is the All-Knower of everything.
102. Such is **Allah**, your **Lord**! La ilaha illa Huwa (none has the right to be worshipped but He), the Creator of all things. So, worship Him, and He is the Wakil (Disposer of affairs) over all things,
103. No vision can grasp Him, but He grasps all visions. He is Al-Latif (the Most subtle), Well-Acquainted with all things. (Darussalam, 1999)

Chapter Al-Anfal   Chapter 8 Verses 38~40
38. Say to those who have disbelieved, if they cease, their past will be forgiven. But if they return, then the examples of those before them have already preceded.

39. And fight them until there is no more fitnah and the religion will all be for **Allah** Alone. But if they cease, then certainly, **Allah** is All-Seer of what they do.
40. And if they turn away, then know that **Allah** is your Maula (Protector) - an excellent Maula (Protector), and an Excellent Helper! (Darussalam, 1999)

Chapter At-Taubah   Chapter 9 Verse 116
Verily, **Allah**! Unto Him belongs the dominion of the heavens and the earth, He gives life and He causes death. And besides **Allah** you have neither any Wali (Protector) nor any helper. (Darussalam, 2000)

Chapter Yunus   Chapter 10 Verse 3
Surely, your **Lord** is **Allah** Who created the heavens and the earth in six days and then rose over (Istawa) the Throne, disposing the affairs of all things. No intercessor except after His leave. That is **Allah**, your **Lord**; so, worship Him. Then, will you not remember? (Darussalam, 2000)

Chapter Yunus   Chapter 10 Verse 56
It is He Who gives life, and causes death, and to Him you shall return. (Darussalam, 2000)

Chapter Yunus   Chapter 10 Verse 68
They say: "**Allah** has begotten son." Glory is to Him! He is Rich. His is all that is in the heavens and all that is in the earth. No warrant you have for this. Do you say against **Allah** what you know not? (Darussalam, 2000)

Chapter Hud   Chapter 11 Verse 90
"And ask forgiveness of your **Lord** and turn unto Him in repentance. Verily, my **Lord** is Most Merciful, Most Loving." (Darussalam, 2000)

Chapter Hud   Chapter 11 Verse 123
And to **Allah** belongs the Ghaib (Unseen) of the heavens and the earth, and to Him return all affairs. So, worship Him and put your trust in Him. And your **Lord** is not unaware of what you do. (Darussalam, 2000)

Chapter Ar-Ra'd   Chapter 13 Verse 9
All-Knower of the unseen and the seen, the Most Great, the Most High. (Darussalam, 2000)

Chapter Al-Hijr   Chapter 15 Verse 49
Declare unto my slaves, that truly, I am the Oft-Forgiving, the Most Merciful. (Darussalam, 2000)

Chapter Al-Hijr   Chapter 15 Verse 86
Verily, your **Lord** is the All-Knowing Creator. (Darussalam, 2000)

Chapter An-Nahl   Chapter 16 Verse 3
He has created the heavens and the earth with truth. High is He, Exalted above all that they associate as partners with Him. (Darussalam, 2000)

Chapter Al-Isra   Ayat Sajada   Chapter 17 Verse 111
110. Say: Invoke **Allah** or invoke the Most Gracious, by whatever name you invoke Him, for to Him belong the Best Names, and offer your Salat (prayer) neither aloud nor in a low voice, but follow a way between.
111. And say: "All the praises and thanks be to **Allah**, Who has not begotten a son, and Who has no partner in Dominion, nor He is low to have a Wali (Protector). And magnify Him with all magnificence." (Darussalam, 2000)

Chapter Al-Kahf   Chapter 18 Verse 44
There, Al-Walayah (power and authority) will be for **Allah**, the True God. He is the best for reward and the best for the final end. (Darussalam, 2000)

Chapter Maryam   Chapter 19 Verse 35-36
35. It befits not **Allah** that He should beget a son. Glorified be He. When He decrees a thing, He only says to it: "Be!"– and it is.
36. And verily, **Allah** is my **Lord** and your **Lord**. So worship Him. That is the Straight Path. (Darussalam, 2000)

Chapter Maryam   Chapter 19 Verse 92-93
92. But it is not suitable for the Most Gracious that He should beget a son.
93. There is none in the heavens and the earth but comes unto the Most Gracious as a slave. (Darussalam, 2000)

Chapter Ta-Ha   Chapter 20 Verse 8
Allah! La ilaha illa Huwa (none has the right to be worshipped but He)! To Him belong the Best Names. (Darussalam, 2000)

Chapter Ta-Ha　　　　　　　　　　　　　　Chapter 20 Verse 14-15

14. "Verily, I am **Allah**! La ilaha illa Ana (none has the right to be worshipped but I), so worship Me, and perform As-Salat (prayer) for My remembrance."
15. "Verily, the Hour is coming - and I am almost hiding it - that every person may be rewarded for that which he strives. (Darussalam, 2000)

Chapter Ta-Ha　　　　　　　　　　　　　　　Chapter 20 Verse 98

Your Ilah (God) is only **Allah**, La ilaha illa Huwa (none has the right to be worshipped but He). He has full knowledge of all things. (Darussalam, 2000)

Chapter Al Anbiya　　　　　　　　　　　　Chapter 21 Verses 1~4

1. Draws near for mankind their reckoning, while they turn away in heedlessness.
2. Comes not unto them an admonition from their **Lord** as a recent revelation but they listen to it while they play.
3. With their hearts occupied. Those who do wrong, conceal their private counsels (saying): "Is this more than a human being like you? Will you submit to magic while you see it?"
4. He said: "My **Lord** knows word in the heavens and on the earth. And He is the All-Hearer, the All- Knower." (Darussalam, 2000)

Chapter Al-Hajj　　　　　　　　　　　　　　Chapter 22 Verse 5-6

5. O mankind! If you are in doubt about the Resurrection, then verily! We have created you from dust, then from a Nutfah (sperm-drop), then from a clot then from a little lump of flesh - some formed and some unformed - that We may make clear to you. And We cause whom We will to remain in the wombs for an appointed term, then We bring you out as infants, then that you may reach your age of full strength. And among you there is he who dies, and among you there is he who is brought back to the miserable old age, so that he knows nothing after having known. And you see the earth barren, but when We send down water on it, it is stirred (to life), it swells and puts forth every lovely kind (of growth).
6. That is because **Allah**: He is the Truth, and it is He Who gives life to the dead, and it is He Who is Able to do all things. (Darussalam, 2000)

Chapter Al-Hajj　　　　　　　　　　　　　　Chapter 22 Verse 64

To Him belongs all that is in the heavens and all that is on the earth. And verily, **Allah** He is Rich, Worthy of all praise. (Darussalam, 2000)

Chapter Al-Mu'minun Chapter 23 Verse 92
All-Knower of the unseen and the seen! Exalted be He over all that they associate as partners to Him! (Darussalam, 2000)

Chapter Al-Mu'minun Chapter 23 Verse 116
So Exalted be **Allah**, the True King: La ilaha illa Huwa (none has the right to be worshipped but He), the **Lord** of the Supreme Throne! (Darussalam, 2000)

Chapter An-Nur Chapter 24 Verse 42
And to **Allah** belongs the sovereignty of the heavens and the earth, and to **Allah** is the return (of all). (Darussalam, 2000)

Chapter An-Nur Chapter 24 Verse 64
Certainly, to **Allah** belongs all that is in the heavens and the earth. Surely, He knows your condition and the Day when they will be brought back to Him, then He will inform them of what they did, and **Allah** is All-Knower of everything. (Darussalam, 2000)

Chapter Al-Furqan Chapter 25 Verse 1-2
1. Blessed be He Who sent down the criterion to His slave that he may be a warner to the 'Alamin (worlds).
2. He to Whom belongs the dominion of the heavens and the earth, and Who has begotten no son and for Whom there is no partner in the dominion. He has created everything, and has measured it exactly according to its due measurements. (Darussalam, 2000)

Chapter Al-Furqan Chapter 25 Verse 58
And put your trust in the Ever living One Who dies not, and glorify His Praises, and Sufficient is He as the All-Knower of the sins of His slaves. (Darussalam, 2000)

Chapter Ash-Shu`ara Chapter 26 Verse 9
And verily, your **Lord**, He is truly, the All- Mighty, the Most Merciful. (Darussalam, 2000)

Chapter Ash-Shu`ara Chapter 26 Verse 220
Verily, He, only He, is the All-**H**earer, the All-Knower. (Darussalam, 2000)

Chapter An-Naml Chapter 27 Verse 26
Allah, La ilaha illa Huwa (none has the right to be worshipped but He), the **Lord** of the Supreme Throne. (Darussalam, 2000)

Chapter Al-Qasas   Chapter 28 Verse 70
And He is **Allah**; La ilaha illa Huwa (none has the right to be worshipped but He), all praises and thanks be to Him in the first and in the Last. And for Him is the Decision, and to Him shall you be returned. (Darussalam, 2000)

Chapter Al-Qasas   Chapter 28 Verse 88
And invoke not any other ilah (god) along with **Allah**, La ilaha illa Huwa (none has the right to be worshipped but He). Everything will perish save His face. His is the Decision, and to Him you shall be returned. (Darussalam, 2000)

Chapter Ar-Rum   Chapter 30 Verse 11
Allah originates the creation, then He will repeat it, then to Him you will be returned. (Darussalam, 2000)

Chapter Ar-Rum   Chapter 30 Verse 27
And He it is Who originates the creation, then He will repeat it, and this is easier for Him. His is the highest description in the heavens and in the earth. And He is the All-Mighty, the All-Wise. (Darussalam, 2000)

Chapter Ar-Rum   Chapter 30 Verse 40
Allah is He Who created you, then provided food for you, then will cause you to die, then He will give life. Is there any of your partners that do anything of that? Glory be to Him! And Exalted be He above all that they associate. (Darussalam, 2000)

Chapter Luqman   Chapter 31 Verse 26
To **Allah** belongs whatsoever is in the heavens and the earth. Verily, **Allah**, He is Al-Ghani (All-Rich), Worthy of all Praise. (Darussalam, 2000)

Chapter Luqman   Chapter 31 Verse 30
That is because **Allah**, He is the truth, and that which they invoke besides Him is al-Batil (falsehood); and that **Allah**, He is the Most High, the Most Great. (Darussalam, 2000)

Chapter As-Sajdah   Chapter 32 Verses 4~6
4. **Allah** it is He Who has created the heavens and the earth, and all that is between them in six days. Then He rose over (Istawa) the Throne. You have none, besides Him, as a Wali (Protector) or an intercessor, will you not then remember?

5. He manages and regulates affair from the heavens to the earth, then it will go up to Him, in one Day, the space whereof is a thousand years of your reckoning.
6. That is He, the All-Knower of the unseen and the seen, the All-Mighty, the Most Merciful. (Darussalam, 2000)

Chapter Al-AhzabChapter 33 Verse 3
And put your trust in **Allah**, and Sufficient is **Allah** as a Wakil (Trustee). (Darussalam, 2000)

Chapter SabaChapter 34 Verse 1
All the praises and thanks be to **Allah**, to Whom belongs all that is in the heavens and all that is in the earth. His is all the praises and thanks in the Hereafter, and He is the All-Wise, the All-Aware. (Darussalam, 2000)

Chapter FatirChapter 35 Verse 38
Verily, **Allah** is the All-Knower of the Unseen of the heavens and the earth. Verily, He is the All-Knower of that is in the breasts. (Darussalam, 2000)

Chapter As-SaffatChapter 37 Verse 4-5
4. Verily, your Ilah (God) is indeed One;
5. **Lord** of the heavens and of the earth, and all that is between them, and **Lord** of every point of the sun's risings. (Darussalam, 2000)

Chapter As-SaffatChapter 37 Verse 182
And all the praises and thanks be to **Allah, Lord** of the 'Alamin (worlds). (Darussalam, 2000)

Chapter SadChapter 38 Verse 66
"The **Lord** of the heavens and the earth and all that is between them, the All-Mighty, the Oft-Forgiving." (Darussalam, 2000)

Chapter Az-ZumarChapter 39 Verse 44
Say: "To **Allah** belongs all intercession. His is the Sovereignty of the heavens and the earth. Then to Him you shall be brought back." (Darussalam, 2000)

Chapter Az-ZumarChapter 39 Verse 46
Say: "O **Allah**! Creator of the heavens and the earth! All-Knower of the Ghaib (Unseen) and the seen! You will judge between your slaves about that wherein they used to differ." (Darussalam, 2000)

Chapter Az-Zumar   Chapter 39 Verse 62
Allah is the Creator of all things, and He is the Wakil (Disposer of affairs) over all things. (Darussalam, 2000)

Chapter Az-Zumar   Chapter 39 Verse 67
They made not a just estimate of **Allah** such as is due to Him. And on the Day of Resurrection the whole of the earth will be grasped by His hand and the heavens will be rolled up in His Right Hand. Glorified be He, and High be He above all that they associate as partners with Him. (Darussalam, 2000)

Chapter Ghafir   Chapter 40 Verse 2-3
2. The revelation of the book is from **Allah**, the All-Mighty, the All-Knower.
3. The Forgiver of sin, the Acceptor of repentance, the Severe in punishment, the Bestower. La ilaha illa Huwa (none has the right to be worshipped but He), to Him is the final return. (Darussalam, 2000)

Chapter Ghafir   Chapter 40 Verse 62
That is **Allah**, your **Lord**; the Creator of all things, La ilaha illa Huwa (none has the right to be worshipped but He). How then are you turning away? (Darussalam, 2000)

Chapter Ghafir   Chapter 40 Verse 65
He is the Ever Living, La ilaha illa Huwa (none has the right to be worshipped but He); so, invoke Him making your worship pure for Him alone. All the praises and thanks be to **Allah**, the **Lord** of the 'Alamin (worlds). (Darussalam, 2000)

Chapter Ghafir   Chapter 40 Verse 68
It is He Who gives life and causes death. And when He decides upon a thing, He says to it only: "Be!" and it is. (Darussalam, 2000)

Chapter Fussilat   Chapter 41 Verse 2
A revelation from the Most Gracious, the Most Merciful. (Darussalam, 2000)

Chapter Ash-Shura   Chapter 42 Verse 4
To Him belongs all that is in the heavens and all that is in the earth, and He is the Most High, the Most Great. (Darussalam, 2000)

Chapter Ash-Shura   Chapter 42 Verses 7~9
7. And thus We have revealed to you a Qur'an in Arabic that you may warn the mother of the Towns and all around it, and warn of the Day of

Assembling, of which there is no doubt, when a party will be in Paradise and a party in the blazing Fire.
8. And if **Allah** had willed, He could have made them one nation, but He admits whom He wills to His Mercy. And the Zalimun (wrong-doers) will have neither a Wali (protector) nor a helper.
9. Or have they taken Auliya' (guardians) besides Him? But **Allah** – He Alone is the Wali (Protector). And it is He Who gives life to the dead, and He is Able to do all things. (Darussalam, 2000)

Chapter Ash-Shura   Chapter 42 Verse 19
Allah is very Gracious and Kind to His slaves. He gives provisions to whom He wills. And He is the All-Strong, the All-Mighty. (Darussalam, 2000)

Chapter Az-Zukhruf   Chapter 43 Verse 64
"Verily, **Allah**! He is my **Lord** and your **Lord**. So, worship Him. This is the Straight Path." (Darussalam, 2000)

Chapter Az-Zukhruf   Chapter 43 Verse 82
Glorified be the **Lord** of the heavens and the earth, the **Lord** of the Throne! Exalted be He from all that they ascribe. (Darussalam, 2000)

Chapter Az-Zukhruf   Chapter 43 Verse 84-85
84. It is He Who is the only Ilah (God) in the heaven and the only Ilah (God) on the earth. And He is the All-Wise, the All-Knower.
85. And Blessed be He to Whom belongs the kingdom of the heavens and the earth, and all that is between them, and with Whom is the knowledge of the hour, and to Whom you will be returned. (Darussalam, 2000)

Chapter Ad-Dukhan   Chapter 44 Verse 7-8
7. The **Lord** of the heavens and the earth and all that is between them, if you have a faith with certainty.
8. La ilaha illa Huwa (none has the right to be worshipped but He). It is He Who gives life and causes death - your **Lord** and the **Lord** of your forefathers. (Darussalam, 2000)

Chapter Al-Jathiyah   Chapter 45 Verse 36-37
36. So all the praises and thanks be to **Allah**, the **Lord** of the heavens and the **Lord** of the earth, and the **Lord** of the 'Alamin (worlds).
37. And His is the Majesty in the heavens and the earth, and He is the All-Mighty, the All-Wise. (Darussalam, 2000)

Chapter Al-Fath   Chapter 48 Verse 7

And to **Allah** belong the hosts of the heavens and the earth. And **Allah** is Ever All-Mighty, All-Wise. (Darussalam, 2000)

Chapter Al-Fath   Chapter 48 Verse 14

And to **Allah** belongs the sovereignty of the heavens and the earth. He forgives whom He wills, and punishes whom He wills. And **Allah** is Ever Oft-Forgiving, Most Merciful. (Darussalam, 2000)

Chapter Al-Hujurat   Chapter 49 Verse 18

Verily, **Allah** knows the Unseen of the heavens and the earth. And **Allah** is the All-Seer of what you do. (Darussalam, 2000)

Chapter Al-Dhariyat   Chapter 51 Verse 58

Verily, **Allah** is the All-Provider, Owner of Power, the Most Strong. (Darussalam, 2000)

Chapter Al-Najm   Chapter 53 Verse 25

But to **Allah** belongs the last and the first. (Darussalam, 2000)

Chapter Ar-Rahman   Chapter 55 Verse 78

Blessed be the name of your **Lord**, the Owner of Majesty and Honour. (Darussalam, 2000)

Chapter Al-Waqi`ah   Chapter 56 Verse 74

Then glorify with praises the Name of your **Lord**, the Most Great. (Darussalam, 2000)

Chapter As-Saff   Chapter 61 Verse 1

Whatsoever is in the heavens and whatsoever is on the earth glorifies **Allah**. And He is the All-Mighty, the All-Wise. (Darussalam, 2000)

Chapter At-Taghabun   Chapter 64 Verse 1

Whatsoever is in the heavens and whatsoever is on the earth glorifies **Allah**. His is the dominion, and to Him belong all the praises and thanks, and He is Able to do all things. (Darussalam, 2000)

Chapter At-Taghabun   Chapter 64 Verse 4

He knows what is in the heavens and on earth, and He knows what you conceal and what you reveal. And **Allah** is the All-Knower of what is in the breasts (of men). (Darussalam, 2000)

Chapter At-Taghabun   Chapter 64 Verse 13
Allah! La ilaha illa Huwa (none has the right to be worshipped but He). And in **Allah** therefore let the believers put their trust. (Darussalam, 2000)

Chapter At-Taghabun   Chapter 64 Verse 18
All-Knower of the unseen and seen, the All-Mighty, the All-Wise. (Darussalam, 2000)

Chapter Al-Mulk   Chapter 67 Verse 1
Blessed be He in Whose hands is the dominion; and He is Able to do all things. (Darussalam, 2000)

Chapter Al-Haqqah   Chapter 69 Verse 52
So, glorify the name of your **Lord**, the Most Great. (Darussalam, 2000)

Chapter Al-Jinn   Chapter 72 Verse 3
And He, exalted be the Majesty of our **Lord**, has taken neither a wife nor a son. (Darussalam, 2000)

Chapter Al-Muzzammil   Chapter 73 Verse 9
The **Lord** of the east and the west; La ilaha illa Huwa (none has the right to be worshipped but He). So, take him Alone as Wakil (Disposer of your affairs). (Darussalam, 2000)

Chapter Al-A'la   Chapter 87 Verse 1
Glorify the name of your **Lord**, the Most High. (Darussalam, 2000)

Chapter Al-Alaq   Chapter 96 Verses 1~3
1. Read! In the Name of your Lord Who has created.
2. He has created man from a clot.
3. Read! And your **Lord** is the Most Generous. (Darussalam, 2000)

Chapter Al-Falaq   Chapter 113 Verse 1
Say: "I seek refuge with, the **Lord** of the daybreak. (Darussalam, 2000)

Chapter An-Nas   Chapter 114 Verses 1~3
1. Say: "I seek refuge with the **Lord** of mankind.
2. "The King of mankind.
3. "The Ilah (God) of mankind." (Darussalam, 2000)

Section II

Signs of Allah mentioned in the Quran

Signs of Allah mentioned in the Quran

In the name of Allah, the Most Gracious, the Most Merciful.

Chapter Al-Baqarah   Chapter 2 Verses 21-22
21. O Mankind! Worship your **Lord**, Who created you and those who were before you so that you may become Al-Muttaqun (the pious).
22. Who has made the earth a resting place for you, and the sky as a canopy, and sent down water from the sky and brought forth therewith fruits as a provision for you. Then do not set up rivals unto **Allah** while you know. (Darussalam, 1999)

Chapter Al-Baqarah   Chapter 2 Verses 28-29
28. How can you disbelieve in **Allah**? Seeing that you were dead and He gave you life. Then He will give you death, then again will bring you to life and then unto Him you will return.
29. He it is Who created for you all that is on earth. Then He rose over (Istawa) towards the heaven and made them seven heavens and He is the All-Knower of everything. (Darussalam, 1999)

Chapter Al-Baqarah   Chapter 2 Verse 107
Know you not that it is **Allah** to whom belongs the dominion of the heavens and the earth? And besides **Allah** you have neither any Wali (protector or guardian) nor any helper. (Darussalam, 1999)

Chapter Al-Baqarah   Chapter 2 Verse 284
To **Allah** belongs all that is in the heavens and all that is on the earth, and whether you disclose what is in your own selves or conceal it, **Allah** will call you to account for it. Then He forgives whom He wills and punishes whom He wills, and **Allah** is Able to do all things. (Darussalam, 1999)

Chapter Al-Imran   Chapter 3 Verse 5
Truly, nothing is hidden from **Allah**, in the earth or in the heaven. (Darussalam, 1999)

Chapter Al-Imran   Chapter 3 Verses 26-27

26. Say: "O **Allah**! Possessor of the kingdom, You give the kingdom to whom You will, and You take the kingdom from whom You will, and You endue with honour whom You will, and You humiliate whom You will. In your hand is the good. Verily, You are Able to do all things.
27. You make the night to enter into the day, and You make the day to enter into the night, You bring the living out of the dead, and You bring the dead out of the living. And You give wealth and sustenance to whom You will, without limit. (Darussalam, 1999)

Chapter Al-Imran   Chapter 3 Verse 29

Say; "Whether you hide what is in your breasts or reveal it, **Allah** knows it, and He knows what is in the heavens and what is in the earth. And **Allah** is Able to do all things." (Darussalam, 1999)

Chapter Al-Imran   Chapter 3 Verse 83

Do they seek other than the religion of **Allah**, while to Him submitted all creatures in the heavens and the earth, willingly or unwillingly. And to Him shall they all be returned. (Darussalam, 1999)

Chapter Al-Imran   Chapter 3 Verse 109

And to **Allah** belongs all that is in the heavens and all that is in the earth. And all matters go back to **Allah**. (Darussalam, 1999)

Chapter Al-Imran   Chapter 3 Verse 129

And to **Allah** belongs all that is in the heavens and all that is in the earth. He forgives whom He wills, and punishes whom He wills. And **Allah** is Oft-Forgiving, Most Merciful. (Darussalam, 1999)

Chapter An-Nisa   Chapter 4 Verse 126

And to **Allah** belongs all that is in the heavens and all that is in the earth. And **Allah** is Ever encompassing all things. (Darussalam, 1999)

Chapter An-Nisa   Chapter 4 Verse 132

And to **Allah** belongs all that is in the heavens and all that is in the earth. And **Allah** is Ever All-Sufficient as Disposer of affairs. (Darussalam, 1999)

Chapter Al-Ma'idah   Chapter 5 Verse 40

Know you not that to **Allah** belongs the dominion of the heavens and the earth! He punishes whom He wills and He forgives whom He wills. And **Allah** is Able to do all things. (Darussalam, 1999)

Chapter Al-Ma'idah — Chapter 5 Verse 120

To **Allah** belongs the dominion of the heavens and the earth and all that is therein, and He is Able to do all things. (Darussalam, 1999)

Chapter Al-An'am — Chapter 6 Verses 1~3

1. All praises and thanks be to **Allah**, Who created the heavens and the earth, and originated the darkness and light; yet those who disbelieve hold others as equal with their **Lord**.
2. He it is Who has created you from clay, and then has decreed a term. And there is with Him another determined term, yet you doubt.
3. And He is **Allah** in the heavens and on the earth; He knows what you conceal and what you reveal, and He knows what you earn. (Darussalam, 1999)

Chapter Al-An'am — Chapter 6 Verse 14

Say: "Shall I take as a Wali (a guardian, protector) any other then **Allah**, the Creator of the heavens and the earth? And it is He Who feeds but is not fed." Say; "Verily, I am commanded to be the first of those who submit themselves to **Allah**." And be not you of the Mushrikun (polytheists). (Darussalam, 1999)

Chapter Al-An'am — Chapter 6 Verses 60~62

60. It is He, Who takes your souls by night, and has knowledge of all that you have done by day, then He raises you up again that a term appointed be fulfilled, then unto Him will be your return. Then He will inform you of that which you used to do.
61. He is the Irresistible (Supreme), over His slaves, and He sends guardians over you, until when death approaches one of you, Our messengers take his soul, and they never neglect their duty.
62. Then they are returned to **Allah**, their True Maula (Lord). Surely, for Him is the judgment and He is the swiftest in taking account. (Darussalam, 1999)

Chapter Al-An'am — Chapter 6 Verse 73

It is He Who has created the heavens and the earth in truth, and on the Day, He will say: "Be!" and it is! His word is the Truth. His will be the dominion on the Day when the Trumpet will be blown. All-Knower of the unseen and the seen. He is the All-Wise, Well-Aware. (Darussalam, 1999)

| Chapter Al-An'am | Chapter 6 Verses 95~99 |

95. Verily, it is **Allah** Who causes the seed grain and the fruit stone to split and sprout. He brings forth the living from the dead, and it is He Who brings forth the dead from the living. Such is **Allah**, then how are you deluded away from the truth?

96. Cleaver of the daybreak. He has appointed the night for resting, and the sun and the moon for reckoning. Such is the measuring of the All-Mighty, the All-Knowing.

97. It is He Who has set the stars for you, so that you may guide your course with their help through the darkness of the land and the sea. We have explained in detail our Ayat (signs) for people who know.

98. It is He Who has created you from a single person, and has given you a place of residing and a place of storage. Indeed, We have explained in detail our Revelations for people who understand.

99. It is He Who sends down water from the sky, and with it We bring forth vegetation of all kinds, and out of it We bring forth green stalks, from which We bring forth thick clustered grain. And out of the date palm and its spathe come forth clusters of dates hanging low and near, and gardens of grapes, olives and pomegranates, each similar yet different. Look at their fruits when they begin to bear, and the ripeness thereof. Verily, in these things there are signs for people who believe. (Darussalam, 1999)

| Chapter Al-An'am | Chapter 6 Verse 133 |

And your **Lord** is Rich, full of mercy; if He wills, He can destroy you, and in your place make whom He wills as your successors, as He raised you from the seed of other people. (Darussalam, 1999)

| Chapter Al-An'am | Chapter 6 Verse 165 |

And it is He Who has made you generations coming after generations, replacing each other on the earth. And He has raised you in ranks, some above others that He may try you in that which He has bestowed on you. Surely, your **Lord** is Swift in retribution, and certainly He is Oft-Forgiving, Most Merciful. (Darussalam, 1999)

| Chapter Al-A'raf | Chapter 7 Verse 54 |

Indeed, your **Lord** is **Allah**, Who created the heavens and the earth in Six Days, and then He rose over (Istawa) the Throne. He brings the night as a cover over the day, seeking it rapidly, and the sun, the moon, the starts subjected to His Command. Surely, His is the creation and commandment. Blessed is **Allah**, the **Lord** of the 'Alamin! (worlds). (Darussalam, 1999)

Chapter Al-A'raf   Chapter 7 Verse 57

And it is He Who sends the winds as heralds of glad tidings, going before His mercy. Till when they have carried a heavy-laden cloud, We drive it to a land that is dead, then We cause water to descend thereon. Then We produce every kind of fruit therewith. Similarly, We shall raise up the dead, so that you may take heed. (Darussalam, 1999)

Chapter Yunus   Chapter 10 Verses 5-6

5. It is He Who made the sun a shining thing and the moon as a light and measured out for it stages that you might know the number of years and the reckoning. **Allah** did not create this but in truth. He explains the Ayat (verses) in detail for people who have knowledge.
6. Verily, in the alternation of the night and the day and in all that **Allah** has created in the heavens and the earth are Ayat (signs) for those people who keep their duty to **Allah**, and fear Him much. (Darussalam, 2000)

Chapter Yunus   Chapter 10 Verse 31

Say: "Who provides for you from the sky and the earth? Or who owns hearing and sight? And who brings out the living from the dead and brings out the dead from the living? And who disposes the affairs?" They will say: "**Allah.**" Say: "Will you not then be afraid of **Allah**'s punishment?" (Darussalam, 2000)

Chapter Yunus   Chapter 10 Verses 34-35

34. Say: "Is there of your partners one that originates the creation and then repeats it?" Say: "**Allah** originates the creation and then He repeats it. Then how are you deluded away?"
35. Say: "Is there of your partners one that guides to the truth?" Say: "It is **Allah** Who guides to the truth. Is then He Who guides to the truth more worthy to be followed, or he Who finds not guidance unless he is guided? Then, what is the matter with you? How judge you?" (Darussalam, 2000)

Chapter Yunus   Chapter 10 Verse 55

No doubt, surely, all that is in the heavens and the earth belongs to **Allah**. No doubt, surely, **Allah**'s Promise is true. But Most of them know not. (Darussalam, 2000)

Chapter Yunus   Chapter 10 Verse 67

He it is Who has appointed for you the night that you may rest therein, and the day to make things visible. Verily, in this are Ayat (signs), for a people who listen. (Darussalam, 2000)

Chapter Yunus   Chapter 10 Verse 107
And if **Allah** touches you with harm, there is none who can remove it but He; and if He intends any good for you, there is none who can repel His Favour which He causes it to reach whomsoever of His slaves He wills. And He is the Oft-Forgiving, the Most Merciful. (Darussalam, 2000)

Chapter Hud   Chapter 11 Verses 6-7
6. And no moving creature is there on earth but its provision is due from **Allah**. And He knows its dwelling place and its deposit. All is in a clear book.
7. And He it is Who has created the heavens and the earth in six Days and His Throne was on the water, that He might try you, which of you is the best in deeds. But if you were to say to them; "You shall indeed be raised up after death," those who disbelieve would be sure to say. "This is nothing but obvious magic." (Darussalam, 2000)

Chapter Hud   Chapter 11 Verse 56
"I put my trust in **Allah**, my **Lord** and your **Lord**! There is not a moving creature but He has the grasp of its forelock. Verily, my **Lord** is on the Straight Path." (Darussalam, 2000)

Chapter Ar-Ra`d   Chapter 13 Verses 2~4
2. **Allah** is He Who raised the heavens without any pillars that you can see. Then, He rose above the Throne. He has subjected the sun and the moon, each running for a term appointed. He manages and regulates all affairs; He explains the Ayat (Verses) in detail, that you may believe with certainty in the Meeting with your **Lord**.
3. And it is He Who spread out the earth, and place therein-firm mountains and rivers and of every kind of fruits He made Zawjain Ithnain (two in pairs). He brings the night as a cover over the day. Verily, in these things, there are Ayat (signs) for people who reflect.
4. And in the earth are neighboring tracts, and gardens of vines, and green crops, and date palms, growing into two or three from a single stem root, or otherwise, watered with the same water; yet some of them We make more excellent than others to eat. Verily, in these things there are Ayat (signs) for the people who understand. (Darussalam, 2000)

Chapter Ar-Ra`d   Chapter 13 Verse 8
Allah knows what every female bears, and by how much the wombs fall short or exceed. Everything with Him is in proportion. (Darussalam, 2000)

Chapter Ar-Ra'd — Chapter 13 Verses 12-13

12. It is He Who shows you the lightning, as fear and as a hope. And it is He Who brings up the clouds, heavy.

13. And Ar-Ra'd (thunder) glorifies and praises Him, and so do the angels because of His awe. He sends the thunderbolts, and there with He strikes whom He wills, yet they dispute about **Allah**. And He is Mighty in strength and Severe in punishment. (Darussalam, 2000)

Chapter Ibrahim — Chapter 14 Verses 19-20

19. Do you not see that **Allah** has created the heavens and the earth with truth? If He wills, He can remove you and bring a new creation!

20. And for **Allah** that is not hard or difficult. (Darussalam, 2000)

Chapter Ibrahim — Chapter 14 Verses 32~34

32. **Allah** is He Who has created the heavens and the earth and sends down water from the sky, and thereby brought forth fruits as provision for you; and He has made the ships to be of service to you, that they may sail through the sea by His Command; and He has made rivers to be of service to you.

33. And He has made the sun and the moon, both constantly pursing their courses, to be of service to you; and He has made the night and the day, to be of service to you.

34. And He gave you of all that you asked for, and if you count the Blessings of **Allah**, never will you be able to count them. Verily, man is indeed an extreme wrongdoer, a disbeliever. (Darussalam, 2000)

Chapter Ibrahim — Chapter 14 Verse 38

O our **Lord**! Certainly, You know what we conceal and what we reveal. Nothing on the earth or in the heaven is hidden from **Allah**. (Darussalam, 2000)

Chapter Al-Hijr — Chapter 15 Verses 23~25

23. And certainly We! We it is Who give life, and cause death, and We are the Inheritors.

24. And indeed, We know the first generations of you who had passed away, and indeed, We know the present generations of you, and also those who will come afterwards.

25. And verily, your **Lord** will gather them together. Truly, He is All-Wise, All-Knowing. (Darussalam, 2000)

Chapter An-Nahl Chapter 16 Verses 10~18

10. He it is Who sends down water from the sky; from it you drink and from it (grows) the vegetations on which you send your cattle to pasture.
11. With it He causes to grow for you the crops, the olives, the date palms, the grapes, and every kind of fruit. Verily, in this is indeed an evident proof and a manifest sign for people who give thought.
12. And He has subjected to you the night and the day, and the sun and the moon; and the stars are subjected by His Command. Surely, in this are proofs for people who understand.
13. And whatsoever He has created for you on the earth of varying colours. Verily, in this is a sign for people who remember.
14. And He it is Who has subjected the sea, that you eat thereof fresh tender meat, and that you bring forth out of it ornaments to wear. And you see the ships ploughing through it, that you may seek of His Bounty and that you may be grateful.
15. And He has affixed into the earth mountains standing firm, lest it should shake with you; and rivers and roads, that you may guide yourselves.
16. And landmarks and by the stars, they guide themselves.
17. Is then He, Who creates as one who creates not? Will you not then remember?
18. And if you would count the Favours of Allah, never could you be able to count them. Truly, Allah is Oft-Forgiving, Most Merciful. (Darussalam, 2000)

Chapter An-Nahl Chapter 16 Verse 40
Verily, Our word unto a thing when We intend it, is only that We say unto it; "Be!" and it is. (Darussalam, 2000)

Chapter An-Nahl Chapter 16 Verses 51-52
51. And **Allah** said: "Take not ilahain (two gods). Verily, He is only One Ilah (God). Then, fear Me much.
52. To Him belongs all that is in the heavens and the earth and Ad-Din (religion) Wasiba (always) is His. Will you then fear any other than **Allah**? (Darussalam, 2000)

Chapter An-Nahl Chapter 16 Verse 65
And **Allah** sends down water from the sky, then He reviews the earth therewith after its death. Verily, in this is a sign for people who listen. (Darussalam, 2000)

Chapter An-Nahl   Chapter 16 Verse 70
And **Allah** has created you and then He will cause you to die; and of you there are some who are send back to senility (age), so that they know nothing after having known. Truly, **Allah** is All-Knowing, All-Powerful. (Darussalam, 2000)

Chapter An-Nahl   Chapter 16 Verses 77~81
77. And to **Allah** belongs the Unseen of the heavens and the earth. And the matter of the hour is not but as a twinkling of the eye, or even nearer. Truly, **Allah** is Able to do all things.
78. And **Allah** has brought you out from the wombs of your mothers while you know nothing. And He gave you hearing, sight, and hearts that you might give thanks.
79. Do they not see the birds held in the midst of the sky? None holds them but **Allah**. Verily, in this are clear Ayat (signs) for people who believe.
80. And **Allah** has made for you in your homes an abode, and made for you out of the hides of the cattle dwelling, which you find so light when you travel and when you stay; and of their wool, fur, and hair, furnishings and articles of convenience, comfort for a while.
81. And **Allah** has made for you out of that which He has created shades, and has made for you places of refuge in the mountains, and has made for you garments to protect you from the heat, and coats of mail to protect you from your violence. Thus, does He perfect His Favour unto you, that you may submit yourselves to His Will. (Darussalam, 2000)

Chapter Al-Isra   Chapter 17 Verse 30
Truly, your **Lord** enlarges the provision for whom He wills and straitens. Verily, He is Ever All-Knower, All-Seer of His slaves. (Darussalam, 2000)

Chapter Al-Isra   Chapter 17 Verse 44
The seven heavens and the earth and all that is therein, glorify Him and there is not a thing but glorifies His Praise. But you understand not their glorification. Truly, He is Ever Forbearing, Oft-Forgiving. (Darussalam, 2000)

Chapter Al-Isra   Chapter 17 Verse 66
Your **Lord** is He Who drives the ship for you through the sea, in order that you may seek of His Bounty. Truly, He is Ever Most Merciful towards you. (Darussalam, 2000)

Chapter Maryam — Chapter 19 Verse 65

Lord of the heavens and the earth, and all that is between them, so worship Him and be constant and patient in His worship. Do you know of any who is similar to Him? (Darussalam, 2000)

Chapter Ta-Ha — Chapter 20 Verses 4~7

4. A Revelation from Him Who has created the earth and high heavens.
5. The Most Gracious rose over (Istawa) the Throne.
6. To Him belongs all that is in the heavens and all that is on the earth, and all that is between them, and all that is under the soil.
7. And if you speak aloud, then verily, He knows the secret and that which is yet more hidden. (Darussalam, 2000)

Chapter Al-Anbiya — Chapter 21 Verses 31~33

31. And We have place on the earth firm mountains, lest it should shake with them, and We placed therein-broad highways for them to pass through, that they may be guided.
32. And We have made the heaven a roof, safe and well-guarded. Yet they turn away from its signs.
33. And He it is Who has created the night and day, and the sun and the moon, each in an orbit floating. (Darussalam, 2000)

Chapter Al-Anbiya — Chapter 21 Verses 51~56

51. And indeed We bestowed aforetime on Ibrahim his guidance, and We were Well-Acquainted with him.
52. When he said to his father and his people: "What are these images, to which you are devoted?"
53. They said: "We found our fathers worshipping them."
54. He said: "Indeed you and your fathers have been in manifest error."
55. They said: "Have you brought us the Truth, or are you one of those who play about?"
56. He said: "Nay, your **Lord** is the **Lord** of the heavens and the earth, Who created them and to that I am one of the witnesses. (Darussalam, 2000)

Chapter Al-Hajj — Chapter 22 Verses 61~66

61. That is because **Allah** merges the night into the day, and He merges the day into the night. And verily, **Allah** is All-**H**earer, All-Seer.
62. That is because **Allah** He is the Truth, and what they invoke besides Him, it is Batil (Falsehood). And verily, **Allah** He is the Most High, the Most Great.

63. See you not that **Allah** sends down water from the sky, and then the earth becomes green? Verily, **Allah** is the Most Kind and Courteous, Well-Acquainted with all things.
64. To Him belongs all that is in the heavens and all that is on the earth. And verily, **Allah** He is Rich, Worthy of all praise.
65. See you not that **Allah** has subjected to you all that is on the earth, and the ships that sail through the sea by His Command? He withholds the heaven from falling on the earth except by His Leave. Verily, **Allah** is for mankind full of Kindness, Most Merciful.
66. It is He, Who gave you life, and then will cause you to die, and will again give you life. Verily, man is indeed an ingrate. (Darussalam, 2000)

Chapter Al-Hajj   Chapter 22 Verse 70
Know you not that **Allah** knows all that is in the heaven and on the earth. Verily, it is in the Book. Verily, that is easy for **Allah**. (Darussalam, 2000)

Chapter Al-Mu'minun   Chapter 23 Verses 78~80
78. It is He Who has created for you hearing, eyes, and hearts. Little thanks you give.
79. And it is He Who has created you on the earth, and to Him you shall be gathered back.
80. And it is He Who gives life and causes death, and His is the alternation of night and day. Will you not then understand? (Darussalam, 2000)

Chapter Al-Mu'minun   Chapter 23 Verse 91
No son did **Allah** beget, nor is there any ilah (god) along with Him. (If there had been many gods) then each god would have taken away what he had created, and some would have tried to overcome others! Glorified be **Allah** above all that they attribute to Him! (Darussalam, 2000)

Chapter Al-Furqan   Chapter 25 Verses 53-54
53. And it is He Who has let free the two seas, this is palatable and sweet, and that is salt and bitter; and He has set a barrier and a complete partition between them.
54. And it is He Who has created man from water, and has appointed for him kindred by blood, and kindred by marriage. And your **Lord** is Ever All-Powerful to do what He wills. (Darussalam, 2000)

| Chapter Al-Furqan | Chapter 25 Verse 59 |

Who created the heavens and the earth and all that is between them in six Days. Then He rose over (Istawa) the Throne. The Most Gracious! Ask Him, as He is Al-Khabir (All-Knower). (Darussalam, 2000)

| Chapter Al-Furqan | Chapter 25 Verses 61-62 |

61. Blessed be He Who has placed in the heaven big stars, and has placed therein a great lamp, and a moon giving light.
62. And He it is Who has put the night and the day in succession, for such who desires to remember or desires to show his gratitude. (Darussalam, 2000)

| Chapter As-Shu'ara | Chapter 26 Verses 78~83 |

78. Who has created me, and it is He Who guides me.
79. And it is He Who feeds me and gives me to drink.
80. And when I am ill, it is He Who cures me.
81. And Who will cause me to die, and then will bring me to life.
82. And Who, I hope, will forgive me my faults on the Day of Recompense.
83. My **Lord**! Bestow Hukm (religious knowledge) on me, and join me with the righteous. (Darussalam, 2000)

| Chapter An-Naml | Ayat Sajada | Chapter 27 Verses 25-26 |

25. So they do not worship **Allah**, Who brings to light what is hidden in the heavens and the earth, and knows what you conceal and what you reveal.
26. Allah, La ilaha illa Huwa (none has the right to be worshipped but He), the Lord of the Supreme Throne! (Darussalam, 2000)

| Chapter An-Naml | Chapter 27 Verses 61~65 |

61. Is not He Who has made the earth as a fixed abode, and has placed rivers in its midst, and has placed firm mountains there in, and has set a barrier between the two seas? Is there any ilah (god) with **Allah**? Nay, but most of them know not!
62. Is not He Who responds to the distressed one, when He calls on Him, and Who removes the evil, and makes you inheritors of the earth, generations after generations? Is there any ilah (god) with **Allah**? Little is that you remember!
63. Is not He Who guides you in the darkness of the land and the sea, and Who sends the winds as heralds of glad tidings, going before His mercy? Is there any ilah (god) with **Allah**? High exalted be **Allah** above all that they associate as partners!

64. Is not He Who originates creation, and shall thereafter repeat it, and Who provides for you from heaven and earth? Is there any ilah (god) with **Allah**? Say: "Bring forth your proofs, if you are truthful."
65. Say: "None in the heavens and the earth knows the Ghaib (Unseen) except **Allah**, nor can they perceive when they shall be resurrected." (Darussalam, 2000)

Chapter An-Naml   Chapter 27 Verse 86
See they not that We have made the night for them to rest therein, and the day sight-giving? Verily, in this are Ayat (signs) for the people who believe. (Darussalam, 2000)

Chapter Al-Qasas   Chapter 28 Verse 73
It is out of His Mercy that He has made for you the night and the day that you may rest therein and that you may seek of His Bounty – and in order that you may be grateful. (Darussalam, 2000)

Chapter Al-Ankabut   Chapter 29 Verse 44
"**Allah** created the heavens and the earth with truth." Verily, therein is surely, a sign for those who believe. (Darussalam, 2000)

Chapter Al-Ankabut   Chapter 29 Verse 52
Say: "Sufficient is **Allah** for a witness between me and you. He knows what is in the heavens and on earth." And those who believe in Batil (falsehood), and disbelieve in **Allah** and it is they who are the losers. (Darussalam, 2000)

Chapter Al-Ankabut   Chapter 29 Verses 61~63
61. And if you were to ask them: "Who has created the heavens and the earth and subjected the sun and the moon?" They will surely reply: "**Allah**." How then are they deviating?
62. **Allah** enlarges the provision for whom He wills of His slaves, and straitens it for whom (He wills). Verily, **Allah** is the All-Knower of everything.
63. And if you were to ask them: "Who sends down water from the sky, and gives life therewith to the earth after its death"? They will surely reply: "**Allah**" Say: "All the praises and thanks be to **Allah**! "Nay, most of them have no sense. (Darussalam, 2000)

Chapter Ar-Rum	Chapter 30 Verses 19~27

19. He brings out the living from the dead, and brings out the dead from the living. And He revives the earth after its death. And thus, shall you be brought out?

20. And among His signs is this, that He created you from dust, and then behold you are human beings scattered!

21. And among His signs is this, that He created for you wives from among yourselves, that you may find repose in them, and He has put between you affection and mercy. Verily, in that are indeed signs for a people who reflect.

22. And among His signs is the creation of the heavens and the earth, and the difference of your languages and colours. Verily, in that are indeed signs for men of sound knowledge.

23. And among His signs is your sleep by night and by day, and your seeking of His Bounty. Verily, in that are indeed signs for a people who listen.

24. And among His signs is that He shows you the lightning, for fear and for hope, and He sends down water from the sky, and therewith revives the earth after its death. Verily, in that are indeed signs for a people who understand.

25. And among His signs is that the heaven and the earth stand by His Command. Then afterwards when He will call you by a single call, behold, you will come out from the earth.

26. To Him belongs whatever is in the heavens and the earth. All are obedient to Him.

27. And He it is Who originates the creation, then He will repeat it; and this is easier for Him. His is the highest description in the heavens and in the earth. And He is the All-Mighty, the All-Wise. (Darussalam, 2000)

Chapter Ar-Rum	Chapter 30 Verse 46

And among His signs is this, that He sends the winds as glad tidings, giving you a taste of His mercy, and that the ships may sail at His Command, and that you may seek of His Bounty, in order that you may be thankful. (Darussalam, 2000)

Chapter Ar-Rum	Chapter 30 Verse 48

Allah is He Who sends the winds, so that they raise clouds, and spread them along the sky as He wills, and then break them into fragments, until you see rain drops come forth from their midst! Then when He has made them fall on whom of His slaves as He wills, lo, they rejoice! (Darussalam, 2000)

Chapter Ar-Rum   Chapter 30 Verse 50
Look then at the effects of **Allah**'s Mercy, how He revives the earth after its death. Verily, that (**Allah**) shall indeed raise the dead, and He is Able to do all things. (Darussalam, 2000)

Chapter Ar-Rum   Chapter 30 Verse 54
Allah is He Who created you in weakness, then gave you strength after weakness, then after strength gave weakness and grey hair. He creates what He wills. And it is He Who is the All-Knowing, the All-Powerful. (Darussalam, 2000)

Chapter Luqman   Chapter 31 Verse 10
He has created the heavens without any pillars that you see, and has set on the earth firm mountains lest it should shake with you. And He has scattered therein moving creatures of all kinds. And We send down water from the sky, and We cause (plants) of every goodly kind to grow therein. (Darussalam, 2000)

Chapter Luqman   Chapter 31 Verse 16
"O my son (Luqman's son)! If it be equal to the weight of a grain of mustard seed, and though it be in a rock, or in the heavens or in the earth, **Allah** will bring it forth. Verily, **Allah** is Subtle, Well-Aware. (Darussalam, 2000)

Chapter Luqman   Chapter 31 Verse 20
See you not that **Allah** has subjected for you whatsoever is in the heavens and whatsoever is in the earth, and has completed and perfected His Graces upon you, apparent and hidden? Yet of mankind is He who disputes about **Allah** without knowledge or guidance or a book giving light! (Darussalam, 2000)

Chapter Luqman   Chapter 31 Verses 25~29
25. And if you ask them: "Who has created the heavens and the earth", they will certainly say: "**Allah**", say: "All the praises and thanks be to **Allah**!" but most of them know not.
26. To **Allah** belongs whatsoever is in the heavens and the earth. Verily, **Allah**, He is Al-Ghani (Rich, Free of all wants), Worthy of all praise.
27. And if all the trees on the earth were pens and the sea, with seven seas behind it to add to it, yet the words of **Allah** would not be exhausted. Verily, **Allah** is All-Mighty, All-Wise.
28. The creation of you all and the resurrection of you all are only as a single person. Verily, **Allah** is All-Hearer, All-Seer.

29. See you not that **Allah** merges the night into the day, and merges the day into the night, and has subjected the sun and the moon, each running its course for a term appointed; and that **Allah** is All-Aware of what you do. (Darussalam, 2000)

Chapter Luqman   Chapter 31 Verse 34
Verily, **Allah**, with Him is the knowledge of the hour, He sends down the rain, and knows that which is in the wombs. No person knows what He will earn tomorrow, and no person knows in what land He will die. Verily, **Allah** is All-Knower, All-Aware. (Darussalam, 2000)

Chapter Sajdah   Chapter 32 Verses 5~9
5. He manages and regulates affair from the heavens to the earth; then it will go up to Him, in one day, the space whereof is a thousand years of your reckoning.
6. That is He, the All-Knower of the unseen and the seen, the All-Mighty, the Most Merciful.
7. Who made everything He has created good and He began the creation of man from clay.
8. Then He made his offspring from semen of despised water.
9. Then He fashioned him in due proportion, and breathed into him the soul, and He gave you hearing, sight and hearts. Little is the thanks you give! (Darussalam, 2000)

Chapter Al-Ahzab   Chapter 33 Verse 17
Say: "Who is He who can protect you from **Allah** if He intends to harm you, or intends mercy on you? And they will not find, besides **Allah**, for themselves any Wali (protector) or any helper. (Darussalam, 2000)

Chapter Saba   Chapter 34 Verse 2
He knows that which goes into the earth and that which comes forth from it, and that which descends from the heaven and that which ascends to it. And He is the Most Merciful, the Oft-Forgiving. (Darussalam, 2000)

Chapter Saba   Chapter 34 Verse 22
Say: "Call upon those whom you assert besides **Allah**, they possess not even an atom's weight either in the heavens or on the earth, nor have they any share in either, nor there is for Him any supporter from among them. (Darussalam, 2000)

Chapter Fatir   Chapter 35 Verses 1~3

1. All the praises and thanks be to **Allah**, the originator of the heavens and the earth, Who made the angels Messengers with wings, two or three or four. He increases in creation what He wills. Verily, **Allah** is Able to do all things.
2. Whatever of mercy, **Allah** may grant to mankind, none can withhold it; and whatever He may withhold, none can grant it thereafter. And He is the All-Mighty, the All-Wise.
3. O Mankind! Remember the Grace of **Allah** upon you! Is there any Creator other than **Allah** Who provides for you from the sky and the earth? La ilaha illa Huwa (none has the right to be worshipped but He). How then are you turning away? (Darussalam, 2000)

Chapter Fatir   Chapter 35 Verses 9~13

9. And it is **Allah** Who sends the winds, so that they raise up the clouds, and We drive them to a dead land, and revive therewith the earth after its death. As such the Resurrection!
10. Whosoever desires honour, power and glory then to **Allah** belong all honour, power and glory. To Him ascend the goodly words, and the righteous deeds exalt it, but those who plot evils, theirs will be a severe torment. And the plotting of such will perish.
11. And **Allah** did create you from dust, then from Nutfah (semen), then He made you pairs. And no female conceives or gives birth, but with His Knowledge, and no aged man is granted a length of life nor is a part cut off from his life, but is in a Book. Surely, that is easy for **Allah**.
12. And the two seas are not alike: this is palatable, sweet and pleasant to drink, and that is salt and bitter. And from them both you eat fresh tender meat, and derive the ornaments that you wear. And you see the ships cleaving, that you may seek of His Bounty, and that you may give thanks.
13. He merges the night into the day, and He mergers the day into the night. And He has subjected the sun and the moon, each runs its course for a term appointed. Such is **Allah**, your **Lord**, His is the kingdom. And those, whom you invoke or call upon instead of Him, own not even a Qitmir (The thin membrane over the date stone). (Darussalam, 2000)

Chapter Fatir   Chapter 35 Verses 27-28

27. See you not that **Allah** sends down water from the sky, and We produce therewith fruits of various colours, and among the mountains are streaks white and red, or varying colours and very black.
28. And likewise, men and Ad-Dawabb (beasts) and cattle are of various colours. It is only those who have knowledge among His slaves that fear **Allah.** Verily, **Allah** is All-Mighty, Oft-Forgiving. (Darussalam, 2000)

Chapter Fatir   Chapter 35 Verse 41

41. Verily, **Allah** grasps the heavens and the earth lest they should move away from their places, if they were to move away from their places, there is not one that could grasp them after Him. Truly, He is Ever Most-Forbearing, Oft-Forgiving. (Darussalam, 2000)

Chapter Fatir   Chapter 35 Verse 44

Have they not traveled in the land, and seen what was the end of those before them-though they were superior to them in power? **Allah** is not such that anything in the heavens or in the earth escapes Him. Verily, He is All-Knowing, All-Omnipotent. (Darussalam, 2000)

Chapter Ya-sin   Chapter 36 Verses 33~44

33. And a sign for them is the dead land. We give it life, and We bring forth from it grains, so that they eat thereof.
34. And We have made therein gardens of date palms and grapes, and We have caused springs water to gush forth therein.
35. So that they may eat of the fruit there of – and their hands made it not. Will they not then give thanks?
36. Glory to be Him Who has created all the pairs of that which the earth produces, as well as of their own kind, and of that which they know not.
37. And a sign for them is the night. We withdraw there from the day, and behold, they are in darkness.
38. And the sun runs on its fixed course for a term. That is the Decree of the All-Mighty, the All-Knowing.
39. And the moon, We have measured for its mansions till it returns like the old dried curved date stalk.
40. It is not for the sun to overtake the moon, nor does the night outstrip the day. They all float, each in an orbit.
41. And an Ayah (sign) for them is that We bore their offspring in the laden ship.
42. And We have created for them of the like thereunto, on which they ride.
43. And if We will, We shall drown them, and there will be no shout for them, nor will they be saved.
44. Unless it be a mercy from Us, and an enjoyment for a while. (Darussalam, 2000)

Chapter Az-Zumar   Chapter 39 Verses 5-6

5. He has created the heavens and the earth with truth. He makes the night to go in the day and makes the day to go in the night, and He has subjected the

sun and the moon, each running for an appointed term. Verily, He is the All-Mighty, the Oft-Forgiving.
6. He created you from a single person; then made from him his wife. And He has sent down for you of cattle eight pairs. He creates you in the wombs of your mothers, creation after creation in three veils of darkness. Such is **Allah** your **Lord**. His is the kingdom. La ilaha illa Huwa (none has the right to be worshipped but He). How then are you turned away? (Darussalam, 2000)

Chapter Az-Zumar   Chapter 39 Verse 21
See you not that **Allah** sends down water from the sky, and causes it to penetrate the earth, as water springs, and afterward thereby produces crops of different colours, and afterward they wither and you see them turn yellow; then He makes them dry and broken pieces. Verily, in this is a reminder for men of understanding. (Darussalam, 2000)

Chapter Az-Zumar   Chapter 39 Verse 42
It is **Allah** Who takes away the souls at the time of their death, and those that die not during their sleep. He keeps those (souls) for which He has ordained death and sends the rest for a term appointed. Verily, in this are signs for a people who think deeply. (Darussalam, 2000)

Chapter Az-Zumar   Chapter 39 Verse 52
Do they not know that **Allah** enlarges the provision for whom He wills, and straitens it? Verily, in this are signs for the folk who believe! (Darussalam, 2000)

Chapter Ghafir   Chapter 40 Verse 13
It is He Who shows you His Ayat (signs) and sends down provision for you from the sky. And none remembers but those who turn (to **Allah**) in repentance. (Darussalam, 2000)

Chapter Ghafir   Chapter 40 Verse 16
The day when they will come out, nothing of them will be hidden from **Allah**. Whose is the kingdom this day? It is **Allah**'s the one, the Irresistible! (Darussalam, 2000)

Chapter Ghafir   Chapter 40 Verses 61~64
61. **Allah**, it is He Who has made the night for you that you may rest therein and the day for you to see. Truly, **Allah** is full of Bounty to mankind; yet, most of mankind gives no thanks.

62. That is **Allah**, your **Lord**; the Creator of all things, La ilaha illa Huwa (none has the right to be worshipped but He). How then are you turning away?
63. Thus were turned away those who used to deny the Ayat (verses) of Allah.
64. **Allah**, it is He Who has made for you the earth as a dwelling place and sky as a canopy, and has given you shape and made your shapes good and has provided you with good things. That is **Allah**, your **Lord**, so blessed be **Allah**, the **Lord** of the 'Alamin (worlds). (Darussalam, 2000)

Chapter Ghafir   Chapter 40 Verses 79-80
79. **Allah**, it is He Who has made cattle for you, that you may ride on some of them, and of some you eat.
80. And you have benefits from them, and that you may reach by their means a desire that is in your breasts, and on them and on ships you are carried. (Darussalam, 2000)

Chapter Fussilat   Chapter 41 Verses 9~12
9. Say, "Do you verily disbelieve in Him Who created the earth in two Days? And you set up rivals with Him? That is the **Lord** of the 'Alamin (worlds).
10. He place therein firm mountains from above it, and He blessed it, and measured therein its sustenance in four days equal for all those who ask.
11. Then He rose over (Istawa) towards the heaven when it was smoke, and said to it and to the earth: "Come both of you willingly or unwillingly." They both said: "We come willingly."
12. Then He completed and finished from their creation seven heavens in two Days and He made in each heaven its affair. And We adorned the nearest heaven with lamps to be an adornment as well as to guard. Such is the decree of Him, the All-Mighty, the All-Knower. (Darussalam, 2000)

Chapter Fussilat   Chapter 41 Verse 39
And among His signs, that you see the earth barren, but when We send down water to it, it is stirred to life and growth. Verily, He Who gives it life, surely is Able to give life to the death. Indeed, He is Able to do all things. (Darussalam, 2000)

Chapter Fussilat   Chapter 41 Verse 47
To Him is referred the knowledge of the Hour. No fruit comes out of its sheath, nor does a female conceive nor brings forth, except by His knowledge. And on the Day when He will call unto them: "Where are my partners?" They will say: "We inform you that none of us bear witness to it!" (Darussalam, 2000)

Chapter Ash-Shura — Chapter 42 Verses 11-12

11. The Creator of the heavens and the earth. He has made for you mates from yourselves, and for the cattle mates. By this means He creates you. There is nothing like Him, and He is the All-**H**earer, the All-Seer.
12. To Him belong the keys of the heavens and the earth. He enlarges provision for whom He wills, and straitens. Verily, He is the All-Knower of everything. (Darussalam, 2000)

Chapter Ash-Shura — Chapter 42 Verses 27~29

27. And if **Allah** were to enlarge the provision for His slaves, they would surely rebel in the earth, but He sends down by measure as He wills. Verily He is, in respect of His slaves, the Well-Aware, the All-Seer.
28. And He it is Who sends down the rain after they have despaired, and spreads His mercy. And He is the Wali (Protector), Worthy of all praise.
29. And among His Ayat (signs) is the creation of the heavens and the earth, and whatever moving creatures He has dispersed in then both. And He is All-Potent over their assembling whenever He wills. (Darussalam, 2000)

Chapter Ash-Shura — Chapter 42 Verses 32~34

32. And among His signs are the ships in the sea like mountains.
33. If He wills, He causes the wind to cease, then they would become motionless on the back. Verily, in this are signs for everyone patient and grateful.
34. Or He may destroy them because of that which their (people) have earned. And He pardons much. (Darussalam, 2000)

Chapter Ash-Shura — Chapter 42 Verses 49-50

49. To **Allah** belongs the kingdom of the heavens and the earth. He creates what He wills. He bestows female upon whom He wills, and bestows male upon whom He wills.
50. Or He bestows both males and females, and He renders barren whom He wills. Verily, He is the All-Knower and is Able to do all things. (Darussalam, 2000)

Chapter Ash-Shura — Chapter 42 Verse 53

The path of **Allah** to whom belongs all that is in the heavens and all that is in the earth. Verily, all matters at the end go to **Allah**. (Darussalam, 2000)

Chapter Az-Zukhruf — Chapter 43 Verses 9~14

9. And indeed if you ask them: "Who has created the heavens and the earth?" They will surely say: "The All-Mighty, the All-Knower created them."

10. Who has made for you the earth like a bed, and has made for you roads therein, in order that you may find your way.
11. And Who sends down water from the sky in due measure. Then We revive a dead land therewith, and even so you will be brought forth.
12. And Who has created all the pairs and has appointed for you ship and cattle on which you ride.
13. In order that you may mount on their backs, and then may remember the Favour of your **Lord** when you mount thereon, and say: "Glory to Him Who has subjected this to us, and we could never have it.
14. And verily, to our **Lord** we indeed are to return!" (Darussalam, 2000)

Chapter Al-Jathiyah   Chapter 45 Verses 3~5
3. Verily, in the heavens and the earth are signs for the believers.
4. And in your creation, and what He scattered of moving creatures are signs for people who have Faith with certainty.
5. And in the alternation of night and day, and the provision that **Allah** sends down from the sky, and revives therewith the earth after its, death, and in the turning about of the winds, are signs for a people who understand. (Darussalam, 2000)

Chapter Al-Jathiyah   Chapter 45 Verses 12-13
12. **Allah**, it is He Who has subjected to you the sea, that ships may sail through it by His command, and that you may seek of His Bounty, and that you may be thankful.
13. And has subjected to you all that is in the heavens and all that is in the earth, it is all as a favour and kindness from Him. Verily, in it are signs for a people who think deeply. (Darussalam, 2000)

Chapter Al-Jathiyah   Chapter 45 Verse 22
And **Allah** has created the heavens and the earth with truth, in order that each person may be recompensed what he has earned, and they will not be wronged. (Darussalam, 2000)

Chapter Al-Jathiyah   Chapter 45 Verses 26-27
26. Say: "**Allah** gives you life, then causes you to die, then He will assemble you on the Day of Resurrection about which there is no doubt. But most of mankind know not."
27. And to **Allah** belongs the kingdom of the heavens and the earth. And on the Day that the hour will be established-on that Day the followers of falsehood shall lose. (Darussalam, 2000)

Chapter Al-Ahqaf   Chapter 46 Verse 3
We created not the heavens and the earth and all that is between them except with truth, and for an appointed term. But those who disbelieve, turn away from that whereof they are warned. (Darussalam, 2000)

Chapter Al-Ahqaf   Chapter 46 Verse 33
Do they not see that **Allah**, Who created the heavens and the earth, and was not wearied by their creation, is Able to give life to the dead? Yes, He surely is Able to do all things. (Darussalam, 2000)

Chapter Qaf   Chapter 50 Verses 7~11
7. And the earth! We have spread it out, and set thereon mountains standing firm, and have produced therein every kind of lovely growth.
8. An insight and a Reminder for every slave who turns to **Allah** in repentance.
9. And We send down blessed water from the sky, then We produce therewith gardens and grain that are reaped.
10. And tall date palms, with ranged clusters.
11. A provision for slaves. And We give life there with to a dead land. Thus, will be the resurrection. (Darussalam, 2000)

Chapter Qaf   Chapter 50 Verse 16
And indeed, We have created man, and We know what his own self whispers to him. And We are nearer to him than his jugular vein. (Darussalam, 2000)

Chapter Qaf   Chapter 50 Verses 38-39
38. And indeed We created the heavens and the earth and all between them in six Days and nothing of fatigue touched us.
39. So bear with patience all that they say, and glorify the Praises of your **Lord**, before the rising of the sun and before setting. (Darussalam, 2000)

Chapter Qaf   Chapter 50 Verse 43
Verily, We it is Who give life and cause death; and to Us is the final return. (Darussalam, 2000)

Chapter Adh-Dhariyat   Chapter 51 Verses 47~51
47. With hands did We construct the heaven. Verily, We are Able to extend the vastness of space thereof.
48. And We have spread out the earth; how excellent Spreader are We!
49. And of everything We have created pairs, that you may remember.
50. So, flee to **Allah**. Verily, I am a plain Warner to you from Him.

51. And set not up any other Ilah (god) along with **Allah**. Verily, I am plain Warner to you from Him. (Darussalam, 2000)

Chapter An-Najm Chapter 53 Verse 31

And to **Allah** belongs all that is in the heavens and all that is in the earth, that He may requite those who do evil with that which they have done, and reward those who do good, with what is best. (Darussalam, 2000)

Chapter An-Najm Chapter 53 Verses 42~48

42. And that to your **Lord** is the End.
43. And that it is He Who makes laugh, and makes weep.
44. And that it is He Who causes death and gives life.
45. And that He creates the pairs, male and female.
46. From Nutfah (semen) when it is emitted.
47. And that upon Him is another bringing forth.
48. And that it is He Who gives much or a little. (Darussalam, 2000)

Chapter Ar-Rahman Chapter 55 Verses 1~8

1. The Most Gracious!
2. He has taught the Quran.
3. He created man.
4. He taught him eloquent speech.
5. The sun and the moon run on their fixed courses calculated with measured out stages for each.
6. And the herbs (or stars) and the trees both prostrate themselves.
7. And the heaven He has raised high, and He has set up the Balance.
8. In order that you may not transgress balance. (Darussalam, 2000)

Chapter Al-Waqi`ah Chapter 56 Verses 57~72

57. We created you, then why do you believe not?
58. Then tell me (about) the (human) semen that you emit.
59. Is it you who create it, or are We the Creator?
60. We have decreed death to you all, and We are not outstripped,
61. To transfigure you and create you in that you know not.
62. And indeed, you have already known the first form of creation, why then do you not remember?
63. Tell Me about the seed that you sow in the ground.
64. Is it you that make it grow, or are We the Grower?
65. Were it Our Will, We could crumble it to dry pieces, and you would be regretful.
66. (Saying): "We are indeed Mughramun (ruined).

67. "Nay, but we are deprived!"
68. Then tell me about the water that you drink.
69. Is it you who cause it from the rain clouds to come down, or are We the Causer of it to come down?
70. If We willed, We verily, could make it salt; why then do you not give thanks?
71. Then tell Me about the fire which you kindle.
72. Is it you who made the tree thereof to grow, or are We the Grower? (Darussalam, 2000)

Chapter Al-Hadid   Chapter 57 Verses 4~6
4. He it is Who created the heavens and the earth in six Days and then rose over (Istawa) the Throne. He knows what goes into the earth and what comes forth from it, and what descends from the heaven and what ascends thereto. And He is with you wheresoever you may be. And **Allah** is the All-Seer of what you do.
5. His is the kingdom of the heavens and the earth. And to **Allah** return all the matters.
6. He merges night into the day, and merges day into night, and He has full knowledge of whatsoever is in the breasts. (Darussalam, 2000)

Chapter Al-Hadid   Chapter 57 Verse 9
It is He Who sends down manifest Ayat (verses) to His slave that He may bring you out from darkness into light. And verily, **Allah** is to you full of kindness, Most Merciful. (Darussalam, 2000)

Chapter Al-Hadid   Chapter 57 Verse 17
Know that **Allah** gives life to the earth after its death! Indeed, We have made clear the Ayat (signs) to you, if you but understand. (Darussalam, 2000)

Chapter Al-Hadid   Chapter 57 Verse 25
Indeed, We have sent our Messengers with clear proofs, and revealed with them the Scripture and the Balance that mankind may keep up justice. And We brought forth iron wherein is mighty power, as well as many benefits for mankind, that **Allah** may test who it is that will help Him and His Messengers in the unseen. Verily, **Allah** is All-Strong, All-Mighty. (Darussalam, 2000)

Chapter Al-Hadid   Chapter 57 Verse 29
So that the people of the Scripture may know that they have no power whatsoever over the Grace of **Allah**, and that Grace is in His hand to bestow

it on whomsoever He wills. And **Allah** is the Owner of Great Bounty. (Darussalam, 2000)

Chapter Al-Mujadilah   Chapter 58 Verse 7
Have you not seen that **Allah** knows whatsoever is in the heavens and whatsoever is on the earth? There is no Najwa (secret counsel) of three but He is their fourth, - nor of the five but He is their sixth, - nor of less than that or more but He is with them wheresoever they may be. And afterwards on the Day of Resurrection He will inform them of what they did. Verily, **Allah** is the All-Knower of everything. (Darussalam, 2000)

Chapter At-Taghabun   Chapter 64 Verses 2-3
2. He it is Who created you, then some of you are disbelievers and some of you are believers. And **Allah** is All-Seer of what you do.
3. He has created the heavens and the earth with truth, and He shaped you and made good your shapes, and to Him is the final Return. (Darussalam, 2000)

Chapter Al-Talaq   Chapter 65 Verse 12
It is **Allah** Who has created seven heavens and of the earth the like thereof. His command descends between them, that you may know that **Allah** has power over all things, and that **Allah** surrounds all things in knowledge. (Darussalam, 2000)

Chapter Al-Mulk   Chapter 67 Verses 1~4
1. Blessed be He in Whose hands is the dominion; and He is Able to do all things.
2. Who has created death and life that He may test which of you is best indeed. And He is the All-Mighty, the Oft-Forgiving;
3. Who has created the seven heavens one above another; you can see no fault in the creation of the Most Gracious. Then look again; "Can you see any rifts?"
4. Then look again and yet again, your sight will return to you in a state of humiliation and worn out. (Darussalam, 2000)

Chapter Al-Mulk   Chapter 67 Verse 19
Do they not see the birds above them, spreading out their wings and folding them in? None upholds them except the Most Gracious. Verily, He is the All-Seer of everything. (Darussalam, 2000)

Chapter Al-Mulk   Chapter 67 Verses 23-24

23. Say it is He Who has created you, and endowed you with hearing and seeing, and hearts. Little thanks you give.
24. Say: "It is He Who has created you on the earth, and to Him shall you be gathered." (Darussalam, 2000)

Chapter Nuh   Chapter 71 Verses 15~20

15. See you not how **Allah** has created the seven heavens one above another?
16. And has made the moon a light therein, and the sun a lamp?
17. And **Allah** has brought you forth from the earth?
18. Afterwards He will return you into it, and bring you forth?
19. And **Allah** has made for you the earth a wide expanse (spread).
20. That you may go about therein in broad roads. (Darussalam, 2000)

Chapter Al-A'la   Chapter 87 Verses 1~7

1. Glorify the name of you **Lord**, the Most High.
2. Who has created, and then proportioned it.
3. And Who has measured; and then guided.
4. And Who brings out the pasturage.
5. And then makes it dark stubble.
6. We shall make you to recite, so you shall not forget.
7. Except what **Allah** may will. He knows what is apparent and what is hidden. (Darussalam, 2000)

Chapter Al-'Alaq   Chapter 96 Verses 1~5

1. Read! In the name of your **Lord** Who has created.
2. He has created man from a clot.
3. Read! And your **Lord** is the Most Generous.
4. Who has taught by the pen.
5. He has taught man that which He knew not. (Darussalam, 2000)

Section III

Names of Allah mentioned in the Quran

Names of Allah mentioned in the Quran- Nine Subsections

SUBSECTION 1

- *Ar-Rahman*   The Most Gracious
- *Ar-Rahim*   The Most Merciful
- *Ar-Rauf*   The Most Kind
- *Al-Barr*   The Most Gracious Benefactor
- *Ar-Kareem*   The Most Generous
- *Al-Wahhab*   The Bestower
- *Ar-Razzaq*   The Ever Providing

SUBSECTION 2

- *Al-Afuww*   The Pardoner
- *Al-Ghafur*   The All-Forgiving
- *Al-Ghaffar*   The Ever Forgiving
- *At-Tawwab*   The Accepter of Repentance
- *Al-Latif*   The Subtle kind
- *Al-Wudud*   The Most Loving
- *Al-Halim*   The Most Forbearing
- *Ash-Shakur*   Most Ready to Appreciate
- *Al-Mujib*   The Responsive

SUBSECTION 3

- *Al-Malik*   The King
- *Maalik-ul-Mulk*   The Owner of All Sovereignty
- *Al-Hameed*   The All-Praiseworthy
- *Al-Majeed*   The All-Glorious
- *Al-Kabir*   The Most Great
- *Al-Azim*   The Most Great
- *Al-Muqit*   The Nourisher
- *Al-Mutaali*   The Most Exalted
- *Al-Muhyi*   The Giver of Life
- *Al-Waaris*   The Inheritor of All
- *Dhu-l-Jalali Wa-l-Ikram*   The Lord of Majesty & Honor

SUBSECTION 4

- *Al-Wahid* — The One
- *Al-Ahad* — The Sole One
- *Al-Samaad* — The Self-Sufficient
- *Al-Haqq* — The Truth
- *Al-Qahhar* — The Irresistible
- *Al-Hayy* — The Ever Living
- *Al-Qayyum* — The Self Subsisting, The Self Existing
- *Al-Ghani* — The All Rich
- *An Nur* — The Light

SUBSECTION 5

- *Al-Alim* — The All-Knowing
- *Al-Khabir* — The All-Aware
- *Al-Hakim* — The Most Wise
- *Al-Basir* — The All-Seeing
- *As-Sami* — The All-Hearing

SUBSECTION 6

- *Al-Khaliq* — The Creator
- *Al-Bari* — The Maker
- *Al-Musawwir* — The Bestower of Forms
- *Al-Badi* — The Originator

SUBSECTION 7

- *Al-Awwal* — The First One
- *Al-Akhir* — The Last
- *Al-Zahir* — The Manifest
- *Al-Batin* — The Hidden

SUBSECTION 8

- *Al-Quddus* — *The Most Holy*
- *Al-Salam* — *The Source of Peace*
- *Al-Mu'min* — *The Giver of Security*
- *Al-Muhaymin* — *The Protector*
- *Al-Hafiz* — *The Guardian*
- *Al-Fattah* — *The Opener*
- *Al-Wasi* — *The All-Sufficient*
- *Al-Hadi* — *The One Who Guides*
- *Al-Waliyy* — *The Protecting Friend*

SUBSECTION 9

- *Al-'Ala* — *The Most High*
- *Al-Aziz* — *The All-Mighty*
- *Al-Qawi* — *The Most Strong*
- *Al-Qadir* — *The All-Capable*
- *Al-Matin* — *The Firm,* The Most Strong
- *Ar-Raqib* — *The Watchful*
- *Al-Hasib* — *The Reckoner*
- *Al-Jaami* — *The Gatherer*
- *Ash-Shahid* — *The Witness*
- *Al-Wakil* — The Trustee, The Best Disposer of affairs
- *Al-Hakam* — *The Judge*
- *Al-Jabbar* — *The Compeller*
- *Al-Mutakabir* — *The Supremely Great*
- *Al-Muqtadir* — The Powerful Determiner

Subsection 1

SUBSECTION 1

- *Ar-Rahman*   The Most Gracious
- *Ar-Rahim*   The Most Merciful
- *Ar-Rauf*   The Most Kind
- *Al-Barr*   The Most Gracious Benefactor
- *Ar-Kareem*   The Most Generous
- *Al-Wahhab*   The Bestower
- *Ar-Razzaq*   The Ever Providing

Ar-Rahman   The Most Gracious

<u>Chapter Al-Fatihah</u>   <u>Chapter 1 Verses 1~3</u>
1. In the Name of **Allah**, the **Most Gracious**, the **Most Merciful**.
2. All the praises and thanks be to **Allah**, the **Lord** of the Alamin (worlds).
3. The **Most Gracious**, the Most Merciful. (Darussalam, 1999)

<u>Chapter Al-Baqarah</u>   <u>Chapter 2 Verse 163</u>
And your Ilah (God) is One Ilah (God), La ilaha illa Huwa (none has the right to be worshipped but He), the **Most Gracious**, the Most Merciful. (Darussalam, 1999)

<u>Chapter Ar-Ra`d</u>   <u>Chapter 13 Verse 30</u>
Thus, have We sent you to a community before whom other communities have passed away, in order that you might recite unto them what We have revealed to you, while they disbelieve in the **Most Gracious.** Say: "He is my **Lord**! La ilaha illa Huwa (none has the right to be worshipped but He)! In Him is my trust, and to Him will be my return with repentance." (Darussalam, 2000)

<u>Chapter Al-Isra   Ayat Sajada   Chapter 17 Verses 110-111</u>
110. Say: Invoke **Allah** or invoke the **Most Gracious**, by whatever name you invoke Him, for to Him belong the Best Names. And offer your Salat (prayer) neither aloud nor in a low voice, but follow a way between.
111. And say: "All the praises and thanks be to **Allah**, Who has not begotten a son, and Who has no partner in Dominion, nor He is low to have a Wali (Protector). And magnify Him with all magnificence." (Darussalam, 2000)

<u>Chapter Maryam</u>   <u>Chapter 19 Verses 16~26</u>
16. And mention in the Book Maryam, when she withdrew in seclusion from her family to a place facing east.
17. She placed a screen from them; then We sent to her Our Ruh (angel Jibrael), and he appeared before her in the form of a man in all respects.
18. She said: "Verily, I seek refuge with the **Most Gracious** from you if you do fear **Allah**."
19. Said: "I am only a messenger from your **Lord**, (to announce) to you the gift of a righteous son"
20. She said: "How can I have a son, when no man has touched me, nor am I unchaste?"

21. He said: "So, your **Lord** said: 'That is easy for Me: And to appoint him as a sign to mankind and a mercy from Us, and it is a matter (already) decreed."
22. So she conceived him, and she withdrew with him to a far place.
23. And the pains of childbirth drove her to the trunk of a date-palm. She said: "Would that I had died before this, and had been forgotten and out of sight!"
24. Then cried unto her from below her, saying: "Grieve not! your **Lord** has provided a water stream under you.
25. "And shake the trunk of date-palm towards you, it will let fall fresh ripe-dates upon you."
26. "So, eat and drink and be glad. And if you see any human being, say: Verily I have vowed a fast unto **Most Gracious** so I shall not speak to any human being this day." (Darussalam, 2000)

Chapter Maryam   Chapter 19 Verses 44~46
44. "O my father! Worship not Shaitan (Satan), verily, Shaitan (Satan) has been a rebel against the **Most Gracious**."
45. "O my father! Verily, I fear lest a torment from the **Most Gracious** should overtake you, so that you become a companion of Shaitan (Satan)."
46. He said: "Do you reject my gods, O Ibrahim? If you stop not, I will indeed stone you. So get away from me safely (before I punish you)." (Darussalam, 2000)

Chapter Maryam   Ayat Sajdah   Chapter 19 Verses 58~61
58. Those were they to whom **Allah** bestowed His Grace from among the Prophets, of the offspring of Adam, and of those whom We carried with Nuh, and of the offspring of Ibrahim and Israel, and from among those whom We guided and chose. When the verses of the **Most Gracious** were recited to them they fell down prostrate and weeping.
59. Then, there has succeeded them a posterity who have given up As-Salat (prayer) and have followed lusts. So they will be thrown in Hell.
60. Except those who repent and believe, and work righteousness. Such will enter Paradise and they will not be wronged in aught.
61. 'Adn paradise, which the **Most Gracious** has promised to His slaves in the Unseen. Verily, His promised must come to pass. (Darussalam, 2000)

Chapter Maryam   Chapter 19 Verses 66~69
66. And man says: "When I am dead, shall I then be raised up alive?"
67. Does not man remember that We created him before, while he was nothing?

68. So by your **Lord**, surely, We shall gather them together, and the Shayatin (Satan), then We shall bring them round Hell on their knees.
69. Then indeed we shall drag out from every sect all those who were worst in obstinate rebellion against the **Most Gracious**. (Darussalam, 2000)

Chapter Maryam Chapter 19 Verses 74-75

74. And how many a generation have We destroyed before them, who were better in wealth, goods and outward appearance?
75. Say: whoever is in error, the **Most Gracious** will extend to him until, when they see that which they were promised, either the torment or the Hour, they will come to know who is worst in position, and who is weaker in forces. (Darussalam, 2000)

Chapter Maryam Chapter19 Verses 77~79

77. Have you seen him who disbelieved in Our Ayat (Verses) and said: "I shall certainly be given wealth and children"
78. Has he known the Unseen or has he taken a covenant from the **Most Gracious**?
79. Nay! We shall record what he says, and We shall increase his torment. (Darussalam, 2000)

Chapter Maryam Chapter 19 Verses 85~93

85. The day we shall gather the Muttaqun (pious) to the **Most Gracious** like a delegation.
86. And We shall drive the Mujrimum (criminals) to Hell, in a thirsty state,
87. None shall have the power of intercession, but such a one as has received permission from the **Most Gracious.**
88. And they say: The **Most Gracious** has begotten a son.
89. Indeed you have brought forth a terrible evil thing.
90. Whereby the heavens are almost torn, and the earth is split asunder, and the mountains fall in ruins.
91. That they ascribe a son to the **Most Gracious**.
92. But it is not suitable for the **Most Gracious** that He should beget a son.
93. There is none in the heavens and the earth but comes to the **Most Gracious** as a slave. (Darussalam, 2000)

Chapter Maryam Chapter 19 Verse 96

Verily, those who believe and work deeds of righteousness, the **Most Gracious** will bestow love for them. (Darussalam, 2000)

Chapter Ta-Ha   Chapter 20 Verses 1~5
1. Ta-Ha
2. We have not sent down the Quran unto you to cause you distress,
3. But only as a Reminder to those who fear.
4. A Revelation from Him Who has created the earth and high heavens.
5. The **Most Gracious** rose over (Istawa) the Throne. (Darussalam, 2000)

Chapter Ta-Ha   Chapter 20 Verses 90-91
90. And Harun indeed had said to them beforehand: "O my people! You are being tried in this, and verily, your **Lord** is the **Most Gracious**, so follow me and obey my order."
91. They said: "We will not stop worshipping it, until Musa returns to us." (Darussalam, 2000)

Chapter Ta-Ha   Chapter 20 Verses 108-109
108. On that Day mankind will follow strictly **Allah's** caller, no crookedness will they show him. And all voice will be humbled for the **Most Gracious**, and nothing shall you hear but the low voice of their footsteps.
109. On that day no intercession shall avail, except the one for whom the **Most Gracious** has given permission and whose word is acceptable to Him. (Darussalam, 2000)

Chapter Al-Anbiya   Chapter 21 Verse 36
And when those who disbelieved see you, they take you not except for mockery: "Is this the one who talks about your gods?" While they disbelieve at the mention of the **Most Gracious**. (Darussalam, 2000)

Chapter Al-Anbiya   Chapter 21 Verse 42
Say: "Who can guard and protect you in the night or in the day from the **Most Gracious**?" Nay, but they turn away from the remembrance of their **Lord**. (Darussalam, 2000)

Chapter Al-Anbiya   Chapter 21 Verse 112
He said: "My **Lord**! Judge You in truth! Our **Lord** is the **Most Gracious**, Whose help is to be sought against that which you attribute!" (Darussalam, 2000)

Chapter Al-Furqan   Chapter 25 Verse 26
The sovereignty on that Day will be the true (sovereignty) belonging to the **Most Gracious**, and it will be a hard day for the disbelievers. (Darussalam, 2000)

| Chapter Al-Furqan | Ayat Sajada | Chapter 25 Verses 59~63 |

59. Who created the heavens and the earth and all that is between them in six days. Then He rose over (Istawa) the Throne. The **Most Gracious**! Ask Him, as He is Khabir (the All-Knower).
60. And when it is said to them: "Prostrate yourselves to the **Most Gracious**!" They say: "And what is the **Most Gracious**? Shall we fall down in prostration to that which you command us? And it increases in them only aversion.
61. Blessed be He Who has placed in the heaven big stars, and has placed therein a great lamp, and a moon giving light.
62. And He it is Who has put the night and the day in succession, for such who desires to remember or desires to show his gratitude.
63. And the slaves of the **Most Gracious** are those who walk on the earth in humility and sedateness, and when the foolish address them they reply back with mild words of gentleness. (Darussalam, 2000)

Chapter Ash-Shu`ara   Chapter 26 Verse 5

And never comes there to them a Reminder as recent revelations from the **Most Gracious**, but they turn away therefrom. (Darussalam, 2000)

Chapter An-Naml   Chapter 27 Verse 30

"Verily, it is from Sulaiman and verily it (reads): In the Name of **Allah**, the **Most Gracious**, the Most Merciful. (Darussalam, 2000)

Chapter Ya-sin   Chapter 36 Verse 11

You can only warn him who follows the Reminder, and fears the **Most Gracious** unseen. Bear you to such one the glad tidings of forgiveness, and a generous reward. (Darussalam, 2000)

Chapter Ya-sin   Chapter 36 Verses 15~17

15. They said: "You are only human beings like ourselves and the **Most Gracious** has revealed nothing. You are only telling lies."
16. The Messengers said:" Our **Lord** knows that we have been sent as Messengers to you.
17. "And our duty is only to convey plainly." (Darussalam, 2000)

Chapter Ya-sin   Chapter 36 Verse 23

"Shall I take besides Him alihah (gods)? If the **Most Gracious** intends me any harm, their intercession will be of no use for me whatsoever, nor can they save me. (Darussalam, 2000)

Chapter Ya-sin   Chapter 36 Verse 52
They will say: "Woe to us! Who has raised us up from our place of sleep"? "This is what the **Most Gracious** had promised, and Messengers spoke truth!" (Darussalam, 2000)

Chapter Fussilat   Chapter 41 Verse 2
A revelation from the **Most Gracious**, the Most Merciful. (Darussalam, 2000)

Chapter Az-Zukhruf   Chapter 43 Verses 17~20
17. And if one of them is informed of the news of that which he sets forth as a parable to the **Most Gracious**, his face becomes dark, and he is filled with grief!
18. A creature who is brought up in adornments and who in dispute cannot make herself clear?
19. And they make the angels who themselves are slaves of the **Most Gracious** females. Did they witness their creation? Their testimony will be recorded, and they will be questioned!
20. And they said: "If it had been the Will of the **Most Gracious**, we should not have worshipped them." They have no knowledge whatsoever of that, they do nothing but lie! (Darussalam, 2000)

Chapter Az-Zukhruf   Chapter 43 Verse 33~36
33. And were it not that mankind would have become one community, We would have provided for those who disbelieve in the **Most Gracious**, silver roofs for their houses, and elevators whereby they ascend,
34. And for their houses, doors (of silver), and thrones (of silver) on which they could recline,
35. And adornments of gold. Yet all this would have been nothing but an enjoyment of this world. And the Hereafter with your **Lord** is only for the Muttaqun (pious).
36. And whosoever turns away blindly from the remembrance of the **Most Gracious**, We appoint for him Shaitan (Satan) to be a Qarin (a companion) to him. (Darussalam, 2000)

Chapter Az-Zukhruf   Chapter 43 Verse 45
And ask those of our Messengers whom we sent before you: "Did we ever appoint alihah (gods) to be worshipped besides the **Most Gracious**?" (Darussalam, 2000)

Chapter Az-Zukhruf | Chapter 43 Verses 81-82
81. Say: "If the **Most Gracious** had a son, then I am the first of worshippers."
82. Glorified be the **Lord** of the heavens and the earth, the **Lord** of the Throne! Exalted be He from all that they ascribe. (Darussalam, 2000)

Chapter Qaf | Chapter 50 Verses 33-34
33. "Who feared the **Most Gracious** in the Ghaib (Unseen) and brought a heart turned in repentance.
34. "Enter You therein in peace and security- this is the Day of eternal life." (Darussalam, 2000)

Chapter Ar-Rahman | Chapter 55 Verse 1
The **Most Gracious**! (Darussalam, 2000)

Chapter Al-Hashr | Chapter 59 Verse 22
He is **Allah**, besides whom La ilaha illa Huwa (none has the right to be worshipped but He), the All-Knower of the unseen and the seen. He is the **Most Gracious**, the Most Merciful. (Darussalam, 2000)

Chapter Al-Mulk | Chapter 67 Verse 3
Who has created the seven heaven one above another: you can see no fault in the creation of the **Most Gracious**. Then look again: "Can you see any rifts? (Darussalam, 2000)

Chapter Al-Mulk | Chapter 67 Verses 19-20
19. Do they not see the birds above them, spreading out their wings and folding them in? None upholds them except the **Most Gracious**. Verily, He is All Seer of everything.
20. Who is he besides the **Most Gracious** that can be an army to you to help you? The disbelievers are in nothing but delusion. (Darussalam, 2000)

Chapter Al-Mulk | Chapter 67 Verse 29
Say: "He is the **Most Gracious**, in Him we believe, and in Him we put our trust. So, you will come to know who it is that is in manifest error." (Darussalam, 2000)

Chapter An-Naba | Chapter 78 Verses 37-38
37. The **Lord** of the heavens and the earth, and whatsoever is in between them, the **Most Gracious**, with whom they cannot dare to speak.

38. The Day that Ar-Ruh and the angels will stand forth in rows, they will not speak except him whom the **Most Gracious** allows, and they will speak what is right. (Darussalam, 2000)

Ar-Rahim   The Most Merciful

Chapter Al-Fatihah   Chapter 1 Verses 1~3
1. In the Name of **Allah**, the Most Gracious, the **Most Merciful**.
2. All the praises and thanks be to **Allah**, the **Lord** of the `Alamin (worlds).
3. The Most Gracious, the **Most Merciful**. (Darussalam, 1999)

Chapter Al-Baqarah   Chapter 2 Verses 35~37
35. And We said: "O Adam! Dwell you and your wife in the Paradise and eat both of you freely with pleasure and delight, of things therein as wherever you will, but come not near this tree or you both will be of the Zalimun (wrong-doers)."
36. Then the Shaitan (Satan) made them slip therefrom, and got them out from that in which they were. We said: "Get you down, all, with enmity between yourselves. On earth will be a dwelling place for you and an enjoyment for a time."
37. Then Adam received from his **Lord** Words. And his **Lord** pardoned him. Verily, He is the One who forgives, the **Most Merciful**. (Darussalam, 1999)

Chapter Al-Baqarah   Chapter 2 Verse 54
And when Musa said to his people: "O my people! Verily, you have wronged yourselves by worshipping the calf. So, turn in repentance to your Creator and kill yourselves, that will be better for you with your Creator." Then He accepted your repentance. Truly, He is the One Who accepts repentance, the **Most Merciful**. (Darussalam, 1999)

Chapter Al-Baqarah   Chapter 2 Verses 63- 64
63. And when We took your covenant and We raised above you the Mount: "Hold fast to that which We have given you, and remember that which is therein so that you may become Al-Muttaqun (the pious)."
64. Then after that you turned away. Had it not been for the **Grace and Mercy of Allah** upon you, indeed you would have been among the losers. (Darussalam, 1999)

Chapter Al-Baqarah   Chapter 2 Verse 128

"Our **Lord**! And make us submissive unto You and of our offspring a nation submissive unto You, and show us our Manasik (all the ceremonies of pilgrimage-Hajj and Umrah), and accept our repentance. Truly, You are the One Who accepts repentance, the **Most Merciful**. (Darussalam, 1999)

Chapter Al-Baqarah   Chapter 2 Verse 143

Thus, we have made you, a just nation, that you be witnesses over mankind and the Messenger be a witness over you. And we made the Qiblah (prayer direction) which you used to face, only to test those who followed the Messenger from those who would turn on their heels. Indeed, it was great except for those whom **Allah** guided. And **Allah** would never make your faith to be lost. Truly, **Allah** is Full of kindness, the **Most Merciful** towards mankind. (Darussalam, 1999)

Chapter Al-Baqarah   Chapter 2 Verse 163

And your Ilah (God) is One Ilah (God), La ilaha illa Huwa (none has the right to be worshipped but He), the Most Gracious, the **Most Merciful**. (Darussalam, 1999)

Chapter Al-Baqarah   Chapter 2 Verse 173

He has forbidden you only the Maitah (dead animals), and blood, and the flesh of swine, and that which is slaughtered as a sacrifice for others than **Allah**. But if one is forced by necessity without willful disobedience nor transgressing due limits, then there is no sin on him. Truly **Allah** is Oft-Forgiving, **Most Merciful**. (Darussalam, 1999)

Chapter Al-Baqarah   Chapter 2 Verse 182

But he who fears from a testator some unjust act or wrong-doing, and thereupon he makes peace between the parties concerned, there shall be no sin on him. Certainly, **Allah** is Oft-Forgiving, **Most Merciful**. (Darussalam, 1999)

Chapter Al-Baqarah   Chapter 2 Verses 191-192

191. And kill them wherever you find them, and turn them out from where they have turned you out. And Al-Fitnah is worse than killing. And fight not with them at Al-Masjid Al-Haram, unless they fight you there. But if they attack you, then kill them. Such is the recompense of the disbelievers.
192. But if they cease, then **Allah** is **Oft-Forgiving**, Most Merciful. (Darussalam, 1999)

Chapter Al-Baqarah Chapter 2 Verses 198-199

198. There is no sin on you if you seek the Bounty of your **Lord**. Then when you leave Arafat, remember **Allah** at the (Muzdalifah). And remember Him as He has guided you, and verily, you were, before, of those who were astray.
199. Then depart from the place whence all the people depart and ask **Allah** for His forgiveness. Truly, **Allah** is **Oft-Forgiving**, Most Merciful. (Darussalam, 1999)

Chapter Al-Baqarah Chapter 2 Verse 218

Verily, those who have believed, and those who have emigrated and have striven hard in the way of **Allah**, all these hope for **Allah's Mercy**, and **Allah** is Oft-Forgiving, **Most Merciful**. (Darussalam, 1999)

Chapter Al-Baqarah Chapter 2 Verses 225-226

225. **Allah** will not call you to account for that which is unintentional in your oaths, but He will call you to account for that which your hearts have earned, and **Allah** is **Oft-Forgiving**, Most Forbearing.
226. Those who take an oath not to have sexual relations with their wives must wait for four months, then if they return, verily, **Allah** is Oft-Forgiving, **Most Merciful**. (Darussalam, 1999)

Chapter Al-Imran Chapter 3 Verses 31-32

31. Say: "If you love **Allah**, then follow me, **Allah** will love you and forgive you your sins, and **Allah** is Oft-Forgiving, **Most Merciful**.
32. Say: "Obey Allah and the Messenger." But if they turn away, then Allah does not like the disbelievers. (Darussalam, 1999)

Chapter Al-Imran Chapter 3 Verses 86~89

86. How shall **Allah** guide a people who disbelieved after their Belief and after they bore witness that the Messenger is true and after clear proofs had come unto them? And **Allah** guides not the people who are Dhalimun (wrong-doers).
87. They are those whose recompense is that on them the Curse of **Allah**, of the angels, and of all mankind.
88. They will abide therein. Neither will their torment be lightened, nor will it be delayed or postponed.
89. Except for those who repent after that and do righteous deeds. Verily, **Allah** is Oft-Forgiving, **Most Merciful**. (Darussalam, 1999)

Chapter Al-Imran   Chapter 3 Verse 129
And to **Allah** belongs all that is in the heavens and all that is in the earth, He forgives whom He wills and punishes whom He wills. And **Allah** is Oft-Forgiving, **Most Merciful**. (Darussalam, 1999)

Chapter An-Nisa   Chapter 4 Verse 23
Forbidden to you are: your mothers, your daughters, your sisters, your father's sisters, your mothers' sisters, your brothers' daughters, your sisters' daughters, your foster mothers who gave you suck, your foster milk suckling sisters, your wives' mothers, your stepdaughters under your guardianship, born of your wives to whom you have gone in – but there is no sin on you if you have not gone into them- the wives of your sons from your own loins, and two sisters in wedlock at the same time, except for what has already passed; verily, **Allah** is Oft-Forgiving, **Most Merciful**. (Darussalam, 1999)

Chapter An-Nisa   Chapter 4 Verse 25
And whoever of you have not the means wherewith to wed free believing women, they may wed believing girls from among those whom your right hands possess, and **Allah** has full knowledge about your Faith; you are one from another. Wed them with the permission of their own folk and give them their Mahr (bridal money) according to what is reasonable; they should be chaste, not committing illegal sex, nor taking boyfriends. And after they have been taken in wedlock if they commit illegal sexual intercourse, their punishment is half of that for free women. This is for him among you who is afraid of being harmed in his religion or in his body; but it is better for you that you practice self-restraint, and **Allah** is Oft-forgiving, **Most Merciful**. (Darussalam, 1999)

Chapter An-Nisa   Chapter 4 Verse 29
O you who believe! Eat not up your property among yourselves unjustly except it be a trade amongst you, by mutual consent. And do not kill yourselves. Surely, **Allah** is **Most Merciful** to you. (Darussalam, 1999)

Chapter An-Nisa   Chapter 4 Verse 64
We sent no Messengers, but to be obeyed by **Allah's** Leave. If they, when they had been unjust to themselves, had come to you and begged **Allah's** forgiveness, and the Messenger had begged forgiveness for them; indeed, they would have found **Allah** All-Forgiving, **Most Merciful**. (Darussalam, 1999)

Chapter An-Nisa   Chapter 4 Verse 83
When there comes to them some matter touching safety or fear, they make it known; if only they had referred it to the Messenger or to those charged with authority among them, the proper investigators would have understood it from them. Had it not been for the **Grace and Mercy of Allah** upon you, you would have followed Shaitan (Satan), except a few of you. (Darussalam, 1999)

Chapter An-Nisa   Chapter 4 Verse 96
Degrees of grades from Him, and forgiveness and mercy. And **Allah** is Ever Oft-Forgiving, **Most Merciful**. (Darussalam, 1999)

Chapter An-Nisa   Chapter 4 Verse 100
He who emigrates in the Cause of **Allah**, will find on earth many dwelling places and plenty to live by. And whosoever leaves his home as an emigrant to **Allah** and His Messenger, and death overtakes him, his reward is then surely incumbent upon **Allah**. And **Allah** is Ever Oft-Forgiving, **Most Merciful**. (Darussalam, 1999)

Chapter An-Nisa   Chapter 4 Verse 106
And seek the forgiveness of **Allah**, certainly, **Allah** is Ever Oft-Forgiving, **Most Merciful**. (Darussalam, 1999)

Chapter An-Nisa   Chapter 4 Verse 110
And whoever does evil or wrong himself but afterwards seeks **Allah**'s forgiveness, he will find **Allah** Oft Forgiving, **Most Merciful**. (Darussalam, 1999)

Chapter An-Nisa   Chapter 4 Verse 129
You will never be able to do perfect justice between wives even if it is your ardent desire, so do not incline too much to one of them so as to leave the other hanging. And if you do justice, and do all that is right and fear **Allah**, then **Allah** is Ever Oft-Forgiving, **Most Merciful**. (Darussalam, 1999)

Chapter An-Nisa   Chapter 4 Verse 152
And those who believe in **Allah** and His Messengers and make no distinction between any of them, We shall give them their rewards; and **Allah** is Ever Oft-Forgiving, **Most Merciful**. (Darussalam, 1999)

Chapter An-Nisa   Chapter 4 Verse 175

So as for those who believed in **Allah** and held fast to Him, He will admit them to His **Mercy and Grace**, and guide them to Himself by a Straight Path. (Darussalam, 1999)

Chapter Al-Ma'idah   Chapter 5 Verse 3

Forbidden to you are Al-Maitah (dead animals), blood, the flesh of swine, and that on which **Allah**'s name has not been mentioned while slaughtering and that which has been killed by strangling, or by a violent blow or by a headlong fall, or by the goring of horns – and that which has been eaten by a wild animal- unless you are able to slaughter it and that which is sacrificed on An-Nusub (stone altars). (Forbidden) also is to use arrows seeking luck or decision; that is fisqun (disobedience of **Allah** and sin). This day, those who disbelieved have given up all hope of your religion; so fear them not, but fear Me. This day, I have perfected your religion for you, completed My Favour upon you, and have chosen for you Islam as your religion. But as for him who is forced by severe hunger, with no inclination to sin, then surely, **Allah** is Oft-Forgiving, **Most Merciful**. (Darussalam, 1999)

Chapter Al-Ma'idah   Chapter 5 Verses 33-34

33. The recompense of those who wage war against **Allah** and His Messenger and do mischief in the land is only that they shall be killed or crucified or their hands and their feet be cut off on the opposite sides, or be exiled from the land. That is their disgrace in this world, and a great torment is theirs in the Hereafter.
34. Except for those who came back with repentance before they fall into your power; in that case, know that **Allah** is Oft-Forgiving, **Most Merciful**. (Darussalam, 1999)

Chapter Al-Ma'idah   Chapter 5 Verses 38-39

38. And the male thief and the female thief, cut off their hands as a recompense for that which they committed, a punishment by way of example from **Allah**. And **Allah** is All-Powerful, All-Wise.
39. But whosoever repents after his crime and does righteous good deeds, then verily; **Allah** will pardon him. Verily, **Allah** is Oft-forgiving, **Most Merciful**. (Darussalam, 1999)

Chapter Al-Ma'idah   Chapter 5 Verse 74

73. Surely, disbelievers are those who said: "**Allah** is the third of the three. "But there is no Ilah (god) but One Ilah (God). And if they cease not from

what they say, verily, a painful torment will befall on the disbelievers among them.
74. Will they not turn with repentance to **Allah** and ask His forgiveness? For **Allah** is Oft-Forgiving, **Most Merciful**. (Darussalam, 1999)

Chapter Al-Ma'idah   Chapter 5 Verse 98
Know that **Allah** is Severe in punishment and that **Allah** is Oft-Forgiving, **Most Merciful**. (Darussalam, 1999)

Chapter Al-An`am   Chapter 6 Verse 12
Say: "To whom belongs all that is in the heavens and the earth?" Say: "To Allah. He has prescribed **Mercy** for Himself. Indeed, He will gather you together on the Day of Resurrection, about which there is no doubt. Those who have lost themselves will not believe. (Darussalam, 1999)

Chapter Al-An`am   Chapter 6 Verse 54
When those who believe in Our Ayat (verse) come to you, say: "Salamun Alaikum (peace be on you); your **Lord** has written **Mercy** for Himself, so that if any of you does evil in ignorance, and thereafter repents and does righteous good deeds, then surely, He is Oft-Forgiving, **Most Merciful**. (Darussalam, 1999)

Chapter Al-An`am   Chapter 6 Verse 133
And your **Lord** is Rich, **full of Mercy**; if He wills, He can destroy you, and in your place make whom He wills as your successors, as He raised you from the seed of other people. (Darussalam, 1999)

Chapter Al-An`am   Chapter 6 Verse 145
Say: "I find not in that which has been related to me anything forbidden to be eaten by one who wishes to eat it, unless it be Maitah (dead animals) or blood poured forth, or the flesh of swine; for that surely, is impure or impious meat which is slaughtered as a sacrifice for others than **Allah**. But whosoever is forced by necessity without willful disobedience, nor transgressing due limits; certainly, your **Lord** is Oft-Forgiving, **Most Merciful**. (Darussalam, 1999)

Chapter Al-An`am   Chapter 6 Verse 165
And it is He who has made you generations coming after generations, replacing each other on the earth. And He has raised you in ranks, some above others that He may try you in that which He has bestowed on you. Surely,

your **Lord** is Swift in retribution, and certainly He is Oft-Forgiving, **Most Merciful**. (Darussalam, 1999)

Chapter Al-A`raf Chapter 7 Verses 151~153
151. Musa said: "O my **Lord**! Forgive me and my brother, and admit us into Your Mercy. For you are the **Most Merciful** of those who show mercy."
152. Certainly, those who took the calf (for worship), wrath from their **Lord** and humiliation will come upon them in the life of this world. Thus, do We recompense those who invent lies.
153. But those who committed evil deeds and then repented afterwards and believed, verily, your **Lord** after that is indeed Oft-Forgiving, **Most Merciful**. (Darussalam, 1999)

Chapter Al-A`raf Chapter 7 Verse 167
And when your **Lord** declared that He would certainly keep on sending against them, till the day of Resurrection, those who would afflict them with a humiliating torment. Verily your **Lord** is Quick in Retribution and certainly He is Oft-Forgiving, **Most Merciful**. (Darussalam, 1999)

Chapter Al-Anfal Chapter 8 Verses 69-70
69. So, enjoy what you have gotten of booty in war, lawful and good, and be afraid of **Allah**. Certainly, **Allah** is Oft-Forgiving, **Most Merciful**.
70. O Prophet! Say to the captives that are in your hands: "If **Allah** knows any good in your hearts, He will give you something better than what has been taken from you, and He will forgive you, and **Allah** is Oft-Forgiving, **Most Merciful**." (Darussalam, 1999)

Chapter At-Taubah Chapter 9 Verse 5
Then when the Sacred months have passed, then kill the Mushrikun (polytheists) wherever you find them, and capture them and besiege them, and lie in wait for them in every ambush. But if they repent and perform As-Salat (prayer), and give Zakat (charity-alms), then leave their way free. Verily, **Allah** is Oft-Forgiving, **Most Merciful**. (Darussalam, 1999)

Chapter At-Taubah Chapter 9 Verses 26-27
26. Then **Allah** did send down His Sakinah (peace) on the Messenger, and on the believers, and sent down forces which you saw not, and punished the disbelievers. Such is the recompense of disbelievers.
27. Then after that **Allah** will accept the repentance of whom He wills. And **Allah** is Oft-Forgiving, **Most Merciful**. (Darussalam, 1999)

Chapter At-Taubah   Chapter 9 Verses 90-91
90. And those who made excuses from the bedouins came asking your permission to exempt them, and those who had lied to **Allah** and His Messenger sat at home; a painful torment will seize those of them who disbelieve.
91. There is no blame on these who are weak or ill or who find no resources to spend, if they are sincere and true to **Allah** and His Messenger. No ground can there be against the Mushinun (good-doers). And **Allah** is Oft-Forgiving, **Most Merciful**. (Darussalam, 1999)

Chapter At-Taubah   Chapter 9 Verse 99
And of the bedouins there are some who believe in **Allah** and the Last Day, and look upon what they spend in **Allah**'s Cause as means of nearness to **Allah**, and a cause of receiving the Messengers' invocations. Indeed, these are a means of nearness for them. **Allah** will admit them to His Mercy. Certainly, **Allah** is Oft-Forgiving, **Most Merciful**. (Darussalam, 2000)

Chapter At-Taubah   Chapter 9 Verses 102~104
102. And others who have acknowledged their sins, they have mixed a deed that was righteous with another that was evil. Perhaps **Allah** will turn to them in forgiveness. Surely, **Allah** is Oft-Forgiving, **Most Merciful**.
103. Take Sadaqah (alms) from their wealth in order to purify them and sanctify them with it, and invoke **Allah** for them. Verily! Your invocations are a source of security for them, and **Allah** is All-Hearer, All-Knower.
104. Know they not that **Allah** accepts repentance from His slaves and takes the Sadaqat (alms), and that **Allah** alone is the one Who forgives and accepts repentance, **Most Merciful**. (Darussalam, 2000)

Chapter At-Taubah   Chapter 9 Verses 117-118
117. **Allah** has forgiven the Prophet, the Muhajirun (emigrants) and the Ansar (the helpers) who followed him in the time of distress, after the hearts of a party of them had nearly deviated, but He accepted their repentance. Certainly, He is unto them Full of Kindness, **Most Merciful**.
118. And the three who did not join till for them the earth, vast as it is, was straitened and their own selves were straitened to them, and they perceived that there is no fleeing from **Allah**, and no refuge but with Him. Then, He forgave them, that they might beg for His pardon. Verily, **Allah** is the One Who forgives and accepts repentance, **Most Merciful**. (Darussalam, 2000)

Chapter Yunus   Chapter 10 Verse 107
And if **Allah** touches you with harm, there is none who can remove it but He; and if He intends any good for you, there is none who can repel His Favour which He causes it to reach whom so ever of His slaves He wills. And He is the Oft-Forgiving, the **Most Merciful**. (Darussalam, 2000)

Chapter Hud   Chapter 11 Verse 41
And he (Nuh) said: "Embark therein: in the Name of **Allah** will be its course and its anchorage. Surely, my **Lord** is Oft-Forgiving, **Most Merciful**. (Darussalam, 2000)

Chapter Hud   Chapter 11 Verse 90
And ask forgiveness of your **Lord** and turn to Him in repentance. Verily, my **Lord** is **Most Merciful**, Most Loving. (Darussalam, 2000)

Chapter Yusuf   Chapter 12 Verses 51~53
51. Said: "What was your affair when you did seek to seduce Yusuf?" The women said: "**Allah** forbid! No evil know we against him!" The wife of Al-'Aziz said: "Now the truth is manifest (to all), it was I who sought to seduce him, and he is surely of the truthful."
52. In order that he (Al-'Aziz) may know that I betrayed him not in absence. And, verily! **Allah** guides not the plot of the betrayers.
53. And I free not myself. Verily the self is inclined to evil, except when my **Lord** bestows His mercy. Verily, my **Lord** is Oft-Forgiving, **Most Merciful**. (Darussalam, 2000)

Chapter Yusuf   Chapter 12 Verses 63-64
63. So, when they returned to their father, they said: "O our father! No more measure of grain shall we get. So send our brother with us, and we shall get our measure and truly we will guard him."
64. He said: "Can I entrust him to you except as I entrusted his brother to you aforetime? But **Allah** is the Best to Guard, and He is the **Most Merciful** of those who show mercy." (Darussalam, 2000)

Chapter Yusuf   Chapter 12 Verse 92
He said: "No reproach on you this day; may **Allah** forgive you, and He is the **Most Merciful** of those who show mercy! (Darussalam, 2000)

<u>Chapter Yusuf</u>　　　　　　　　　　　　　　Chapter 12 Verse 98
He said: "I will ask my **Lord** for forgiveness for you, verily, He! Only He is the Oft-Forgiving, the **Most Merciful**. (Darussalam, 2000)

<u>Chapter Ibrahim</u>　　　　　　　　　　　Chapter 14 Verses 35-36
35. And when Ibrahim said: "O my **Lord**! Make this city one of peace and security, and keep me and my sons away from worshipping idols.
36. "O my **Lord**! They have indeed led astray many among mankind. But whoso follows me, he verily is of me. And whoso disobeys me, still You are indeed Oft-Forgiving, **Most Merciful**. (Darussalam, 2000)

<u>Chapter Al-Hijr</u>　　　　　　　　　　　　　Chapter 15 Verse 49
Declare unto my slaves that truly I am the Oft-Forgiving, the **Most Merciful**. (Darussalam, 2000)

<u>Chapter An Nahl</u>　　　　　　　　　　　Chapter 16 Verses 5~7
5. And the cattle, He has created them for you; in them there is warmth, and numerous benefits, and of them you eat.
6. And wherein is beauty for you, when you bring them home in the evening, and as you lead them forth to pasture in the morning.
7. And they carry your loads to a land that you could not reach except with great trouble to yourselves. Truly, your **Lord** is full of Kindness, **Most Merciful**. (Darussalam, 2000)

<u>Chapter An Nahl</u>　　　　　　　　　　　　Chapter 16 Verse 18
And if you would count the Favours of **Allah**, never could you be able to count them. Truly, **Allah** is Oft-Forgiving, **Most Merciful**. (Darussalam, 2000)

<u>Chapter An Nahl</u>　　　　　　　　　　　Chapter 16 Verses 45~47
45. Do then those who devise evil plots feel secure that **Allah** will not sink them into the earth, or that the torment will not seize them from directions they perceive not?
46. Or that He may catch them in the midst of their going to and fro, so that there be no escape for them?
47. Or that He may catch them with gradual wasting? Truly, your **Lord** is indeed full of Kindness, **Most Merciful**. (Darussalam, 2000)

Chapter An Nahl   Chapter 16 Verse 110
Then, verily, your **Lord** - for those who emigrated after they had been put to trials and thereafter strove hard and fought and were patient, verily your **Lord**, afterward, is Oft-Forgiving, **Most Merciful**. (Darussalam, 2000)

Chapter An Nahl   Chapter 16 Verse 115
He has forbidden you only Al-Maitah (dead animals), blood, the flesh of swine, and any animal which is slaughtered as a sacrifice for others than **Allah**. But if one is forced by necessity, without willful disobedience, and not transgressing, - then, **Allah** is Oft- Forgiving, **Most Merciful**. (Darussalam, 2000)

Chapter An Nahl   Chapter 16 Verse 119
Then, verily, your **Lord** - for those who do evil in ignorance and afterward repent and do righteous deeds, verily, your **Lord** thereafter, is Oft-Forgiving, **Most Merciful**. (Darussalam, 2000)

Chapter Al-Isra   Chapter 17 Verse 66
Your **Lord** is He Who drivers the ship for you through the sea, in order that you may seek of His Bounty. Truly, He is Ever **Most Merciful** towards you. (Darussalam, 2000)

Chapter Al-Anbiya   Chapter 21 Verse 83
And Ayyub, when he cried to his **Lord**: "Verily, distress has seized me, and You are the **Most Merciful** of all those who show mercy." (Darussalam, 2000)

Chapter Al-Hajj   Chapter 22 Verse 65
See you not that **Allah** has subjected to you all that is on the earth, and the ships that sail through the sea by His command? He withholds the heaven from falling on the earth except by His leave. Verily, **Allah** is for mankind full of kindness, **Most Merciful**. (Darussalam, 2000)

Chapter Al-Mu'minun   Chapter 23 Verse 109
Verily, there was a party of My salves who used to say: "Our **Lord**! We believe so forgive us and have mercy on us, for You are the **Best of all who show mercy**." (Darussalam, 2000)

Chapter Al-Mu'minun   Chapter 23 Verse 118
And say: "My **Lord**! Forgive and have mercy for You are the **Best of those who show mercy!**" (Darussalam, 2000)

Chapter An-Nur   Chapter 24 Verses 4-5

4. And those who accuse chaste women, and produce not four witnesses, flog them with eighty stripes, and reject their testimony forever. They indeed are the Fasiqun (disobedient).
5. Except those who repent thereafter and do righteous deeds; verily, **Allah** is Oft-Forgiving, **Most Merciful**. (Darussalam, 2000)

Chapter An-Nur   Chapter 24 Verses 20~22

20. And had it not been for the Grace of **Allah** and His mercy on you. And that **Allah** is full of Kindness, **Most Merciful**.
21. O you who believe! Follow not the footsteps of Shaitan (Satan). And whosoever follows the footsteps of Shaitan (Satan), then, verily he commands Al-Fahsha (immorality), and Al-Munkar (evil). And had it not been for the Grace of **Allah** and His Mercy on you, not one of you would ever have been pure from sins. But **Allah** purifies whom He wills, and **Allah** is All-Hearer, All-Knower.
22. And let not those among you who are blessed with graces and wealth swear not to give to their kinsmen, Al-Masakin (the poor), and those who left their homes for **Allah**'s Cause. Let them pardon and forgive. Do you not love that **Allah** should forgive you? And **Allah** is Oft-Forgiving, **Most Merciful**. (Darussalam, 2000)

Chapter An-Nur   Chapter 24 Verse 33

And let those who find not the financial means for marriage keep themselves chaste, until **Allah** enriches them of His Bounty. And such of your slaves as seek a writing, give them such writing, if you find that there is good and honesty in them. And give them something out of the wealth of **Allah** which He has bestowed upon you. And force not your maids to prostitution, if they desire chastity, in order that you make a gain in the goods of this worldly life. But if anyone compels them, then after such compulsion, **Allah** is Oft-Forgiving, **Most Merciful**. (Darussalam, 2000)

Chapter An-Nur   Chapter 24 Verse 62

The true believers are only those who believe in **Allah** and His Messengers and when they are with him on some common matter, they go not away until they have asked his permission. Verily, those who ask your permission, those are they who believe in **Allah** and His Messenger. So if they ask your permission for some affairs of theirs, give permission to whom you will of them and ask **Allah** for their forgiveness. Truly, **Allah** is Oft-Forgiving, **Most Merciful**. (Darussalam, 2000)

Chapter Al-Furqan   Chapter 25 Verse 6
Say: "It has been sent down by Him Who knows the secret of the heavens and the earth. Truly, He is Ever Oft-Forgiving, **Most Merciful**." (Darussalam, 2000)

Chapter Al-Furqan   Chapter 25 Verses 68~70
68. And those who invoke not any other ilah (god) along with **Allah**, nor kill such person as **Allah** has forbidden, except for just cause, nor commit illegal sexual intercourse and whoever does this, shall receive the punishment.
69. The torment will be doubled to him on the Day of Resurrection, and he will abide therein in disgrace;
70. Except those who repent and believe and do righteous deeds; for those, **Allah** will change their sins into good deeds, and **Allah** is Ever Oft-Forgiving, **Most Merciful**. (Darussalam, 2000)

Chapter Ash-Shu`ara   Chapter 26 Verses 7~9
7. Do they not observe the earth how much of every good kind We cause to grow therein?
8. Verily, in this is an Ayah (sign), yet most of them are not believers.
9. And verily, your **Lord**, He is truly, the All-Mighty, the **Most Merciful**. (Darussalam, 2000)

Chapter Ash-Shu`ara   Chapter 26 Verses 61~68
61. And when the two hosts saw each other, the companions of Musa said: "We are sure to be overtaken."
62. Said "Nay, verily, with me is my **Lord**. He will guide me."
63. Then We revealed to Musa: "Strike the sea with your stick." And it parted, and each separate part become like huge mountain.
64. Then We brought near the others to that place.
65. And We save Musa and all those with him.
66. Then We drowned the others.
67. Verily, in this is indeed a sign, yet most of them are not believers.
68. And verily, your **Lord**, He is truly, the All-Mighty, the **Most Merciful**. (Darussalam, 2000)

Chapter Ash-Shu`ara   Chapter 26 Verses 91~104
91. And the Fire will be place in full view of the erring.
92. And it will be said to them: "Where are those that you used to worship."
93. "Instead of **Allah**? Can they help you or help themselves?"

94. Then they will be thrown on their faces into the (fire), they and the Ghawun (erring).
95. And the whole hosts of Iblis (Satan) together.
96. They will say while contending therein,
97. By **Allah**, we were truly in manifest error,
98. When we held you as equals with the **Lord** of the 'Alamin (worlds);
99. And none has brought us into error except the Mujrimun (criminals).
100. Now we have no intercessors,
101. Nor a close friend.
102. If we only had a chance to return, we shall truly be among the believers!
103. Verily, in this is indeed a sign, yet most of them are not believers.
104. And verily, your **Lord**, He is truly, the All-Mighty, the **Most Merciful**. (Darussalam, 2000)

Chapter Ash-Shu`ara   Chapter 26 Verses 116~122
116. They said: "If you cease not, O Nuh you will surely, be among those stoned."
117. He said: "My **Lord**! Verily, my people have belied me.
118. Therefore judge you between me and them, and save me and those of the believers who are with me."
119. And We saved him and those with him in the laden ship.
120. Then We drowned the rest thereafter.
121. Verily, in this is indeed a sign, yet most of them are not believers.
122. And verily, your **Lord**, He is indeed the All-Mighty, the **Most Merciful**. (Darussalam, 2000)

Chapter Ash-Shu`ara   Chapter 26 Verses 136~140
136. They said: "It is the same to us whether you preach or be not of those who preach."
137. "This is no other than the false tales and religion of the ancients."
138. "And we are not going to be punished."
139. So they belied him, and We destroyed them. Verily, in this is indeed a sign, yet most of them are not believers.
140. And verily, your **Lord**, He is indeed the All-Mighty, the **Most Merciful**. (Darussalam, 2000)

Chapter Ash-Shu`ara   Chapter 26 Verses 155~159
155. He said: "Here is a she camel: it has a right to drink, and you have a right to drink on a day known.
156. "And touch her not with harm, lest the torment of a great day should seize you."

157. But they killed her, and then they became regretful.
158. So the torment overtook them. Verily, in this is indeed a sign, yet most of them are not believers.
159. And verily, your **Lord**, He is indeed the All-Mighty, the **Most Merciful**. (Darussalam, 2000)

Chapter Ash-Shu`ara   Chapter 26 Verses 167~175

167. They said: "If you cease not. O Lot! Verily, you will be one of those who are driven out!"
168. He said: "I am, indeed of those who disapprove with severe anger and fury your action."
169. "My **Lord**! Save me and my family from what they do."
170. So We saved him and his family, all.
171. Except an old woman among those who remained behind.
172 Then afterward We destroyed the others.
173. And We rained on them a rain. And how evil was the rain of those who had been warned!
174. Verily, in this is indeed a sign, yet most of them are not believers.
175. And verily, you **Lord**; He is indeed the All-Mighty, the **Most Merciful**. (Darussalam, 2000)

Chapter Ash-Shu`ara   Chapter 26 Verses 185~191

185. They said: "You are only one of those bewitched!"
186. "You are but a human being like us and verily, we think that you are one of the liars!"
187. "So cause a piece of the heaven to fall on us, if you are of the truthful!"
188. He said: "My **Lord** is the best Knower of what you do."
189. But they belied him, so the torment of the Day of Shadow seized them. Indeed, that was the torment of a Great Day.
190. Verily, in this is indeed a sign, yet most of them are not believers.
191. And verily, your **Lord**, He is indeed the All-Mighty, The **Most Merciful**. (Darussalam, 2000)

Chapter Ash-Shu`ara   Chapter 26 Verses 213~217

213. So invoke not with **Allah** another ilah (god) lest you should be among those who receive punishment.
214. And warn your tribe of near kindred.
215. And be kind and humble to the believers who follow you.
216. Then if they disobey you, say: "I am innocent of what you do."
217. And put your trust in the All-Mighty, the **Most Merciful**. (Darussalam, 2000)

Chapter An-Naml   Chapter 27 Verses 10-11

10. "And throw down your stick!" But when he saw it moving as if it were a snake, he turned in flight, and did not look back. "O Musa! Fear not, verily! The Messengers fear not in front of Me.
11. Except him who has done wrong and afterwards has changed evil for good; then surely, I am Oft-Forgiving, **Most Merciful**. (Darussalam, 2000)

Chapter An-Naml   Chapter 27 Verse 30

"Verily, it is from Sulaiman, and verily it (reads): In the Name of **Allah**, the Most Gracious, the **Most Merciful**. (Darussalam, 2000)

Chapter Al-Qasas   Chapter 28 Verses 15-16

15. And he entered the city at a time of unawareness of its people: and he found there two men fighting, - one of his party, and the other of his foes. The man of his party asked him for help against his foe, so Musa struck him with his fist and killed him. He said: "This is of Shaitan's (Satan) doing, verily, he is a plain misleading enemy."
16. He said: "My **Lord**! Verily, I have wronged myself so forgive me." Then He forgave him. Verily, He is the Oft-Forgiving, the **Most Merciful**. (Darussalam, 2000)

Chapter Ar-Rum   Chapter 30 Verses 1~5

1. Alif-Lam-Mim
2. The Romans have been defeated.
3. In the nearest land, and they, after their defeat, will be victorious.
4. Within three to nine years. The decision of the matter, before and after is only with **Allah**. And on that Day, the believers will rejoice,
5. With the Help of **Allah**. He helps whom He wills, and He is the All-Mighty, the **Most Merciful**. (Darussalam, 2000)

Chapter As-Sajdah   Chapter 32 Verse 6

That is, He the All-knower of the unseen and the seen, the All-Mighty, the **Most Merciful**. ((Darussalam, 2000)

Chapter Al-Ahzab   Chapter 33 Verses 4-5

4. **Allah** has not put for any man two hearts inside his body. Neither has He made your wives whom you declare to be like your mothers' backs, your real mothers. Nor has He made your adopted sons your real sons. That is but your saying with your mouths. But **Allah** says the truth, and He guides to the (Right) Way.

5. Call them by their fathers, that is more just with **Allah**, but if you know not their fathers your brothers in Faith and Mawalikun (your freed slaves), and there is no sin on you concerning that in which you made a mistake, except in regard to what your hearts deliberately intend. And **Allah** is Ever Oft-Forgiving, **Most Merciful**. (Darussalam, 2000)

Chapter Al-Ahzab   Chapter 33 Verse 24
That **Allah** my reward the men of truth for their truth and punish the hypocrites, if He wills, or accept their repentance by turning to them. Verily, **Allah** is Ever Oft-Forgiving, **Most Merciful.** (Darussalam, 2000)

Chapter Al-Ahzab   Chapter 33 Verse 43
He it is who sends Salat (His blessings) on you, and His angels too, that He may bring you out from darkness into light. And He is Ever **Most Merciful** to the believers. ((Darussalam, 2000)

Chapter Al-Ahzab   Chapter 33 Verse 50
O Prophet! Verily, we have made lawful to you your wives, to whom you have paid their Mahr (bridal money), and those whom your right hand possesses- whom **Allah** has given to you, and the daughters of your Amm (paternal uncles) and the daughters of your Ammat (paternal aunts) and the daughters of your khal (maternal uncles) and the daughters of your khalat (maternal aunts) who migrated with you, and a believing woman if she offers herself to the Prophet, and the Prophet wishes to marry her- a privilege for you only, not for the (rest of) the believers. Indeed, We know what We have enjoined upon them about their wives and those whom their right hands possess, in order that there should be no difficulty on you. And **Allah** is Ever Oft-Forgiving, **Most Merciful**. (Darussalam, 2000)

Chapter Al-Ahzab   Chapter 33 Verse 59
O Prophet! Tell your wives and your daughters and the women of the believers to draw their cloaks all over their bodies. That will be better that they should be known so as not to be annoyed. And **Allah** is Ever Oft-Forgiving, **Most Merciful**. (Darussalam, 2000)

Chapter Al-Ahzab   Chapter 33 Verses 72~73
72. Truly, we did offer Al-Amanah (the trust) to the heavens and the earth, and the mountains, but they declined to bear it and were afraid of it. But man bore it. Verily, he was unjust and ignorant.
73. So that **Allah** will punish the hypocrites, men and women, and the men and women who are Al- Mushrikun (polytheists). And **Allah** will pardon the

true believers of Islamic Monotheism, men and women. And **Allah** is Ever Oft-Forgiving, **Most Merciful.** (Darussalam, 2000)

Chapter Saba — Chapter 34 Verse 2
He knows that which goes into the earth and that which comes forth from it, and that which descends from the heaven and that which ascends to it. And He is the **Most Merciful,** the Oft-Forgiving. (Darussalam, 2000)

Chapter Ya-sin — Chapter 36 Verses 3~5
3. Truly, you are one of the Messengers.
4. On a Straight Path.
5. (This is a Revelation) sent down by the All-Mighty, **the Most Merciful**. (Darussalam, 2000)

Chapter Ya-sin — Chapter 36 Verse 58
Salam (peace be on you)-a Word from the **Lord**, **Most Merciful.** (Darussalam, 2000)

Chapter Az-Zumar — Chapter 39 Verse 53
Say: "O Ibadi who have transgressed against themselves! Despair not of the **Mercy** of **Allah**, verily, **Allah** forgives all sins. Truly, He is Oft-Forgiving, **Most Merciful.** (Darussalam, 2000)

Chapter Fussilat — Chapter 41 Verse 2
A revelation from the Most Gracious, the **Most Merciful**. (Darussalam, 2000)

Chapter Fussilat — Chapter 41 Verse 32
"An entertainment from the Oft-Forgiving, **Most Merciful**." (Darussalam, 2000)

Chapter Ash-Shura — Chapter 42 Verse 5
Nearly the heavens might be rent asunder from above them, and the angels glorify the praises of their **Lord**, and ask for forgiveness for those on the earth. Verily, **Allah** is the Oft-Forgiving, **the Most Merciful**. (Darussalam, 2000)

Chapter Ad-Dukhan — Chapter 44 Verses 40~42
40. Verily, the Day of Judgment is the time appointed for all of them.
41. The Day when a Maula (a near relative) cannot avail a Maula (a near relative) in aught, and no help can they receive.

42. Except, him on whom **Allah** has mercy. Verily, He is the All-Mighty, **the Most Merciful.** (Darussalam, 2000)

Chapter Al-Ahqaf   Chapter 46 Verse 8

Or say they: "He has fabricated it." Say: "If I have fabricated it, still you have no power to support me against **Allah**. He knows best of what you say among yourselves concerning it! Sufficient is He for a witness between me and you! And He is the Oft-Forgiving, **the Most Merciful.** (Darussalam, 2000)

Chapter Al-Fath   Chapter 48 Verse 14

And to **Allah** belongs the Sovereignty of the heavens and the earth. He forgives whom He wills, and punishes whom He wills. And **Allah** is Ever Oft-Forgiving, **Most Merciful.** (Darussalam, 2000)

Chapter Al-Hujurat   Chapter 49 Verses 4-5

4. Verily, those who call you from behind the dwelling, most of them have no sense.
5. And if they had patience till you could come out to them, it would have been better for them. And **Allah** is Oft-Forgiving, **Most Merciful.** (Darussalam, 2000)

Chapter Al-Hujurat   Chapter 49 Verse 12

O you who believe! Avoid much suspicion; indeed, some suspicions are sins. And spy not, neither backbite one another. Would one of you like to eat the flesh of his dead brother? You would hate it. And fear **Allah**. Verily, **Allah** is the one who forgives and accepts repentance, **Most Merciful**. (Darussalam, 2000)

Chapter Al-Hujurat   Chapter 49 Verse 14

The bedouins say: "We believe." Say: "You believe not but you only say. "We have surrendered, 'for Faith has not yet entered your hearts. But if you obey **Allah** and His Messenger, He will not decrease anything in reward for your deeds. Verily, **Allah** is Oft-Forgiving, **Most Merciful.** (Darussalam, 2000)

Chapter At-Tur   Chapter 52 Verses 25~28

25. And some of them draw near to others, questioning.
26. Saying: "Aforetime, we were afraid in the midst of our families.
27. "So **Allah** has been Gracious to us, and has saved us from the torment of the fire.

28. "Verily, we used to invoke Him before. Verily, He is Al-Barr (the Most Subtle), **the Most Merciful.** (Darussalam, 2000)

Chapter Al-Hadid   Chapter 57 Verse 9
It is He who sends down manifest Ayat (verses) to His slave that He may bring you out from darkness into light. And verily, **Allah** is to you full of Kindness, **Most Merciful.** (Darussalam, 2000)

Chapter Al-Hadid   Chapter 57 Verse 28
O you who believe! Fear **Allah** and believe in His Messenger, He will give you a double portion of His mercy, and He will give you a light by which you shall walk. And He will forgive you. And **Allah** is Oft-Forgiving, **Most Merciful.** (Darussalam, 2000)

Chapter Al-Mujadilah   Chapter 58 Verse 12
O you who believe! When you consult the Messenger in private, spend something in charity before your private consultation. That will be better and purer for you. But if you find not, then verily, **Allah** is Oft-Forgiving, **Most Merciful.** ((Darussalam, 2000)

Chapter Al-Hashr   Chapter 59 Verse 10
And those who came after them say: "Our **Lord**! Forgive us and our brethren who have proceeded us in Faith, and put not in our hearts any hatred against those who have believed. Our **Lord**! You are indeed full of kindness, **Most Merciful.** (Darussalam, 2000)

Chapter Al-Hashr   Chapter 59 Verse 22
He is **Allah**, besides whom La ilaha illa Huwa (none has the right to be worshipped but He), the All-Knower of the unseen and the seen. He is the Most Gracious, the **Most Merciful.** (Darussalam, 2000)

Chapter Al-Mumtahanah   Chapter 60 Verse 7
Perhaps **Allah** will make friendship between you and those whom you hold as enemies. And **Allah** has power (over all things), and **Allah** is Oft-Forgiving, **Most Merciful.** (Darussalam, 2000)

Chapter Al-Mumtahanah   Chapter 60 Verse 12
O Prophet! When believing women comes to you to give you the Bai'ah (pledge), that they will not associate anything in worship with **Allah**, that they will not steal, that they will not commit illegal sexual intercourse, that they will not kill their children, that they will not utter slander, intentionally

forgiving falsehood, and that they will not disobey you in Ma'ruf (just matter), then accept their Bai'ah (pledge), and ask **Allah** to forgive them. Verily, **Allah** is Oft-Forgiving, **Most Merciful**. (Darussalam, 2000)

<u>Chapter At-Taghabun</u>   Chapter 64 Verse 14
O you who believe! Verily among your wives and your children there are enemies for you; therefore, be aware of them! But if you pardon and overlook, and forgive, then verily, **Allah** is Oft-Forgiving, **Most Merciful**. (Darussalam, 2000)

<u>Chapter At-Tahrim</u>   Chapter 66 Verse 1
O Prophet! Why do you forbid that which **Allah** has allowed to you, seeking to please your wives? And **Allah** is Oft-Forgiving, **Most Merciful**. (Darussalam, 2000)

<u>Chapter Al-Muzzammil</u>   Chapter 73 Verse 20
Verily, your **Lord** knows that you do stand a little less than two-thirds of the night, or half the night, or a third of the night, and also a party of those with you. And **Allah** measures the night and the day. He knows that you are unable to pray the whole night, so He has turned to you. So, recite you of the Quran as much as may be easy for you. He knows that there will be some among you sick, others traveling through the land, seeking of **Allah**'s Bounty, yet others fighting in **Allah**'s Cause. So, recite as much of the Quran as may be easy, and perform As-Salat (prayer) and give Zakat (charity-alms), and lend to **Allah** a goodly loan. And whatever good you send before you for yourselves, you will certainly find it with **Allah**, better and greater in reward. And seek forgiveness of **Allah**. Verily, **Allah** is Oft-Forgiving, **Most Merciful**. (Darussalam, 2000)

Ar-Rauf   The Most Kind

<u>Chapter Al-Baqarah</u>   Chapter 2 Verse 143
Thus we have made you, a just nation, that you be witnesses over mankind and the Messenger be a witness over you. And We made the Qiblah (prayer direction), which you used to face, only to test those who followed the Messenger from those who would turn on their heels. Indeed, it was great except for those whom **Allah** guided. And **Allah** would never make your faith to be lost. Truly, **Allah** is **Full of Kindness**, the Most Merciful towards mankind. (Darussalam, 1999)

Chapter Al-Baqarah   Chapter 2 Verse 207
And of mankind is he who would sell himself, seeking the Pleasure of **Allah**. And **Allah** is **Full of Kindness** to (His) slaves. (Darussalam, 1999)

Chapter Al-Imran   Chapter 3 Verse 30
On the day when every person will be confronted with all the good, he has done, and all the evil he has done, he will wish that there was a great distance between him and his evil. And **Allah** warns you against Himself and **Allah** is **Full of Kindness** to (His) slaves. (Darussalam, 1999)

Chapter At-Taubah   Chapter 9 Verse 117
Allah has forgiven the Prophet, the Muhajirun (emigrants) and the Ansar (the helpers) who followed him in the time of distress, after the hearts of a party of them had nearly deviated, but He accepted their repentance. Certainly, He is unto them **Full of Kindness**, Most Merciful. (Darussalam, 2000)

Chapter An-Nahl   Chapter 16 Verses 5~7
5. And the cattle, He has created them for you; in them there is warmth, and numerous benefits, and of them you eat.
6. And wherein is beauty for you, when you bring them home in the evening, and as you lead them forth to pasture in the morning.
7. And they carry your loads to a land that you could not reach except with great trouble to yourselves. Truly, your **Lord** is **Full of Kindness**, Most Merciful. (Darussalam, 2000)

Chapter An-Nahl   Chapter 16 Verses 45~47
45. Do then those who devise evil plots feel secure that **Allah** will not sink them into the earth, or that the torment will not seize them from directions they perceive not?
46. Or that He may catch them in the midst of their going to and fro, so that there be no escape for them?
47. Or that He may catch them with gradual wasting. Truly, your **Lord** is indeed **Full of Kindness**, Most Merciful? (Darussalam, 2000)

Chapter Al-Hajj   Chapter 22 Verse 65
See you not that **Allah** has subjected to you all that is on the earth, and the ships that sail through the sea by His Command? He withholds the heaven from falling on the earth except by His leave. Verily, **Allah** is, for mankind, **Full of Kindness**, Most Merciful. (Darussalam, 2000)

| Chapter An-Nur | Chapter 24 Verses 19~21 |

19. Verily, those who like that illegal sexual intercourse should be propagated among those who believe, they will have a painful torment in this world and in the Hereafter. And **Allah** knows and you know not.
20. And had it not been for the Grace of **Allah** and His Mercy on you. And that **Allah** is **Full of Kindness**, Most Merciful.
21. O you who believe! Follow not the footsteps of Shaitan (Satan). And whosoever follows the footsteps of Shaitan (Satan), then, verily he commands Al-Fahsha (immorality), and Al-Munkar (evil). And had it not been for the Grace of **Allah** and His Mercy on you, not one of you would ever have been pure from sins. But **Allah** purifies whom He wills, and **Allah** is All-Hearer, All-Knower. (Darussalam, 2000)

| Chapter Al-Hadid | Chapter 57 Verse 9 |

It is He Who sends down manifest Ayat (Verses) to His slave that He many bring you out from darkness into light. And verily, **Allah** is to you **Full of kindness**, Most Merciful. (Darussalam, 2000)

| Chapter Hashr | Chapter 59 Verse 10 |

And those who came after them say: "Our **Lord**! Forgive us and our brethren who have preceded us in Faith, and put not in our hearts any hatred against those who have believed. Our **Lord**! You are indeed **Full of Kindness**, Most Merciful. (Darussalam, 2000)

Al-Barr   The Gracious Benefactor

| Chapter At-Tur | Chapter 52 Verses 25~28 |

25. And some of them draw near to others, questioning.
26. Saying: "Aforetime, we were afraid in the midst of our families.
27. "So **Allah** has been gracious to us, and has saved us from the torment of the fire.
28. "Verily, we used to invoke Him before. Verily, He is **Al-Barr (the Most Subtle, kind, Courteous, and Generous**), the Most Merciful. (Darussalam, 2000)

Al-Kareem   The Most Generous

Chapter An-Naml   Chapter 27 Verses 38-40
38. He Said: "O chiefs! Which of you can bring me her throne before they come to me surrendering themselves in obedience?"
39. An Ifrit (strong one) from the jinn said: "I will bring it to you before you rise from your place. And verily, I am indeed strong and trustworthy for such work."
40. One with whom was knowledge of the Scripture said: "I will bring it to you within the twinkling of an eye!" Then when he saw it placed before him, he said: "This is by the Grace of my **Lord** to test me whether I am grateful or ungrateful! And whoever is grateful, truly, his gratitude is for his own self; and whoever is ungrateful. Certainly, my **Lord** is Rich, **Bountiful.** (Darussalam, 2000)

Chapter Al-Infitar   Chapter 82 Verses 6~8
6. O man! What has made you careless about your **Lord**, the **Most Generous**?
7. Who created you, fashioned you perfectly, and gave you due proportion.
8. In whatever form He willed, He put you together. (Darussalam, 2000)

Chapter Al-Alaq   Chapter 96 Verses 1~3
1. Read! In the name of your **Lord** Who has created.
2. He has created man from a clot.
3. Read! And your **Lord** is the **Most Generous.** (Darussalam, 2000)

Al-Wahhab   The Bestower

Chapter Al-Imran   Chapter 3 Verse 8
"Our **Lord**! Let not our hearts deviate after you have guided us, and grant us mercy from You. Truly, You are the **Bestower**." (Darussalam, 1999)

Chapter Sad   Chapter 38 Verses 6~10
6. And the leaders among them went about: "Go on, and remain constant to your alihah (gods)! Verily, this is a thing designed!
7. "We have not heard of this in the religion of these later days. This is nothing but an invention!

8. "Has the Reminder been sent down to him from among us? Nay, but they are in doubt about My Reminder! Nay, but they have not tasted Torment!
9. Or have they the treasures of the Mercy of your **Lord**, the All-Mighty, the Real **Bestower**?
10. Or is it that the dominion of the heavens and the earth and all that is between them is theirs? If so, let them ascend up with means! (Darussalam, 2000)

Chapter Sad   Chapter 38 Verses 34~38
34. And indeed, We did try Sulaiman and We placed on his throne Jasad and he did return.
35. He said: "My **Lord**! Forgive me, and bestow upon me a kingdom such as shall not belong to any other after me: Verily, You are the **Bestower**."
36. So, We subjected to him the wind; it blew gently by his order wherever he willed.
37. And also the Shayatin (Satan) from the jinn every kind of builder and diver,
38. And also others bound in fetters. (Darussalam, 2000)

Ar-Razzaq   The Ever Providing

Chapter Al-Baqarah   Chapter 2 Verse 212
Beautified is the life of this world for those who disbelieve, and they mock at those who believe. But those who obey **Allah**'s Orders and keep away from what He has forbidden, will be above them on the Day of Resurrection. And **Allah gives to whom He wills without limit.** (Darussalam, 1999)

Chapter Al-Imran   Chapter 3 Verses 35~37
35. When the wife of 'Imran said: "O my **Lord**! I have vowed to You what is in my womb to be dedicated for Your services, so accept this, from me. Verily, You are the All-Hearer, the All-Knowing."
36. Then when she gave birth to her, she said: "O my **Lord**! I have given birth to a female child," - and **Allah** knew better what she brought forth, - "And the male is not like the female, and I have named her Maryam, and I seek refuge with You for her and for her offspring from Shaitan (Satan), the outcast."
37. So, her **Lord** accepted her with goodly acceptance. He made her grow in a good manner and put her under the care of Zakariya. Every time he entered Al-Mihrab to her, he found her supplied with sustenance. He said: "O

Maryam! From where have you got this? She said, "This is from **Allah**." Verily **Allah provides sustenance to whom He wills**, without limit. (Darussalam, 1999)

Chapter Al-Ma'idah   Chapter 5 Verse 114
Isa, son of Maryam, said: "O **Allah**, our **Lord**! Send us from the heaven a table spread that there may be for us – for first and the last of us- festival and a sign from You: and provide us with sustenance, for You are the **Best of sustainers**." (Darussalam, 1999)

Chapter Al-A`raf   Chapter 7 Verse 50
And the dwellers of the Fire will call to the dwellers of Paradise: "Pour on us some water or anything that **Allah has provided you with**." They will say: "Both **Allah** has forbidden to the disbelievers." (Darussalam, 1999)

Chapter Yunus   Chapter 10 Verse 31
Say: "**Who provides for you** from the sky and the earth? Or who owns hearing and sight? And who brings out the living from the dead and brings out the dead from the living? And who disposes the affairs? They will say? "**Allah**" Say: "Will you not then be afraid of **Allah**'s punishment?" (Darussalam, 2000)

Chapter Ta-Ha   Chapter 20 Verses 132
And enjoin As-Salat (prayer) on your family, and be patient in offering them. We ask not of you a provision: **We provide for you.** And the good end is for the Muttaqun (pious). (Darussalam, 2000)

Chapter An-Nur   Chapter 24 Verses 37-38
37. Men whom neither trade nor sale diverts them from the remembrance of **Allah**, nor from performing As-Salat (prayer), nor from giving the Zakat (charity-alms). They fear a Day when hearts and eyes will be overturned.
38. That **Allah** may reward them according to the best of their deeds, and add even more for them out of His Grace. And **Allah provides without measure to whom He wills**. (Darussalam, 2000)

Chapter An-Naml   Chapter 27 Verse 64
Is not He Who originates creation, and shall thereafter repeat it, and **Who provides for you** from heaven and earth? Is there any ilah (god) with **Allah**? Say: "Bring forth your proofs, if you are truthful." (Darussalam, 2000)

Chapter Al-Ankabut   Chapter 29 Verse 60

And so many a moving creature carries not its own provision! **Allah provides for it and for you.** And He is the All-Hearer, the All-Knower. (Darussalam, 2000)

Chapter Saba   Chapter 34 Verses 24~27

24. Say: "**Who gives you provision** from the heavens and the earth?" say: "**Allah**. And verily, we or you are rightly guided or in the plain error."
25. Say: "You will not be asked about our sins, nor shall we be asked of what you do."
26. Say: "Our **Lord** will assemble us all together, then He will judge between us with truth. And He is the Just Judge, the All-Knower of the true state of affairs."
27. Say: "Show me those whom you have joined with Him as partners. Nay! But He is **Allah**, the All-Mighty, the All-Wise." (Darussalam, 2000)

Chapter Fatir   Chapter 35 Verse 3

O mankind! Remember the Grace of **Allah** upon you! Is there any creator other than **Allah** who **provides for you** from the sky and the earth? La ilaha illa Huwa (none has the right to be worshipped but He). How then are you turning away? (Darussalam, 2000)

Chapter Ash-Shura   Chapter 42 Verse 19

Allah is very Gracious and kind to His slaves. **He gives provisions to whom He wills.** And He is the All-Strong, the All-Mighty. (Darussalam, 2000)

Chapter Adh-Dhariyat   Chapter 51 Verse 58

Verily, **Allah** is the **All-Provider**, Owner of Power, the Most Strong. (Darussalam, 2000)

Chapter Al-Mulk   Chapter 67 Verses 20-21

20. Who is He besides the Most Gracious that can be an army to you to help you? The disbelievers are in nothing but delusion.
21. Who is he that can provide for you if He should withhold His **provision**? Nay, but they continue to be in pride, and flee. (Darussalam, 2000)

Subsection 2

SUBSECTION 2

- *Al-Afuww*   The Pardoner
- *Al-Ghafur*   The All-Forgiving
- *Al-Ghaffar*   The Ever Forgiving
- *At-Tawwab*   The Accepter of Repentance
- *Al-Latif*   The Subtle kind
- *Al-Wudud*   The Most Loving
- *Al-Halim*   The Most Forbearing
- *Ash-Shakur*   Most Ready to Appreciate
- *Al-Mujib*   The Responsive

Al-Afuww   The Pardoner

Chapter Al-Baqarah   Chapter 2 Verse 187
It is made lawful for you to have sexual relations with your wives on the night of As Saum (the fasts). They are Libas (clothing, garments) for you and you are the same for them. **Allah** knows that you used to deceive yourselves, so He turned to you and **forgave** you. So now have sexual relations with them and seek that which **Allah** has ordained for you, and eat and drink until the white thread of down appears to you distinct from the black thread, then complete your Saum (fasts) till the nightfall. And do not have sexual relations with them while you are in I'tikaf in the mosques. These are the limits by **Allah**, so approach them not. Thus does **Allah** make clear His Ayat (verse) to mankind that they may become Al-Muttaqun (the pious). (Darussalam, 1999)

Chapter Al-Imran   Chapter 3 Verse 152
And **Allah** did indeed fulfill His promise to you when you were killing them with His permission; until you lost your courage and fell to disputing about the order, and disobeyed after He showed you which you love. Among you are some that desire this world and some that desire the hereafter. Then He made you flee from them, that He might test you. But surely, He **forgave** you, and **Allah** is Most Gracious to the believers. (Darussalam, 1999)

Chapter Al-Imran   Chapter 3 Verse 155
Those of you who turned back on the day the two hosts met, it was Shaitan (Satan) who caused them to backslide because of some they had earned. But **Allah**, indeed, has **forgiven** them. Surely, **Allah** is Oft-Forgiving, Most Forbearing. (Darussalam, 1999)

Chapter An-Nisa   Chapter 4 Verse 43
O you who believe! Approach not As-Salat (prayer) when you are in a drunken state until you know of what you utter, nor when you are in a state of Janaba (i.e., in a state of sexual impurity and have not yet taken a bath), except when traveling on the road, till you wash your whole body. And if you are ill, or a journey, or one of you comes after answering the call of nature, or you have been in contact with women and you find no water, perform Tayammum with clear earth and rub therewith your faces and hands. Truly, **Allah** is Ever **Oft-Pardoning**, Oft-Forgiving. (Darussalam, 1999)

Chapter An-Nisa   Chapter 4 Verses 97~99

97. Verily, as for those whom the angels take while they are wronging themselves, they say: "In what were you? They reply: "We were weak and oppressed on the earth. "They say: "Was not the earth of **Allah** spacious enough for you to emigrate therein? "Such men will find their abode in Hell-what an evil destination.
98. Except the weak ones among men, women and children who cannot devise a plan, nor are they able to direct their way.
99. These are they whom **Allah** is likely to forgive them, and **Allah** is Ever **Oft-Pardoning**, Oft-Forgiving. (Darussalam, 1999)

Chapter An-Nisa   Chapter 4 Verse 149

Whether you disclose a good deed, or conceal it, or pardon an evil, verily, **Allah** is Ever **Oft-Pardoning**, All-Powerful. (Darussalam, 1999)

Chapter Al-Ma'idah   Chapter 5 Verse 95

O you who believe! Kill not the game while you are in a state of Ihram, and whosoever of you kills it intentionally, the penalty is an offering, brought to the ka'bah, of an eatable animal equivalent to the one he killed, as adjudged by two just men among you; or, for expiation, he should feed Masakin (poor persons), or its equivalent in saum (fasting), that he may taste the heaviness of his deed. **Allah** has **forgiven** what is past, but whosoever commits it again, **Allah** will take retribution from him. And **Allah** is All-Mighty, All-Able of Retribution. (Darussalam, 1999)

Chapter Al-Ma`idah   Chapter 5 Verse 101

O you who believe! Ask not about things, which, if made plain to you, may cause you trouble. But if you ask about them while the Quran is being revealed, they will be made plain to you. **Allah** has **forgiven** that, and **Allah** is Oft-Forgiving, Most Forbearing. (Darussalam, 1999)

Chapter Al-Hajj   Chapter 22 Verse 60

That is so. And whoever has retaliated with the like of that which he was made to suffer, and then has again been wronged, **Allah** will surely help him. Verily, **Allah** indeed is **Oft-Pardoning**, Oft-Forgiving. (Darussalam, 2000)

Chapter Al-Mujadilah   Chapter 58 Verse 2

Those among you who make their wives unlawful to them by Zihar (saying to them "you are like my mother's back"), they cannot be their mothers. None can be their mothers except those who gave them birth. And verily, they utter an ill word and a lie. And verily, **Allah** is **Oft-Pardoning**, Oft-Forgiving. (Darussalam, 2000)

Al-Ghafur   The All-Forgiving

Chapter Al-Baqarah   Chapter 2 Verse 173
He has forbidden you only the Maitah (dead animals), and blood, and the flesh of swine, and that, which is slaughtered as a sacrifice for others than **Allah**. But if one is forced by necessity without willful disobedience nor transgressing due limits, then there is no sin on him. Truly, **Allah** is **Oft-Forgiving**, Most Merciful. (Darussalam, 1999)

Chapter Al-Baqarah   Chapter 2 Verse 182
But He who fears from a testator some unjust act or wrongdoing, and thereupon he makes peace between the parties concerned, there shall be no sin on him. Certainly, **Allah** is **Oft-Forgiving**, Most Merciful. (Darussalam, 1999)

Chapter Al-Baqarah   Chapter 2 Verses 191-192
191. And kill them wherever you find them, and turn them out from where they have turned you out. And Al-Fitnah is worse than killing. And fight not with them at Al-Masjid Al-Haram, unless they fight you there. But if they attack you, then kill them. Such is the recompense of the disbelievers.
192. But if they cease, then **Allah** is **Oft-Forgiving**, Most Merciful. (Darussalam, 1999)

Chapter Al-Baqarah   Chapter 2 Verses 198-199
198. There is no sin on you if you seek the Bounty of your **Lord**. Then when you leave Arafat, remember **Allah** at the (Muzdalifah). And remember Him as He has guided you, and verily, you were, before, of those who were astray.
199. Then depart from the place whence all the people depart and ask **Allah** for His forgiveness. Truly, **Allah** is **Oft-Forgiving**, Most Merciful. (Darussalam, 1999)

Chapter Al-Baqarah   Chapter 2 Verse 218
Verily, those who have believed, and those who have emigrated and have striven hard in the way of **Allah**, all these hope for **Allah**'s Mercy. And **Allah** is **Oft-Forgiving**, Most-Merciful. (Darussalam, 1999)

Chapter Al-Baqarah   Chapter 2 Verses 225-226

225. **Allah** will not call you to account for that which is unintentional in your oaths, but He will call you to account for that which your hearts have earned. And **Allah** is **Oft-Forgiving**, Most Forbearing.
226. Those who take an oath not to have sexual relations with their wives must wait for four months, then if they return, verily, **Allah** is **Oft-Forgiving**, Most Merciful. (Darussalam, 1999)

Chapter Al-Baqarah   Chapter 2 Verse 235
And there is no sin on you if you make a hint of betrothal or conceal it in yourself, **Allah** knows that you will remember them, but do not make a promise of contract with them in secret except that you speak an honourable saying according to the Islamic law. And do not consummate the marriage until the term prescribed is fulfilled. And know that **Allah** knows what is in your minds, so fear Him. And know that **Allah** is **Oft-Forgiving**, Most Forbearing. (Darussalam, 1999)

Chapter Al-Imran   Chapter 3 Verse 31-32
31. Say: "If you love **Allah**, then follow me, **Allah** will love you and forgive you your sins. And **Allah** is **Oft-Forgiving**, Most Merciful.
32. Say: "Obey Allah and the Messenger." But if they turn away, then Allah does not like the disbelievers. (Darussalam, 1999)

Chapter Al-Imran   Chapter 3 Verses 86~89
86. How shall **Allah** guide a people who disbelieved after their Belief and after they bore witness that the Messenger is true and after clear proofs had come unto them? And **Allah** guides not the people who are Dhalimun (wrong-doers).
87. They are those whose recompense is that on them the Curse of **Allah**, of the angels, and of all mankind.
88. They will abide therein. Neither will their torment be lightened, nor will it be delayed or postponed.
89. Except for those who repent after that and do righteous deeds. Verily, **Allah** is **Oft-Forgiving**, Most Merciful. (Darussalam, 1999)

Chapter Al-Imran   Chapter 3 Verse 129
And to **Allah** belongs all that is in the heavens and all that is in the earth. He forgives whom He wills, and punishes whom He wills. And **Allah** is **Oft-Forgiving**, Most Merciful. (Darussalam, 1999)

Chapter Al-Imran   Chapter 3 Verse 155

Those of you who turned back on the day the two hosts met, it was Shaitan (Satan) who caused them to backslide because of some they had earned. But **Allah**, indeed, has forgiven them. Surely, **Allah** is **Oft-Forgiving**, Most forbearing. (Darussalam, 1999)

Chapter An-Nisa   Chapter 4 Verse 23

Forbidden to you are: your mothers, your daughters, your sisters, your father's sisters, your mother's sisters, your brother's daughters, your sister's daughters, your foster mothers who gave you suck, your foster milk suckling sisters, your wives' mothers, your stepdaughters under your guardianship, born of your wives to whom you have gone in but there is no sin on you if you have not gone in them, -- the wives of your sons who from your own loins, and two sisters in wedlock at the same time, except for what has already passed; verily, **Allah** is **Oft-Forgiving**, Most Merciful. (Darussalam, 1999)

Chapter An-Nisa   Chapter 4 Verse 25

And whoever of you have not the means wherewith to wed free believing women, they may wed believing girls from among those whom your right hands possess, and **Allah** has full knowledge about your Faith; you are one from another. Wed them with the permission of their own folk and give them their Mahr (bridal money) according to what is reasonable; they should be chaste, not committing illegal sex, nor taking boyfriends. And after they have been taken in wedlock, if they commit illegal sexual intercourse, their punishment is half of that for free women, this is for him among you who is afraid of being harmed in his religion or in his body; but it is better for you that you practice self-restraint, and **Allah** is **Oft-Forgiving**, Most Merciful. (Darussalam, 1999)

Chapter An-Nisa   Chapter 4 Verse 43

O you who believe! Approach not As-Salat (prayer) when you are in a drunken state until you know of what you utter, nor when you are in a state of Janaba (i.e., in a state of sexual impurity and have not yet taken a bath), except when traveling on the road, till you wash your whole body. And if you are ill, or on a journey, or one of you comes after answering the call of nature, or you have been in contact with women and you find no water, perform Tayammum with clean earth and rub therewith your faces and hand. Truly, **Allah** is Ever Oft-Pardoning, **Oft-Forgiving**. (Darussalam, 1999)

Chapter An-Nisa   Chapter 4 Verse 48

Verily, **Allah** forgives not that partners should be set up with him, but He forgives except that to whom He wills; and whoever sets up partners with **Allah** in worship, He has indeed invented a tremendous sin. (Darussalam, 1999)

Chapter An-Nisa   Chapter 4 Verses 95~100

95. Not equal are those of the believers who sit, except those who are disabled, and those who strive hard and fight in the cause of **Allah** with their wealth and their lives. **Allah** has preferred in grades those who strive hard and fight with their wealth and their lives above those who sit. Unto each, **Allah** has promised good, but **Allah** has preferred those who strive hard and fight, above those who sit by a huge reward.
96. Degrees of grades from Him, and forgiveness and mercy. And **Allah** is Ever **Oft-Forgiving**, Most Merciful.
97. Verily, as for those whom the angels take while they are wronging themselves, they say: "In what were you?" They reply: "We were weak and oppressed on the earth." They say: "Was not the earth of **Allah** spacious enough for you to emigrate therein?" Such men will find their abode in Hell- what an evil destination!
98. Except the weak ones among men, women and children who cannot devise a plan, nor are they able to direct their way.
99. These are they whom **Allah** is likely to forgive them, and **Allah** is Ever Oft-Pardoning, **Oft-Forgiving**.
100. He who emigrates in the cause of **Allah**, will find on earth many dwelling places and plenty to live by. And whosoever leaves his home as an emigrant unto **Allah** and His Messenger, and death overtakes him, his reward is then surely, incumbent upon **Allah**. And **Allah** is Ever **Oft-Forgiving**, Most Merciful. (Darussalam, 1999)

Chapter An-Nisa   Chapter 4 Verse 106

And seek the forgiveness of **Allah**, certainly, **Allah** is Ever **Oft-Forgiving**, Most Merciful. (Darussalam, 1999)

Chapter An-Nisa   Chapter 4 Verse 110

And whoever does evil or wrongs himself but afterwards seeks **Allah**'s forgiveness, he will find **Allah Oft-Forgiving**, Most Merciful. (Darussalam, 1999)

Chapter An-Nisa   Chapter 4 Verse 116
Verily, **Allah** forgives not setting up partners with Him, but He forgives whom He wills, sins other than that, and whoever sets up partners in worship with **Allah** has indeed strayed far away. (Darussalam, 1999)

Chapter An-Nisa   Chapter 4 Verse 129
You will never be able to do perfect justice between wives even if it is your ardent desire, so do not incline too much to one of them so as to leave the other hanging. And if you do justice, and do all that is right and fear **Allah** by keeping away from all that is wrong, then **Allah** is Ever **Oft-Forgiving**, Most Merciful. (Darussalam, 1999)

Chapter An-Nisa   Chapter 4 Verse 152
And those who believe in **Allah** and His Messengers and make no distinction between any of them, We shall give them their rewards; and **Allah** is Ever **Oft-Forgiving**, Most Merciful. (Darussalam, 1999)

Chapter Al-Ma'idah   Chapter 5 Verse 3
Forbidden to you are Al-Maitah (dead animals), blood, the flesh of swine, and that on which **Allah**'s name has not been mentioned while slaughtering and that which has been killed by strangling, or by a violent blow or by a headlong fall, or by the goring of horns – and that which has been eaten by a wild animal- unless you are able to slaughter it and that which is sacrificed on An-Nusub (stone altars). (Forbidden) also is to use arrows seeking luck or decision; that is fisqun (disobedience of Allah and sin). This day, those who disbelieved have been given up all hope of your religion; so fear them not, but fear Me. This day, I have perfected your religion for you, completed My Favour upon you, and have chosen for you Islam as your religion. But as for him who is forced by severe hunger, with no inclination to sin, then surely, **Allah** is Oft-Forgiving, **Most Merciful**. (Darussalam, 1999)

Chapter Al-Ma'idah   Chapter 5 Verses 33-34
33. The recompense of those who wage war against **Allah** and His Messenger and do mischief in the land is only that they shall be killed or crucified or their hands and their feet be cut off from opposite sides, or be exiled from the land. That is their disgrace in this world. And a great torment is theirs in the Hereafter.
34. Except for those who came back with repentance before they fall into you power; in that case, know that **Allah** is **Oft-Forgiving**, Most Merciful. (Darussalam, 1999)

Chapter Al-Ma'idah — Chapter 5 Verses 38~40

38. And the male thief and the female thief, cut off their hands as a recompense for that which they committed, a punishment by way of example from **Allah**. And **Allah** is All-Powerful, All-Wise.
39. But whosoever repents after his crime and does righteous good deeds, then verily, **Allah** will pardon him. Verily, **Allah** is **Oft-Forgiving**, Most Merciful.
40. Know you not that to **Allah** belongs the dominion of the heavens and the earth! He punishes whom He wills and He forgives whom He wills. And **Allah** is Able to do all things. (Darussalam, 1999)

Chapter Al-Ma'idah — Chapter 5 Verses 73-74

73. Surely, disbelievers are those who said: "**Allah** is the third of the three." "But there is no Ilah (god) but One Ilah (God). And if they cease not from what they say, verily, a painful torment will befall on the disbelievers among them.
74. Will they not turn with repentance to **Allah** and ask His forgiveness? For **Allah** is **Oft-Forgiving**, Most Merciful. (Darussalam, 1999)

Chapter Al-Ma'idah — Chapter 5 Verse 98

Know that **Allah** is Severe in punishment and that **Allah** is **Oft-Forgiving**, Most Merciful. (Darussalam, 1999)

Chapter Al-Ma'idah — Chapter 5 Verse 101

O you who believe! Ask not about things, which if made plain to you, may cause you trouble. But if you ask about them while the Quran is being revealed, they will be made plain to you. **Allah** has forgiven that, and **Allah** is **Oft-Forgiving**, Most Forbearing. (Darussalam, 1999)

Chapter Al-An`am — Chapter 6 Verse 54

When those who believe in Our Ayat (verse) come to you, say: "Salamun Alaikum (peace be on you); your **Lord** has written **Mercy** for Himself, so that if any of you does evil in ignorance, and thereafter repents and does righteous good deeds, then surely, He is **Oft-Forgiving**, Most Merciful. (Darussalam, 1999)

Chapter Al-An`am — Chapter 6 Verse 145

Say: "I find not in that which has been revealed to me anything forbidden to be eaten by one who wishes to eat it, unless it be Maitah (dead animals) or blood poured forth, or the flesh of swine; for that surely, is impure or impious meat which is slaughtered as a sacrifice for others than **Allah**. But whosoever is forced by necessity without willful disobedience, nor transgressing due limits; certainly, your **Lord** is **Oft-Forgiving**, Most Merciful. (Darussalam, 1999)

Chapter Al-An`am   Chapter 6 Verse 165
And it is He who has made you generations coming after generations, replacing each other on the earth. And He has raised you in ranks. Some above others that He may try you in that which He has bestowed on you. Surely, your **Lord** is swift in retribution, and certainly He is **Oft-Forgiving**, Most Merciful. (Darussalam, 1999)

Chapter Al-A`raf   Chapter 7 Verses 152-153
152. Certainly, those who took the calf, wrath from their **Lord** and humiliation will come upon them in the life of this world. Thus, do we recompense those who invent lies.
153. But those who committed evil deeds and then repented afterwards and believed, verily, your **Lord** after that is indeed **Oft-Forgiving**, Most Merciful. (Darussalam, 1999)

Chapter Al-A`raf   Chapter 7 Verse 167
167. And when your **Lord** declared that He would certainly keep on sending against them, till the Day of Resurrection, those who would afflict them with a humiliating torment. Verily, your **Lord** is Quick in Retribution and certainly He is **Oft-Forgiving**, Most Merciful. (Darussalam, 1999)

Chapter Al-Anfal   Chapter 8 Verses 69-70
69. So, enjoy what you have gotten of booty in war, lawful and good, and be afraid of **Allah**. Certainly, **Allah** is **Oft-Forgiving**, Most Merciful.
70. O Prophet! Say to the captives that are in your hands. "If **Allah** knows any good in your hearts, He will give you something better than what has been taken from you, and He will Forgive you, and **Allah** is **Oft-Forgiving**, Most Merciful. (Darussalam, 1999)

Chapter At-Taubah   Chapter 9 Verse 5
Then when the Sacred Months have passed, then kill the Mushrikun (polytheists) wherever you find them, and capture them and besiege them, and lie in wait for them in each and every ambush. But if they repent and perform As-Salat (prayer), and give Zakat (charity-alms), then leave their way free. Verily, **Allah** is **Oft-Forgiving**, Most Merciful. (Darussalam, 1999)

| Chapter At-Taubah | Chapter 9 Verses 26-27 |

26. Then **Allah** did send down his Sakinah (peace) on the Messenger, and on the believers, and sent down forces which you saw not, and punished the disbelievers. Such is the recompense of disbelievers.

27. Then after that **Allah** will accept the repentance of whom He wills. And **Allah** is **Oft-Forgiving**, Most Merciful. (Darussalam, 1999)

| Chapter At-Taubah | Chapter 9 Verse 91 |

There is no blame on those who are weak or ill or who find no resources to spend, if they are sincere and true to **Allah** and His Messenger. No ground can there be against the Muhsinun (good-doers). And **Allah** is **Oft-Forgiving**, Most Merciful. (Darussalam, 1999)

| Chapter At-Taubah | Chapter 9 Verse 102 |

And others who have acknowledged their sins, they have mixed a deed that was righteous with another that was evil. Perhaps **Allah** will turn unto them in forgiveness. Surely, **Allah** is **Oft-Forgiving**, Most Merciful. (Darussalam, 2000)

| Chapter Yunus | Chapter 10 Verse 107 |

And if **Allah** touches you with harm, there is none who can remove it but He; and if He intends any good for you, there is none who can repel His favour which He causes it to reach whomsoever of His slaves He wills. And He is the **Oft-Forgiving**, Most Merciful. (Darussalam, 2000)

| Chapter Hud | Chapter 11 Verse 41 |

And he (Nuh) said: "Embark therein in the name of **Allah** will be its course and its anchorage. Surely, my **Lord** is **Oft-Forgiving**, Most Merciful." (Darussalam, 2000)

| Chapter Yusuf | Chapter 12 Verse 53 |

"And I free not myself. Verily, the self is inclined to evil, except when my **Lord** bestows His mercy. Verily, my **Lord** is **Oft-Forgiving**, Most Merciful." (Darussalam, 2000)

| Chapter Yusuf | Chapter 12 Verses 97-98 |

97. They said: "O our father! Ask forgiveness for our sins, indeed we have been sinners."

98. He said: "I will ask my **Lord** for forgiveness for you, verily, He! Only He is the **Oft-Forgiving**, the Most Merciful. (Darussalam, 2000)

Chapter Ibrahim   Chapter 14 Verses 35-36
35. And when Ibrahim said: "O my **Lord**! Make this city one of peace and security, and keep me and my sons away from worshipping idols.
36. "O my **Lord**! They have indeed led astray many among mankind. But whoso follows me, he verily, is of me. And whoso disobeys me, still you are indeed **Oft-Forgiving**, Most Merciful. (Darussalam, 2000)

Chapter Al-Hijr   Chapter 15 Verse 49
Declare unto my slaves, that truly, I am the **Oft-Forgiving**, Most Merciful. (Darussalam, 2000)

Chapter An-Nahl   Chapter 16 Verse 18
And if you would count the Favours of **Allah**, never could you be able to count them. Truly, **Allah** is **Oft-Forgiving**, Most Merciful. (Darussalam, 2000)

Chapter An-Nahl   Chapter 16 Verse 110
Then, verily, your **Lord** – for those who emigrated after they had been put to trials and thereafter strove hard and fought and were patient, verily, your **Lord** afterward is, **Oft-Forgiving**, Most Merciful. (Darussalam, 2000)

Chapter An-Nahl   Chapter 16 Verse 115
He has forbidden you only Al-Maitah (dead animals), blood, the flesh of swine, and any animal which is slaughtered as a sacrifice for others than **Allah**. But if one is forced by necessity, without willful disobedience, and not transgressing, - then, **Allah** is **Oft-Forgiving**, Most Merciful. (Darussalam, 2000)

Chapter An-Nahl   Chapter 16 Verse 119
Then, verily, your **Lord** - for those who do evil in ignorance and afterward repent and do righteous deeds, verily, your **Lord** thereafter, is **Oft-Forgiving**, Most Merciful. (Darussalam, 2000)

Chapter Al-Isra   Chapter 17 Verse 25
Your **Lord** knows best what is in your inner- selves. If you are righteous, then, verily, He is Ever **Most Forgiving** to those who turn unto Him again and again in obedience, and in repentance. (Darussalam, 2000)

Chapter Al-Isra   Chapter 17 Verse 44
The seven heavens and the earth and all that is therein, glorify Him and there is not a thing but glorifies His Praise. But you understand not their

glorification. Truly, He is Ever Forbearing, **Oft-Forgiving**. (Darussalam, 2000)

Chapter Al-Kahf   Chapter 18 Verse 58
And your **Lord** is **Most Forgiving**, Owner of mercy. Were He to call them to account for what they have earned, then surely, He would have hastened their punishment. But they have their appointed time, beyond which they will find no escape. (Darussalam, 2000)

Chapter Al-Hajj   Chapter 22 Verse 60
That is so. And whoever has retaliated with the like of that which he was made to suffer, and then has again been wronged, **Allah** will surely help him. Verily, **Allah** indeed is Oft-Pardoning, **Oft-Forgiving**. ((Darussalam, 2000)

Chapter An-Nur   Chapter 24 Verses 4-5
4. And those who accuse chaste women, and produce not four witnesses, flog them with eighty stripes, and reject their testimony forever. They indeed are the Fasiqun (disobedient).
5. Except those who repent thereafter and do righteous deeds; verily, **Allah** is **Oft-Forgiving**, Most Merciful. (Darussalam, 2000)

Chapter An-Nur   Chapter 24 Verse 22
And let not those among you who are blessed with graces and wealth swear not to give to their kinsmen, Al-Masakin (the poor), and those who left their homes for **Allah**'s Cause. Let them pardon and forgive. Do you not love that **Allah** should forgive you? And **Allah** is **Oft-Forgiving**, Most Merciful. (Darussalam, 2000)

Chapter An-Nur   Chapter 24 Verse 33
And let those who find not the financial means for marriage keep themselves chaste, until **Allah** enriches them of His Bounty. And such of your slaves as seek a writing, give them such writing, if you find that there is good and honesty in them. And give them something out of the wealth of **Allah** which He has bestowed upon you. And force not your maids to prostitution, if they desire chastity, in order that you make a gain in the goods of this worldly life. But if anyone compels them, then after such compulsion, **Allah** is **Oft-Forgiving**, Most Merciful. (Darussalam, 2000)

Chapter An-Nur   Chapter 24 Verse 62
The true believers are only those, who believe in **Allah** and His Messenger; and when they are with him on some common matter, they go not away until

they asked his permission. Verily, those who ask your permission, those are they who believe in **Allah** and His Messenger. So, if they ask your permission for some affairs of theirs, give permission to whom you will of them, and ask **Allah** for their forgiveness. Truly, **Allah** is **Oft-Forgiving**, Most Merciful. (Darussalam, 2000)

Chapter Al-Furqan   Chapter 25 Verse 6
Say: It has been sent down by Him Who knows the secret of the heavens and the earth. Truly, He is **Oft-Forgiving**, Most Merciful. (Darussalam, 2000)

Chapter Al-Furqan   Chapter 25 Verse 70
Except those who repent and believe, and do righteous deeds; for those, **Allah** will change their sins into good deeds, and **Allah** is **Oft-Forgiving**, Most Merciful. (Darussalam, 2000)

Chapter An-Naml   Chapter 27 Verses 10-11
1. "And throw down your stick!" But when he saw it moving as if it were a snake, he turned in flight, and did not look back. O Musa! Fear not: verily, the Messengers fear not in front of Me.
2. Except him who has done wrong and afterwards has changed evil for good; then surely, I am **Oft-Forgiving**, Most Merciful. (Darussalam, 2000)

Chapter Al-Qasas   Chapter 28 Verses 15-16
15. And he entered the city at a time of unawareness of its people; and he found there two men fighting, one of his party, and the other of his foes. The man of his party asked him for help against his foe, so Musa struck him with his fist and killed him. He said: "This is of Shaitan's (Satan) doing, verily, he is a plain misleading enemy."
16. He said: "My **Lord**! Verily, I have wronged myself, so forgive me." Then He forgave him. Verily, He is the **Oft-Forgiving**, the Most Merciful. (Darussalam, 2000)

Chapter Al-Ahzab   Chapter 33 Verses 4-5
4. **Allah** has not made for any man two hearts inside his body. Neither has He made your wives whom you declare to be like your mothers' backs, your real mothers. Nor has He made your adopted sons your real sons. That is but your saying with your mouths. But **Allah** says the truth, and He guides to the way.
5. Call them by their fathers, that is more just with **Allah**, but if you know not their father's your brothers in Faith and Mawalikum (your freed slaves). And there is no sin on you concerning that in which you made a mistake,

except in regard to what your hearts deliberately intend. And **Allah** is Ever **Oft-Forgiving**, Most Merciful. (Darussalam, 2000)

Chapter Al-Ahzab   Chapter 33 Verse 23-24
23. Among the believers are men who have been true to their covenant with **Allah**; of them some have fulfilled their obligations; and some of them are still waiting, but they have never changed in the least.
24. That **Allah** may reward the men of truth for their truth and punish the hypocrites, if He wills, or accept their repentance by turning to them. Verily, **Allah** is **Oft-Forgiving**, Most Merciful. (Darussalam, 2000)

Chapter Al-Ahzab   Chapter 33 Verse 50
O Prophet! Verily, we have made lawful to you your wives, to whom you have paid their Mahr (bridal money), and those whom your right hand possesses- whom **Allah** has given to you, and the daughters of your Amm (paternal uncles) and the daughters of your Ammat (paternal aunts) and the daughters of your khal (maternal uncles) and the daughters of your khalat (maternal aunts) who migrated with you, and a believing woman if she offers herself to the Prophet, and the Prophet wishes to marry her- a privilege for you only, not for the (rest of) the believers. Indeed, We know what We have enjoined upon them about their wives and those whom their right hands possess, in order that there should be no difficulty on you. And **Allah** is **Ever Oft-Forgiving**, Most Merciful. (Darussalam, 2000)

Chapter Al-Ahzab   Chapter 33 Verse 59
O Prophet! Tell your wives and your daughters and the women of the believers to draw their cloaks all over their bodies. That will be better that they should be known so as not to be annoyed. And **Allah** is Ever **Oft-Forgiving**, Most Merciful. (Darussalam, 2000)

Chapter Al-Ahzab   Chapter 33 Verses 72-73
72. Truly, we did offer Al-Amanah (the trust) to the heavens and the earth, and the mountains, but they declined to bear it and were afraid of it. But man bore it. Verily, he was unjust and ignorant.
73. So that **Allah** will punish the hypocrites, men and women, and the men and women who are Al- Mushrikun (polytheists). And **Allah** will pardon the true believers of Islamic Monotheism, men and women. And **Allah** is Ever **Oft-Forgiving**, Most Merciful. (Darussalam, 2000)

Chapter Saba   Chapter 34 Verse 2

He knows that which goes into the earth and that which comes forth from it, and that which descends from the heaven and that which ascends to it. And He is the Most Merciful, the **Oft-Forgiving**. (Darussalam, 2000)

Chapter Saba   Chapter 34 Verse 15

Indeed, there was for Saba a sign in their dwelling place- two gardens on the right hand and on the left; "Eat of the provision of your **Lord**, and be grateful to Him." A Fair land and an **Oft-Forgiving Lord**! (Darussalam, 2000)

Chapter Fatir   Chapter 35 Verses 28~30

28. And likewise, men and Ad-Dawabb (moving creatures) and cattle are of various colours, it is only those who have knowledge among His slaves that fear **Allah**. Verily, **Allah** is All-Mighty. **Oft-Forgiving**.
29. Verily, those who recite the book of **Allah**, and perform As-Salat (prayer), and spend out of what We have provided for them, secretly and openly, they hope for a trade - gain that will never perish.
30. That He may pay them their wages in full, and give them more, out of His Grace. Verily, He is **Oft-Forgiving**, Most Ready to appreciate. (Darussalam, 2000)

Chapter Fatir   Chapter 35 Verses 33-34

33. And Adn (paradise) will they enter, therein will they be adorned with bracelets of gold and pearls, and their garments therein will be of silk.
34. And they will say: "All the praises and thanks be to **Allah** who has removed from us grief. Verily, our **Lord** is indeed **Oft-Forgiving**, Most Ready to appreciate. (Darussalam, 2000)

Chapter Fatir   Chapter 35 Verse 41

Verily, **Allah** grasps the heavens and the earth lest they should move away from their places, and if they were to move away from their places, there is not one that could grasp them after Him. Truly, He is Ever Most Forbearing, **Oft-Forgiving**. (Darussalam, 2000)

Chapter Az-Zumar   Chapter 39 Verse 53

Say: "O' Ibadi (My slaves) who have transgressed against themselves! Despair not of the Mercy of **Allah**, verily, **Allah** forgives all sins. Truly, He is **Oft-Forgiving**, Most Merciful. (Darussalam, 2000)

Chapter Fussilat   Chapter 41 Verses 30-32
30. Verily, those who say: "Our Lord is Allah," and then they stand firm, on them the angels will descend (at the time of their death) (saying): "Fear not, nor grieve! But receive the glad tidings of Paradise which you have been promised!
31. "We have been your friends in the life of this world and are in the Hereafter. Therein you shall have that your inner-selves desire, and therein you shall have for which you ask."
32. "An Entertainment from, the **Oft-Forgiving**, Most Merciful." (Darussalam, 2000)

Chapter Ash-Shura   Chapter 42 Verse 5
Nearly the heavens might be rent asunder from above them, and the angels glorify the praises of their **Lord**, and ask for forgiveness for those on the earth. Verily, **Allah** is the **Oft-Forgiving**, the Most Merciful. (Darussalam, 2000)

Chapter Ash-Shura   Chapter 42 Verses 22-23
22. You will see, the Zalimun (wrong-doers) fearful of that which they have earned, and it will surely befall them. But those who believe and do righteous deeds (will be) in the flowering meadows of the Gardens. They shall have whatsoever they desire with their **Lord**. That is the Supreme Grace.
23. That is whereof **Allah** gives glad tidings to His slaves who believe and do righteous good deeds. Say: "No reward do I ask of you for this except to be kind to me for my kinship with you." And whoever earns a good righteous deed, We shall give him an increase of good in respect thereof. Verily, **Allah** is **Oft-Forgiving**, Most Ready to appreciate. (Darussalam, 2000)

Chapter Al-Ahqaf   Chapter 46 Verse 8
Or say they: "He has fabricated it." Say: "If I have fabricated it, still you have no power to support me against **Allah**. He knows best of what you say among yourselves concerning it! Sufficient is He as a witness between me and you! And He is the **Oft-Forgiving**, the Most Merciful." (Darussalam, 2000)

Chapter Al-Fath   Chapter 48 Verse 14
And to **Allah** belongs the sovereignty of the heavens and the earth. He forgives whom He wills, and punishes whom He wills. And **Allah** is Ever **Oft-Forgiving**, Most Merciful. (Darussalam, 2000)

Chapter Al-Hujurat   Chapter 49 Verses 4-5

4. Verily, those who call you from behind the dwellings, most of them have no sense.
5. And if they had patience till you could come out to them, it would have been better for them. And **Allah** is **Oft-Forgiving**, Most Merciful. (Darussalam, 2000)

Chapter Al-Hujurat   Chapter 49 Verse 14

The bedouins say: "We believe." Say: "You believe not but you only say, We have surrendered, for Faith has not yet entered your hearts. But if you obey **Allah** and His Messenger, He will not decrease anything in reward for your deeds. Verily, **Allah** is **Oft-Forgiving**, Most Merciful." (Darussalam, 2000)

Chapter Al-Hadid   Chapter 57 Verse 28

O you who believe! Fear **Allah**, and believe in His Messenger, He will give you a double portion of His Mercy, and He will give you a light by which you shall walk. And He will forgive you. And **Allah** is **Oft-Forgiving**, Most Merciful. (Darussalam, 2000)

Chapter Al-Mujadilah   Chapter 58 Verse 2

Those among you who make their wives unlawful to them by Zihar (saying to them "you are like my mother's back") they cannot be their mothers. None can be their mothers except those who gave them birth. And verily, they utter an ill word and a lie. And verily, **Allah** is Oft-Pardoning, **Oft-Forgiving**. (Darussalam, 2000)

Chapter Al-Mujadilah   Chapter 58 Verse 12

O you who believe! When you consult the Messenger in private, spend something in charity before your private consultation. That will be better and purer for you. But if you find not, then verily, **Allah** is **Oft-Forgiving**, Most Merciful. (Darussalam, 2000)

Chapter Al-Mumtahanah   Chapter 60 Verses 5~7

5. "Our **Lord**! Make us not a trial for the disbelievers, and forgive us, Our **Lord**! Verily, You, only You, are the All-Mighty, the All-Wise."
6. Certainly, there has been in them an excellent example for you to follow- for those who look forward to **Allah** and the Last Day. And whoever turns away, then verily, **Allah** is Rich, Worthy of all praise.
7. Perhaps **Allah** will make friendship between you and those whom you hold as enemies. And **Allah** has power (over all things), and **Allah** is **Oft-Forgiving**, Most Merciful. (Darussalam, 2000)

Chapter Al-Mumtahanah   Chapter 60 Verse 12

O Prophet! When believing women comes to you to give you the Bai'ah (pledge), that they will not associate anything in worship with **Allah**, that they will not steal, that they will not commit illegal sexual intercourse, that they will not kill their children, that they will not utter slander, intentionally forgiving falsehood, and that they will not disobey you in Ma'ruf (just matter), then accept their Bai'ah (pledge), and ask **Allah** to forgive them. Verily, **Allah** is Oft-Forgiving, **Most Merciful**. (Darussalam, 2000)

Chapter At-Taghabun   Chapter 64 Verse 14

O you who believe! Verily, among your wives and your children there are enemies for you, therefore beware of them! But if you pardon and overlook, and forgive, then verily, **Allah** is **Oft-Forgiving**, Most Merciful. (Darussalam, 2000)

Chapter At-Tahrim   Chapter 66 Verse 1

O Prophet! Why do you forbid that which **Allah** has allowed to you, seeking to please your wives? And **Allah** is **Oft-Forgiving**, Most Merciful. (Darussalam, 2000)

Chapter Al-Mulk   Chapter 67 Verses 1-2

1. Blessed be He in Whose hand is the dominion; and He is Able to do all things.
2. Who has created death and life that He may test you which of you is best in deed. And He is the All-Mighty, the **Oft-Forgiving**. (Darussalam, 2000)

Chapter Al-Muzzammil   Chapter 73 Verse 20

Verily, your **Lord** knows that you do stand a little less than two-thirds of the night, or half the night, or a third of the night, and also a party of those with you. And **Allah** measures the night and the day. He knows that you are unable to pray the whole night, so He has turned to you. So, recite you of the Quran as much as may be easy for you. He knows that there will be some among you sick, others traveling through the land, seeking of **Allah**'s Bounty, yet others fighting in **Allah**'s Cause. So, recite as much of the Quran as may be easy, and perform As-Salat (prayer) and give Zakat (charity-alms), and lend to **Allah** a goodly loan. And whatever good you send before you for yourselves. You will certainly find it with **Allah**, better and greater in reward. And seek forgiveness of **Allah**. Verily, **Allah** is Oft-Forgiving, **Most Merciful.** (Darussalam, 2000)

Chapter Al-Buruj — Chapter 85 Verses 13~16

13. Verily, He is who begins and repeats.
14. And He is **Oft-Forgiving**, Full of love.
15. Owner of the Throne, the Glorious.
16. Doer of whatsoever He intends. (Darussalam, 2000)

Al-Ghaffar   The Ever Forgiving

Chapter Ta-Ha — Chapter 20 Verse 82
And verily, I am indeed **forgiving** to him who repents, believes and does righteous good deeds, and then remains constant in doing them. (Darussalam, 2000)

Chapter Sad — Chapter 38 Verse 66
"The **Lord** of the heavens and the earth and all that is between them, the All-Mighty, the **Oft-Forgiving**." (Darussalam, 2000)

Chapter Az-Zumar — Chapter 39 Verse 5
He has created the heavens and the earth with truth. He makes the night to go in the day and makes the day to go in the night. And He has subjected the sun and the moon. Each running for an appointed term. Verily, He is the All-Mighty, **Oft-Forgiving**. (Darussalam, 2000)

Chapter Ghafir — Chapter 40 Verses 1~3
1. Ha Mim
2. The revelation of the book is from **Allah**, the All-Mighty, the All-Knower.
3. The **Forgiver of sin**, the Acceptor of repentance, the Severe in punishment, the Bestower, La ilaha illa Huwa (none has the right to be worshipped but He), to Him is the final return. (Darussalam, 2000)

Chapter Ghafir — Chapter 40 Verse 42
"You invite me to disbelieve in **Allah**, and to join partners in worship with Him of which I have no knowledge, and I invite you to the All-Mighty, the **Oft-Forgiving**! (Darussalam, 2000)

Chapter Nuh — Chapter 71 Verse 10
"I said: "Ask forgiveness from your **Lord**, verily, He is **Oft-Forgiving**; (Darussalam, 2000)

At-Tawwab   The Accepter of Repentance

Chapter Al-Baqarah   Chapter 2 Verse 37
Then Adam received from his **Lord** Words. And his **Lord** pardoned him. Verily, He is the one **Who Forgives**, the Most Merciful. (Darussalam, 1999)

Chapter Al-Baqarah   Chapter 2 Verse 54
And when Musa said to his people: "O my people! Verily, you have wronged yourselves by worshipping the calf. So, turn in repentance to your Creator and kill yourselves, that will be better for you with your Creator." Then He accepted your repentance. Truly, He is the **One Who accepts repentance**, the Most Merciful. (Darussalam, 1999)

Chapter Al-Baqarah   Chapter 2 Verse 128
"Our **Lord**! And make us submissive unto You and of our offspring a nation submissive unto You, and show us our Manasik (all the ceremonies of pilgrimage-Hajj and Umrah), and accept our repentance. Truly, You are the **One Who accepts repentance**, the Most Merciful. (Darussalam, 1999)

Chapter Al-Baqarah   Chapter 2 Verses 159-160
159. Verily, those who conceal the clear proof, evidences and the guidance, which We have sent down, after we have made it clear for the people in the Book, they are the ones cursed by **Allah** and cursed by the cursers.
160. Except those who repent and do righteous deeds, and openly declare. These, I will accept their repentance. And I am the **One Who accepts repentance**, the Most Merciful. (Darussalam, 1999)

Chapter An-Nisa   Chapter 4 Verse 16
And the two persons among you who commit illegal sexual intercourse, hurt them both. And if they repent and do righteous good deeds, leave them alone. Surely, **Allah** is Ever **All-Forgiving**, Most Merciful. (Darussalam, 1999)

Chapter An-Nisa   Chapter 4 Verse 64
We sent no Messenger, but to be obeyed by **Allah**'s Leave. If they, when they had been unjust to themselves, had come to you and begged **Allah**'s forgiveness, and the Messenger had begged forgiveness for them, indeed, they would have found **Allah All-Forgiving**, Most Merciful. (Darussalam, 1999)

Chapter At-Taubah   Chapter 9 Verse 104
Know they not that **Allah** accepts repentance from His slaves and takes the Sadaqat (alms), and that **Allah** alone is the **One Who forgives and accepts repentance,** Most Merciful. (Darussalam, 2000)

Chapter At-Taubah   Chapter 9 Verse 118
And the three who did not join till for them the earth, vast as it is, was straitened and their own selves were straitened to them, and they perceived that there is no fleeing from **Allah**, and no refuge but with Him. Then, He forgave them, that they might beg for His pardon. Verily, **Allah** is the **One Who forgives and accepts repentance,** Most Merciful. (Darussalam, 2000)

Chapter An-Nur   Chapter 24 Verses 6~10
6. And for those who accuse their wives, but have no witnesses except themselves, let the testimony of one of them be four testimonies by **Allah** that he is one of those who speak the truth.
7. And the fifth the invoking of the Curse of **Allah** on him if he be of those who tell a lie.
8. But it shall avert the punishment from her, if she bears witness four times by **Allah**, that he is telling a lie.
9. And the fifth should be that the Wrath of **Allah** be upon her if he speaks the truth.
10. And had it not been for the Grace of **Allah** and His Mercy on you! And that **Allah** is the **One Who accepts repentance**, the All-Wise. (Darussalam, 2000)

Chapter Al-Hujurat   Chapter 49 Verse 12
O you who believe! Avoid much suspicion; indeed, some suspicions are sins. And spy not, neither backbite one another. Would one of you like to eat the flesh of his dead brother? You would hate it. And fear **Allah.** Verily, **Allah** is the **One Who forgives and accepts repentance**, Most Merciful. (Darussalam, 2000)

Chapter An-Nasr   Chapter 110 Verse 3
So, glorify the Praises of your **Lord**, and ask His forgiveness. Verily, He is the **One Who accepts the repentance and who forgives.** (Darussalam, 2000)

Al-Latif   The Subtle kind

Chapter Al-An'am   Chapter 6 Verse 103

No vision can grasp him, but He grasps all vision. He is **Al-Latif (the Most Subtle and Courteous)**, Well-Acquainted with all things. (Darussalam, 1999)

Chapter Yusuf   Chapter 12 Verse 100

And he (Yusuf) raised his parents to the throne and they fell down before him prostrate. And he said: "O my father! This is the interpretation of my dream aforetime! My **Lord** has made it come true! He was indeed good to me, when He took me out of the prison, and brought you out of the bedouin-life, after Shaitan (Satan) had sown enmity between me and my brothers. Certainly, my **Lord** is **Most Courteous and Kind** unto whom He wills. Truly, He! Only He is the All-Knowing, the All-Wise. (Darussalam, 2000)

Chapter Al-Hajj   Chapter 22 Verse 63

See you not that **Allah** sends down water from the sky, and then the earth becomes green? Verily, **Allah** is **Most kind and Courteous**, Well-Acquainted with all things. (Darussalam, 2000)

Chapter Luqman   Chapter 31 Verse 16

"O my son! If it be equal to the weight of a grain of mustard seed, and though it be in a rock, or in the heavens or in the earth, **Allah** will bring it forth. Verily, **Allah** is **Subtle**, Well-Aware. (Darussalam, 2000)

Chapter Al-Ahzab   Chapter 33 Verse 34

And remember, that which is recited in your houses of the verses of **Allah** and Al-Hikmah (the Wisdom). Verily, **Allah** is **Ever Most Courteous**, Well-Acquainted with all things. (Darussalam, 2000)

Chapter Ash-Shura   Chapter 42 Verse 19

Allah is very **Gracious and Kind** to His slaves. He gives provisions to whom He wills. And He is the All-Strong, the All-Mighty. (Darussalam, 2000)

Chapter Al-Mulk   Chapter 67 Verses 13-14

13. And whether you keep your talk secret or disclose it, verily, He is the All-Knower of what is in the breasts.

14. Should not He Who has created know? And He is the **Most kind and Courteous**, All-Aware. (Darussalam, 2000)

Al-Wudud   The Most Loving

Chapter Hud   Chapter 11 Verse 90
"And ask forgiveness of your **Lord** and turn unto Him in repentance. Verily, my **Lord** is Most Merciful, **Most Loving**." (Darussalam, 2000)

Chapter Al-Buruj   Chapter 85 Verses 13~16
13. Verily, He it is who begins and repeats.
14. And He is Oft-Forgiving, **full of love**.
15. Owner of the Throne, the Glorious.
16. Doer of whatsoever He intends. (Darussalam, 2000)

Al-Halim   The Most Forbearing

Chapter Al-Baqarah   Chapter 2 Verse 225
Allah will not call you to account for that which is unintentional in your oaths, but He will call you to account for that which your hearts have earned. And **Allah** is Oft-Forgiving, **Most Forbearing**. (Darussalam, 1999)

Chapter Al-Baqarah   Chapter 2 Verse 235
And there is no sin on you if you make a hint of betrothal or conceal it in yourself, **Allah** knows that you will remember them, but do not make a promise of contract with them in secret except that you speak an honourable saying according to Islamic law. And do not consummate the marriage until the term prescribed is fulfilled. And know that **Allah** knows what is in your minds, so fear Him. And know that **Allah** is Oft-Forgiving, **Most Forbearing**. (Darussalam, 1999)

Chapter Al-Baqarah   Chapter 2 Verse 263
Kind words and forgiving of faults are better than Sadaqat (alms-charity) followed by injury. And **Allah** is Rich and He is **Most Forbearing**. (Darussalam, 1999)

Chapter Al-Imran   Chapter 3 Verse 155

Those of you who turned back on the day the two hosts met, it was Shaitan (Satan) who caused them to backslide because of some they had earned. But **Allah**, indeed, has forgiven them. Surely, **Allah** is Oft-Forgiving, **Most Forbearing**. (Darussalam, 1999)

Chapter An-Nisa   Chapter 4 Verse 12

In that which your wives leave, your share is a half if they have no child; but if they leave a child, you get a fourth of that which they leave after payment of legacies that they may have bequeathed or debts. In that which you leave, their share is a fourth if you leave no child; but if you leave a child, they get an eight of that which you leave after payment of legacies that you may have bequeathed or debts. If the man or woman whose inheritance is in question has left neither ascendants nor descendants, but has left a brother or a sister, each one of the two gets a sixth; but if more than two, they share in a third, after payment of legacies he may have bequeathed or debts, so that no loss is caused. This is a Commandment from **Allah**; and **Allah** is Ever All-Knowing, **Most Forbearing**. (Darussalam, 1999)

Chapter Al-Ma'idah   Chapter 5 Verse 101

O you who believe! Ask not about things which, if made plain to you, may cause you trouble. But if you ask about them while the Quran is being revealed, they will be made plain to you. **Allah** has forgiven that, and **Allah** is Oft-Forgiving, **Most Forbearing**. (Darussalam, 1999)

Chapter Al-Isra   Chapter 17 Verse 44

The seven heavens and the earth and all that is therein, glorify Him and there is not a thing but glorifies His Praise. But you understand not their glorification. Truly, He is **Ever Forbearing**, Oft-Forgiving. (Darussalam, 2000)

Chapter Al-Hajj   Chapter 22 Verses 58-59

58. Those who emigrated in the Cause of **Allah** and after that were killed or died, surely, **Allah** will provide a good provision for them. And verily, it is **Allah** Who indeed is the Best of those who make provision.

59. Truly, He will make them enter an entrance with which they shall be well-pleased, and verily, **Allah** indeed is All-Knowing, **Most Forbearing**. (Darussalam, 2000)

Chapter Al-Ahzab   Chapter 33 Verse 51
You (O Muhammad) can postpone whom you will of them, and you may receive whom you will. And whomsoever you desire of those whom you have set aside, it is no sin on you; that is better that they may be comforted and not grieved, and may all be pleased with what you give them. **Allah** knows what is in your hearts. And **Allah** is Ever All-Knowing, **Most Forbearing**. (Darussalam, 2000)

Chapter Fatir   Chapter 35 Verse 41
Verily, **Allah** grasps the heavens and the earth lest they should move away from their places, and if they were to move away from their places, there is not one that could grasp them after Him. Truly, He is Ever **Most Forbearing**, Oft-Forgiving. (Darussalam, 2000)

Chapter At-Taghabun   Chapter 64 Verse 17
If you lend to **Allah** a goodly loan, He will double it for you, and will forgive you, and **Allah** is Most Ready to appreciate and to reward, **Most Forbearing**. (Darussalam, 2000)

Ash-Shakur   Most Ready to Appreciate

Chapter Al-Baqarah   Chapter 2 Verse 158
Verily, As-Safa and Al-Marwah (two mountains in Makkah) are of the symbols of **Allah**. So, it is not a sin on him who performs Hajj or Umrah (pilgrimage) of the House to perform the going between them. And whoever does good voluntarily, then **Allah** is **All-Recogniser**, All-Knower. (Darussalam, 1999)

Chapter An-Nisa   Chapter 4 Verse 147
Why should **Allah** punish you if you have thanked and have believed in Him. And **Allah** is Ever **All-Appreciative**, All-Knowing. (Darussalam, 1999)

Chapter Fatir   Chapter 35 Verses 29-30
29. Verily, those who recite the Book of **Allah**, and perform as Salat (prayer), and spend out of what we have provided for them, secretly and openly, they hope for a trade gain that will never perish.
30. That He may pay them their wages in full, and give them more, out of His Grace. Verily, He is Oft-Forgiving, **Most Ready to appreciate**. (Darussalam, 2000)

Chapter Fatir   Chapter 35 Verses 33-34
33. Adn paradise (everlasting Gardens) will they enter, therein will they be adorned with bracelets of gold and pearls, and their garments therein will be of silk.
34. And they will say: "All the praises and thanks be to **Allah** Who has removed from us grief. Verily, our **Lord** is indeed Oft-Forgiving, **Most Ready to Appreciate**. (Darussalam, 2000)

Chapter Ash-Shura   Chapter 42 Verse 23
That is whereof **Allah** gives glad tidings to His slaves who believe and do righteous good deeds. Say: "No reward do I ask of you for this except to be kind to me for my kinship with you." And whoever earns a good righteous deed, We shall give him an increase of good in respect thereof. Verily, **Allah** is Oft-Forgiving, **Most Ready to appreciate**. (Darussalam, 2000)

Chapter At-Taghabun   Chapter 64 Verses 17-18
17. If you lend to **Allah** a goodly loan, He will double it for you, and will forgive you. And **Allah** is **Most ready to appreciate and to reward**, Most Forbearing.
18. All-Knower of the unseen and seen, the All-Mighty, the All-Wise. (Darussalam, 2000)

Al-Mujib   The Responsive

Chapter Hud   Chapter 11 Verse 61
And to Thamud their brother Salih. He said: "O my people! Worship **Allah**: you have no other ilah (god) but Him. He brought you forth from the earth and settled you therein, then ask forgiveness of Him and turn to Him in repentance. Certainly, my **Lord** is Near, **Responsive**." (Darussalam, 2000)

Subsection 3

SUBSECTION 3

- *Al-Malik*   *The King*
- *Maalik-ul-Mulk*   *The Owner of All Sovereignty*
- *Al-Hameed*   *The All-Praiseworthy*
- *Al-Majeed*   *The All-Glorious*
- *Al-Kabir*   *The Most Great*
- *Al-Azim*   *The Most Great*
- *Al-Muqit*   *The Nourisher*
- *Al-Mutaali*   *The Most Exalted*
- *Al-Muhyi*   *The Giver of Life*
- *Al-Waaris*   *The Inheritor of All*
- *Dhu-l-Jalali Wa-l-Ikram*   *The Lord of Majesty & Honor*

Al-Malik   The King

Chapter Al-Fatihah   Chapter 1 Verse 4
The **Only Owner** of the Day of Recompense. (Darussalam, 1999)

Chapter Ta-Ha   Chapter 20 Verse 114
Then High above all be **Allah**, the **True King**. And be not in haste with the Quran before its revelation is completed to you and say: "My **Lord**! Increase me in Knowledge." (Darussalam, 2000)

Chapter Al-Mu'minun   Chapter 23 Verse 116
So Exalted be **Allah**, the True **King**: La ilaha illa Huwa (none has the right to be worshipped but He), the **Lord** of the Supreme Throne! (Darussalam, 2000)

Chapter Al-Qamar   Chapter 54 Verses 54-55
54. Verily, the Muttaqun (pious), will be in the midst of gardens and Rivers.
55. In a seat of truth, near the Omnipotent **King**. (Darussalam, 2000)

Chapter Al-Hashr   Chapter 59 Verse 23
He is **Allah**, besides whom La ilaha illa Huwa (none has the right to be worshipped but He), the **King**, the Holy, the One Free from all defects, the Giver of security, the Watcher over His creatures, the All-Mighty, the Compeller, the Supreme. Glory be to **Allah**! above all that they associate as partners with Him. (Darussalam, 2000)

Chapter Al-Jumu'ah   Chapter 62 Verse 1
Whatsoever is in the heavens and whatsoever is on the earth glorifies **Allah**, the **King**, the Holy, the All-Mighty, the All-Wise. (Darussalam, 2000)

Chapter An-Nas   Chapter 114 Verses 1~3
1. Say: "I seek refuge with the **Lord** of mankind,
2. "The **King** of mankind
3. "The Ilah (God) of mankind. (Darussalam, 2000)

Maalik-ul-Mulk The Owner of All Sovereignty

Chapter Al-Baqarah   Chapter 2 Verse 107
Know you not that it is **Allah** to **Whom belongs the dominion of the heavens and the earth**? And besides **Allah** you have neither any Wali (protector) nor any helper. (Darussalam, 1999)

Chapter Al-Imran   Chapter 3 Verse 26
Say: "O **Allah! Possessor of the kingdom**, You give the kingdom to whom You will, and You take the kingdom from whom You will, and You endue with honour whom You will, and You humiliate whom You will. In Your Hand is the good. Verily, You are Able to do all things. (Darussalam, 1999)

Al-Hameed   The All-Praiseworthy

Chapter Al-Baqarah   Chapter 2 Verse 267
O you who believe! Spend of the good things which you have earned, and of that which we have produced from the earth for you, and do not aim at that which is bad to spend from it, you would not accept it save if you close your eyes and tolerate therein. And know that **Allah** is Rich, and **Worthy of all Praise**. (Darussalam, 1999)

Chapter An-Nisa   Chapter 4 Verse 131
And to **Allah** belongs all that is in the heavens and all that is in the earth. And verily, We have recommended to the people of the Scripture before you, and to you that you fear **Allah**, and keep your duty to Him. But if you disbelieve, then unto **Allah** belongs all that is in the heavens and all that is in the earth, and **Allah** is Ever Rich, **Worthy of all praise**. (Darussalam, 1999)

Chapter Hud   Chapter 11 Verses 69~73
69. And verily, there came Our messengers to Ibrahim with glad tidings. They said: Salam (peace) he answered, Salam (peace) and he hastened to entertain them with a roasted calf.
70. But when he saw their hands went not towards it, he mistrusted them, and conceived a fear of them. They said: "Fear not, we have been sent against the people of Lut."
71. And his wife was standing, and she laughed. But We gave her glad tidings of Ishaq, and after Ishaq, of Ya'qub.

72. She said: "Woe unto me! Shall I have a child while I am an old woman, and here is my husband an old man? Verily, this is a strange thing!"
73. They said: "Do you wonder at the Decree of **Allah**? The Mercy of **Allah** and His blessing be on you, O the family. Surely, **He is All-Praise Worthy**, All-Glorious. (Darussalam, 2000)

Chapter Ibrahim   Chapter 14 Verse 1
Alif-Lam-Ra. A book which We have revealed unto you in order that you might lead mankind out of darkness into light by their **Lord**'s Leave to the path of the All-Mighty, **the Owner of all Praise**. (Darussalam, 2000)

Chapter Ibrahim   Chapter 14 Verse 8
And Musa said: "If you disbelieve, you and all on earth together, then verily, **Allah** is Rich, **Owner of all Praise**. (Darussalam, 2000)

Chapter Al-Hajj   Chapter 22 Verses 23-24
23. Truly, **Allah** will admit those who believe and do righteous good deeds, to Gardens underneath which rivers flow, wherein they will be adorned with bracelets of gold and pearls and their garments therein will be of silk.
24. And they are guided unto goodly speech and they are guided to the path of Him, Who is **Worthy of all Praises**. (Darussalam, 2000)

Chapter Al-Hajj   Chapter 22 Verse 64
To Him belongs all that is in the heavens and all that is on the earth. And verily, **Allah** He is rich, **Worthy of all Praise**. (Darussalam, 2000)

Chapter Luqman   Chapter 31 Verse 12
And indeed, We bestowed upon Luqman Al-Hikmah (wisdom) saying: "Give thanks to **Allah**." And whoever gives thanks, he gives thanks for his own self. And whoever is unthankful, then verily, **Allah** is All-Rich, **Worthy of all praise**. (Darussalam, 2000)

Chapter Luqman   Chapter 31 Verse 26
To **Allah** belongs whatsoever is in the heavens and the earth. Verily, **Allah**, He is Al-Ghani (Rich), **Worthy of all Praise**. (Darussalam, 2000)

Chapter Saba   Chapter 34 Verse 6
And those who have been given knowledge see that what is revealed to you from your **Lord** is the truth, and that it guides to the Path of the Exalted in might, **Owner of all Praise**. (Darussalam, 2000)

Chapter Fatir   Chapter 35 Verse 15
O mankind! It is you who stand in need of **Allah**. But **Allah** is Rich, **Worthy of all Praise.** (Darussalam, 2000)

Chapter Fussilat   Chapter 41 Verses 41-42
41. Verily, those who disbelieved in the Reminder when it came to them. And verily, it is an honourable well-fortified respected Book.
42. Falsehood cannot come to it from before it or behind it, sent down by the All-Wise, **Worthy of all Praise.** (Darussalam, 2000)

Chapter Ash-Shura   Chapter 42 Verse 28
And He it is Who sends down the rain after they have despaired, and spreads His Mercy. And He is the Wali (the Protector), **Worthy of all Praise.** (Darussalam, 2000)

Chapter Al-Hadid   Chapter 57 Verse 24
Those who are misers and enjoin upon people miserliness- (**Allah** is not in need of their charity). And whosoever turns away, then **Allah** is Rich, **Worthy of all praise.** (Darussalam, 2000)

Chapter Al-Mumtahanah   Chapter 60 Verses 5-6
5. "Our **Lord**! Make us not a trial for the disbelievers, and forgive us, Our **Lord**! Verily, You, only You, are the All-Mighty, the All-Wise."
6. Certainly, there has been in them an excellent example for you to follow- for those who look forward to (the Meeting with) **Allah** and the last day. And whosoever turns away, then verily, **Allah** is Rich, **Worthy of all praise**. (Darussalam, 2000)

Chapter At-Taghabun   Chapter 64 Verses 5-6
5. Has not the news reached you of those who disbelieved aforetime? And so they tasted the evil result of their disbelief, and theirs will be a painful torment.
6. That was because there came to them their Messengers with clear proofs, but they said: "Shall mere men guide us?" So they disbelieved and turned away. But **Allah** was not in need (of them). And **Allah** is Rich, **Worthy of all praise**. (Darussalam, 2000)

Chapter Al-Buruj   Chapter 85 Verses 4~8
4. Cursed were the people of the ditch.
5. Fire supplied with fuel,
6. When they sat by it,

7. And they witnessed what they were doing against the believers.
8. And they had no fault except that they believed in **Allah**, the All-Mighty, **Worthy of all praise**! (Darussalam, 2000)

Al-Majeed   The All-Glorious

Chapter Hud   Chapter 11 Verses 69~73

69. And verily, there came Our messengers to Ibrahim with glad tidings. They said: Salam (peace) he answered, Salam (peace) and he hastened to entertain them with a roasted calf.
70. But when he saw their hands went not towards it, he mistrusted them, and conceived a fear of them. They said: "Fear not, we have been sent against the people of Lut."
71. And his wife was standing, and she laughed. But We gave her glad tidings of Ishaq, and after Ishaq, of Ya'qub.
72. She said: "Woe unto me! Shall I have a child while I am an old woman, and here is my husband an old man? Verily, this is a strange thing!"
73. They said: "Do you wonder at the Decree of **Allah**? The Mercy of **Allah** and His blessing be on you, O the family. Surely, He is All-Praiseworthy, **All-Glorious**. (Darussalam, 2000)

Chapter Al-Buruj   Chapter 85 Verses 13~15
13. Verily, He it is who begins and repeats.
14. And He is Oft-Forgiving, Full of love.
15. Owner of the Throne, **the Glorious**. (Darussalam, 2000)

Al-Kabir   The Most Great

Chapter An-Nisa   Chapter 4 Verse 34
Men are the protectors and maintainers of women, because **Allah** has made one of them to excel the other, and because they spend from their means. Therefore, the righteous women are devoutly obedient, and guard in the husband's absence what **Allah** order them to guard. As to those women on whose part you see ill-conduct, admonish them, refuse to share their beds, beat them; but if they return to obedience, seek not against them means. Surely, **Allah** is Ever Most High, **Most Great**. (Darussalam, 1999)

Chapter Ar-Ra`d   Chapter 13 Verses 8-9

8. **Allah** knows what every female bears, and by how much the wombs fall short or exceed. Everything with Him is in proportion.
9. All-Knower of the unseen and the seen, the **Most Great**, the Most High. (Darussalam, 2000)

Chapter Al-Hajj   Chapter 22 Verse 62

That is because **Allah** He is truth, and what they invoke besides Him, it is Batil. And verily, **Allah** He is the Most High, the **Most Great**. (Darussalam, 2000)

Chapter Luqman   Chapter 31 Verse 30

That is because **Allah**, He is the truth, and that which they invoke besides Him is Al-Batil (falsehood); and that **Allah**, He is the Most High, **the Most Great**. (Darussalam, 2000)

Chapter Saba   Chapter 34 Verses 22-23

22. Say: "Call upon those whom you assert besides **Allah**, they possess not even an atom's weight either in the heavens or on the earth, nor have they any share in either, nor there is for Him any supporter from among them. (Darussalam, 2000)
23. Intercession with Him profits not except for him whom He permits. So much so that when fear is banished from their hearts, they say: "What is it that your **Lord** has said?" They say: "The truth and He is the Most High, the **Most Great**." (Darussalam, 2000)

Chapter Ghafir   Chapter 40 Verses 11-12

11. They will say: "Our **Lord**! You have made us to die twice, and You have given us life twice! Now we confess our sins, then is there any way to get out?"
12. "This is because, when **Allah** alone was invoked, you disbelieved, but when partners were joined to Him, you believed! So, the judgment is only with **Allah**, the Most High, the **Most Great**!" (Darussalam, 2000)

Al-Azim   The Most Great

Chapter Al-Baqarah   Chapter 2 Verse 255
Allah! La ilaha illa Huwa (none has the right to be worshipped but He), Al-Hayyul-Qayyum (the Ever Living, the One Who Sustains and Protects all that exists). Neither slumber nor sleep overtakes Him. To Him belongs whatever is in the heavens and whatever is on the earth. Who is he that can intercede with Him except with His permission? He knows what happens to them in this world, and what will happen to them in the Hereafter. And they will never compass anything of His knowledge except that which He wills. His Kursi (Chair) extends over the heavens and the earth, and He feels no fatigue in guarding and preserving them. And He is the Most High, the **Most Great**. (Darussalam, 1999)

Chapter Ash-Shura   Chapter 42 Verses 1~4
1. Ha-Mim
2. Ain-sin-Qaf
3. Likewise **Allah**, the All-Mighty, the All-Wise sends Revelation to you as those before you.
4. To Him belongs all that is in the heavens and all that is in the earth, and He is the Most High, The **Most Great**. (Darussalam, 2000)

Chapter Al-Waqi`ah   Chapter 56 Verses 71~74
71. Then tell me about the fire which you kindle.
72. Is it you who made the tree thereof to grow, or are We the Grower?
73. We have made it a Reminder, and an article of use for the travelers.
74. Then glorify with praises the name of your **Lord**, the **Most Great**. (Darussalam, 2000)

Chapter Al-Haqqah   Chapter 69 Verse 33
Verily, he used not to believe in **Allah**, the **Most Great**. (Darussalam, 2000)

Chapter Al-Haqqah   Chapter 69 Verse 52
So, glorify the Name of your **Lord**, the **Most Great**. (Darussalam, 2000)

Al-Muqit   The Nourisher

Chapter An-Nisa   Chapter 4 Verse 85
Whosoever intercedes for a good cause will have reward thereof, and whosoever intercedes for an evil cause will have a share in its burden. And **Allah** is over everything **Reckoner.** (Darussalam, 1999)

Al-Mutaali   The Most Exalted

Chapter Ar-Ra`d   Chapter 13 Verses 8-9
8. **Allah** knows what every female bears, and by how much the wombs fall short or exceed. Everything with Him is in proportion.
9. All-Knower of the unseen and the seen, the Most Great, **the Most High**. (Darussalam, 2000)

Al-Muhyi   The Giver of Life

Chapter Ar-Rum   Chapter 30 Verse 50
Look then at the effects of **Allah**'s Mercy, how He revives the earth after its death. Verily, that **(Allah) shall indeed raise the dead**, and He is Able to do all things. (Darussalam, 2000)

Chapter Fussilat   Chapter 41 Verse 39
And among His signs, that you see the earth barren, but when We send down water to it, it is stirred to life and growth. Verily, He who gives it life, surely is **Able to give life to the dead**. Indeed, He is Able to do all things. (Darussalam, 2000)

Al-Waaris   The Inheritor of All

Chapter Al-Hijr   Chapter 15 Verse 23
And certainly We! We it is Who give life, and cause death, and **We are the Inheritors**. (Darussalam, 2000)

Chapter Al-Anbiya   Chapter 21 Verse 89
And Zakariya, when He cried to his **Lord**: "O My **Lord**! Leave me not single, though You are the **Best of the Inheritors**." (Darussalam, 2000)

Chapter Al-Qasas   Chapter 28 Verse 58
And how many a town have We destroyed, which was thankless for its means of livelihood! And those are their dwellings, which have not been inhabited after them except a little. And verily, **We have been the Inheritors.** (Darussalam, 2000)

Dhu-l-Jalali Wa-l-Ikram The Lord of Majesty & Honour

Chapter Ar-Rahman   Chapter 55 Verse 27
And the face of your **Lord full of Majesty and Honour** will remain forever. (Darussalam, 2000)

Chapter Ar-Rahman   Chapter 55 Verse 78
Blessed be the name of your **Lord, the Owner of Majesty and Honour**. (Darussalam, 2000)

Subsection 4

SUBSECTION 4

- *Al-Wahid* — **The One**
- *Al-Ahad* — **The Sole One**
- *Al-Samaad* — **The Self-Sufficient**
- *Al-Haqq* — **The Truth**
- *Al-Qahhar* — **The Irresistible**
- *Al-Hayy* — **The Ever Living**
- *Al-Qayyum* — **The Self Subsisting, The Self Existing**
- *Al-Ghani* — **The All Rich**
- *An Nur* — **The Light**

Al- Wahid   The One

Chapter Al-Baqarah   Chapter 2 Verse 133
Or were you witnesses when death approached Yaqub? When he said unto his sons. "What will you worship after me?" They said, "We shall worship your Ilah (God), the Ilah (God) of your fathers, Ibrahim, Ismail, Ishaq, **One Ilah (God)**, and to Him we submit." (Darussalam, 1999)

Chapter Al-Baqarah   Chapter 2 Verse 163
And your Ilah (God) is **One Ilah (God)**, La ilaha illa Huwa (none has the right to be worshipped but He), the Most Gracious, the Most Merciful. (Darussalam, 1999)

Chapter An-Nisa   Chapter 4 Verse 171
O people of the scripture! Do not exceed the limits in your religion, nor say of **Allah** aught but the truth. The Messiah Isa, son of Maryam, was a Messenger of **Allah** and His word, which He bestowed on Maryam and a spirit created by Him; so, believe in **Allah** and His Messenger. Say not: "Three!" cease! Better for you. For **Allah** is **One Ilah (God)**, glory is to Him (For exalted is He) above having a son. To Him belongs all that is in the heavens and all that is in the earth. And **Allah** is All-Sufficient as a Disposer of affairs. (Darussalam, 1999)

Chapter Al-Ma'idah   Chapter 5 Verse 73
Surely, disbelievers are those who said: "**Allah** is third of the three." But there is no Ilah (god) but **One Ilah (God)**. And if they cease not from what they say, verily, a painful torment will befall on the disbelievers among them. (Darussalam, 1999)

Chapter Al-An'am   Chapter 6 Verse 19
Say: "What thing is the most great in witness?" Say" **Allah** is Witness between me and you; this Quran has been revealed to me that I may therewith warn you and whomsoever it may reach. Can you verily, bear witness that besides **Allah** there are other aliha (gods)?" Say: "I bear no witness!" Say: "But in truth He is the only **One Ilah (God)**. And truly, I am innocent of what you join in worship with Him." (Darussalam, 1999)

Chapter At-Taubah   Chapter 9 Verse 31

They took their rabbis and their monks to be their lords besides **Allah**, and Messiah, son of Maryam, while they were commanded to worship none but **One Ilah (God)** La ilaha illa Huwa (none has the right to be worshipped but He). Praise and glory be to Him from having the partners they associate." (Darussalam, 1999)

Chapter Yusuf   Chapter 12 Verses 39-40

39. "O two companions of the prison! Are many different lords better or **Allah**, the **One**, the Irresistible?
40. "You do not worship besides Him but only names which you have named, you and your fathers, for which **Allah** has sent down no authority. The command is for none but **Allah**. He has commanded that you worship none but Him, that is the straight religion, but most men know not. (Darussalam, 2000)

Chapter Ar-Ra`d   Chapter 13 Verse 16

Say: "Who is the **Lord** of the heavens and the earth?" say: "**Allah**." Say: "Have you then taken Auliya (friends and helpers, etc.) other than Him, such as have no power either for benefit or for harm to themselves?" Say: "Is the blind equal to the one who sees? Or darkness equal to light? Or do they assign to **Allah** partners who created the like of His creation, so that the creation seemed alike to them?" Say: "**Allah** is the Creator of all things; and He is the **One**, the Irresistible." (Darussalam, 2000)

Chapter Ibrahim   Chapter 14 Verse 48

On the Day when the earth will be changed to another earth and so will be the heavens, and they will appear before **Allah**, the **One,** the Irresistible. (Darussalam, 2000)

Chapter Ibrahim   Chapter 14 Verse 52

This is a message for mankind, in order that they may be warned thereby, and that they may know that He is the only **One Ilah (God)** and that men of understanding may take heed. (Darussalam, 2000)

Chapter An-Nahl   Chapter 16 Verse 22

Your Ilah (God) is **One Ilah (God)**. But for those who believe not in the Hereafter, their hearts deny, and they are proud. (Darussalam, 2000)

Chapter An-Nahl Chapter 16 Verses 51-52

51. And **Allah** said: "Take not ilahain (two gods). Verily, He is only **One Ilah** (God). Then, fear Me much.
52. To Him belongs all that is in the heavens and the earth and Ad-Din (religion) Wasiba (always) is His. Will you then fear any other than **Allah**? (Darussalam, 2000)

Chapter Al-Kahf Chapter 18 Verse 110

Say: "I am only a man like you. It has been revealed to me that your Ilah (God) is **One Ilah (God)**. So, whoever hopes for the Meeting with His **Lord**, let him work righteousness and associate none as partner in the worship of his **Lord**." (Darussalam, 2000)

Chapter Al-Anbiya Chapter 21 Verse 108

Say: "It is revealed to me that your Ilah (God) is only **One Ilah (God)**. Will you then submit to His will? (Darussalam, 2000)

Chapter Al-Hajj Chapter 22 Verse 34

And for every nation we have appointed religious ceremonies, that they may mention the Name of **Allah** over the beast of cattle that He has given them for food. And your Ilah (God) is **One Ilah (God)**, so you must submit to Him alone. And give glad tidings to the Mukhbitun (to those who obey Allah with humility). (Darussalam, 2000)

Chapter As-Saffat Chapter 37 Verses 4-5

4. Verily, your Ilah (God) is indeed **One**;
5. **Lord** of the heavens and of the earth, and all that is between them, and **Lord** of every point of the suns rising. (Darussalam, 2000)

Chapter Sad Chapter 38 Verses 65-66

65. Say: "I am only a Warner and there is no Ilah (god) except **Allah** the **One**, the Irresistible.
66. The **Lord** of the heavens and the earth and all that is between them, the All-Mighty, the Oft-Forgiving." (Darussalam, 2000)

Chapter Az-Zumar Chapter 39 Verse 4

Had **Allah** willed to take a son, He could have chosen whom He willed out of those whom He created. But glory be to Him! He is **Allah**, the **One**, Irresistible. (Darussalam, 2000)

Chapter Ghafir   Chapter 40 Verse 16
The Day when they will come out, nothing of them will be hidden from **Allah**. Whose is the kingdom this Day? It is **Allah**'s the **One**, the Irresistible! (Darussalam, 2000)

Chapter Fussilat   Chapter 41 Verse 6
Say: "I am only a human being like you. It is revealed to me that your Ilah (God) is **One Ilah (God)**, therefore take straight path to Him and obedience to Him, and seek forgiveness of Him, and woe to Mushrikun (polytheists). (Darussalam, 2000)

Al-Ahad   The Sole One

Chapter Al-Ikhlas   Chapter 112 Verses 1~4
1. Say: "He is **Allah**, (the) **One.**
2. **Allah**-us Samaad (**Allah** the self- Sufficient)
3. "He begets not, nor was He begotten.
4. "And there is none co-equal or comparable unto Him;" (Darussalam, 2000)

Al-Samaad   The Self-Sufficient

Chapter Al-Ikhlas   Chapter 112 Verses 1~4
1. Say: He is **Allah**, (the) One.
2. **Allah-us Samaad (Allah the Self- Sufficient)**
3. He begets not, nor was He begotten.
4. And there is none co-equal or comparable unto Him. (Darussalam, 2000)

Al-Haqq   The Truth

Chapter Al-An'am   Chapter 6 Verses 61-62
61. He is the Irresistible, over His slaves, and He sends guardians over you, until when death approaches one of you, Our messengers take his soul, and they never neglect their duty.
62. Then they are returned to **Allah**, their **True Maula (Lord)**. Surely, for Him is the judgment and He is the swiftest in taking account. (Darussalam, 1999)

Chapter Yunus   Chapter 10 Verses 30~32

30. There! Every person will know what he had earned before and they will be brought back to **Allah**, their rightful **Maula** (**Lord**), and their invented false deities will vanish from them.

31. Say: "Who provides for you from the sky and the earth? Or who owns hearing and sight? And who brings out the living from the dead and brings out the dead from the living? And who disposes the affairs"? They will say: "**Allah**." Say: "Will you not then be afraid of **Allah**'s punishment?

32. Such is **Allah**, your **Lord in truth**. So, after the truth, what else can there be, save error? How then are you turned away? (Darussalam, 2000)

Chapter Al-Kahf   Chapter 18 Verse 44

There, Al-Walayah (power/ authority) will be for **Allah, the True God**. He is the Best for reward and the Best for the final end. (Darussalam, 2000)

Chapter Ta-Ha   Chapter 20 Verse 114

Then High above all be **Allah**, the **True king**. And be not in haste with the Quran before its revelation is completed to you, and say: "My **Lord**! Increase me in knowledge." (Darussalam, 2000)

Chapter Al-Hajj   Chapter 22 Verse 6

That is because **Allah**: **He is the Truth**, and it is He who gives life to the dead, and it is He Who is Able to do all things. (Darussalam, 2000)

Chapter Al-Hajj   Chapter 22 Verse 62

That is because **Allah He is the Truth**, and what they invoke besides Him, it is Batil (falsehood). And verily, **Allah** He is the Most High, the Most Great. (Darussalam, 2000)

Chapter Al-Mu'minun   Chapter 23 Verse 116

So exalted be **Allah**, the **True king**: La ilaha illa Huwa (none has the right to be worshipped but He), the **Lord** of the Supreme Throne! (Darussalam, 2000)

Chapter An-Nur   Chapter 24 Verse 25

On that day **Allah** will pay them the recompense of their deeds in full, and they will know that **Allah**, He is the **Manifest Truth**. (Darussalam, 2000)

Chapter Luqman   Chapter 31 Verse 30

That is because **Allah, He is Truth**, and that which they invoke besides Him is Al-Batil (Falsehood); and that **Allah**, He is the Most High, the Most Great. (Darussalam, 2000)

Al-Qahhar   The Irresistible

Chapter Al-An'am   Chapter 6 Verse 18
And He is the **Irresistible** (Supreme), above His slaves, and He is the All-Wise, Well-Acquainted with all things. (Darussalam, 1999)

Chapter Yusuf   Chapter 12 Verse 39-40
39. "O two companions of the prison! Are many different lords better or **Allah**, the One, the **Irresistible**?
40. "You do not worship besides Him but only names which you have named, you and your fathers, for which **Allah** has sent down no authority. The command is for none but **Allah**. He has commanded that you worship none but Him, that is the straight religion, but most men know not. (Darussalam, 2000)

Chapter Ar-Ra'd   Chapter 13 Verse 16
Say: "Who is **Lord** of the heavens and the earth?" Say: "**Allah**." Say: "Have you then taken Auliya (protectors) other than Him, such as have no power either for benefit or for harm to themselves?" Say: "Is the blind equal to the one who sees? Or darkness equal to light? Or do they assign to **Allah** partners who created the like of His creation, so that the creation seemed alike to them?" Say: "**Allah** is the Creator of all things: and He is One, the **Irresistible**." (Darussalam, 2000)

Chapter Ibrahim   Chapter 14 Verse 48
On the Day when the earth will be changed to another earth and so will be the heavens, and they will appear before **Allah**, the One, the **Irresistible**. (Darussalam, 2000)

Chapter Sad   Chapter 38 Verses 65-66
65. Say: "I am only a Warner and there is no Ilah (god) except **Allah** the One, the **Irresistible**.
66. "The **Lord** of the heavens and the earth and all that is between them, the All-Mighty, the Oft-Forgiving." (Darussalam, 2000)

Chapter Az-Zumar   Chapter 39 Verse 4
Had **Allah** willed to take a son. He could have chosen whom He willed out of those whom He created. But glory be to Him! He is **Allah**, the One, the **Irresistible**. (Darussalam, 2000)

Chapter Ghafir   Chapter 40 Verse 16

The Day when they will come out, nothing of them will be hidden from **Allah**. Whose is the kingdom this Day? It is **Allah**'s the One, the **Irresistible**! (Darussalam, 2000)

Al-Hayy   The Ever Living

Chapter Al-Baqarah   Chapter 2 Verse 255

Allah! La ilaha illa Huwa (none has the right to be worshipped but He), **Al-Hayyul-Qayyum** (the Ever Living, the One Who Sustains and Protects all that exists). Neither slumber nor sleep overtakes Him. To Him belongs whatever is in the heavens and whatever is on the earth. Who is he that can intercede with Him except with His Permission? He knows what happens to them in this world, and what will happen to them in the Hereafter. And they will never compass anything of His knowledge except that which He wills. His Kursi (Chair) extends over the heavens and the earth, and He feels no fatigue in guarding and preserving them. And He is the Most High, the Most Great. (Darussalam, 1999)

Chapter Al-Imran   Chapter 3 Verses 1-2

1. Alif-Lam-Mim
2. **Allah**! La ilaha illa Huwa (none has the right to be worshipped but He), **Al-Hayyul-Qayyum** (the Ever living, the One Who sustains and protects all that exists). (Darussalam, 1999)

Chapter Ta-Ha   Chapter 20 Verse 111

And faces shall be humbled before, **Al-Hayyul-Qayyum** (the Ever living, the One Who sustains and protects all that exists), and he who carried (a burden of) wrong doing, will be indeed a complete failure. (Darussalam, 2000)

Chapter Al-Furqan   Chapter 25 Verses 58-59

58. And put your trust in the **Ever Living** One who dies not, and glorify His praises, and Sufficient is He as the All-Knower of the sins of His slaves.
59. Who created the heavens and the earth and all that is between them in six days. Then He rose over (Istawa) the Throne. The Most Gracious! Ask Him, as He is Al-Khabir (the All-Knower). (Darussalam, 2000)

Chapter Ghafir   Chapter 40 Verse 65
He is the **Ever Living**, La ilaha illa Huwa (none has the right to be worshipped but He); so, invoke Him making your worship pure for Him Alone. All the praises and thanks be to **Allah**, the **Lord** of the 'Alamin (worlds). (Darussalam, 2000)

Al-Qayyum   The Self Subsisting, The Self Existing

Chapter Al-Baqarah   Chapter 2 Verse 255
Allah! La ilaha illa Huwa (none has the right to be worshipped but He), **Al-Hayyul-Qayyum** (the Ever Living, the One Who Sustains and Protects all that exists). Neither slumber nor sleep overtakes Him. To Him belongs whatever is in the heavens and whatever is on the earth. Who is he that can intercede with Him except with His permission? He knows what happens to them in this world, and what will happen to them in the Hereafter. And they will never compass anything of His knowledge except that which He wills. His Kursi (Chair) extends over the heavens and the earth, and He feels no fatigue in guarding and preserving them. And He is the Most High, the Most Great. (Darussalam, 1999)

Chapter Al-Imran   Chapter 3 Verses 1-2
1. Alif-Lam-Mim
2. **Allah**! La ilaha illa Huwa (none has the right to be worshipped but He), **Al-Hayyul-Qayyum** (the Ever living, the One Who sustains and protects all that exists). (Darussalam, 1999)

Chapter Ta-Ha   Chapter 20 Verse 111
And faces shall be humbled before, **Al-Hayyul-Qayyum** (the Ever living, the One Who sustains and protects all that exists), and he who carried (a burden of) wrong doing, will be indeed a complete failure. (Darussalam, 2000)

Al-Ghani   The All Rich

Chapter Al-Baqarah   Chapter 2 Verse 263
Kind words and forgiving of faults are better then Sadaqah (charity-alms) followed by injury. And **Allah** is **Rich** and He is Most-Forbearing. (Darussalam, 1999)

Chapter Al-Baqarah　　　　　　　　　　　　　　　Chapter 2 Verse 267

O you who believe! Spend of the good things which you have earned, and of that which We have produced from the earth for you, and do not aim at that which is bad to spend from it, you would not accept it save if you close your eyes and tolerate therein. And know that **Allah** is **Rich**, and Worthy of all praise. (Darussalam, 1999)

Chapter Al-Imran　　　　　　　　　　　　　　　Chapter 3 Verse 97

In it are manifest signs, the Maqam (place) of Ibrahim; whosoever enters it, he attains security. And Hajj (pilgrimage to Makkah) to the House (Ka'bah) is a duty that mankind owes to **Allah**, those who can afford the expenses and whoever disbelieves, then **Allah stands not in need of any of the 'Alamin (worlds).** (Darussalam, 1999)

Chapter An-Nisa　　　　　　　　　　　　　　　Chapter 4 Verse 131

And to **Allah** belongs all that is in the heavens and all that is in the earth. And verily, We have recommended to the people of the scripture before you, and to you that you fear **Allah**, and keep your duty to Him. But if you disbelieve, then unto **Allah** belongs all that is in the heavens and all that is in the earth, and **Allah** is ever **Rich**, Worthy of all praise. (Darussalam, 1999)

Chapter Al-An'am　　　　　　　　　　　　　　　Chapter 6 Verse 133

And our **Lord** is **Rich**, full Mercy; if He wills, He can destroy you, and in your place make whom He wills as your successors, as He raised you from the seed of other people. (Darussalam, 1999)

Chapter Yunus　　　　　　　　　　　　　　　Chapter 10 Verse 68

They say: "**Allah** has begotten a son." Glory is to him! He is **Rich**. His is all that is in the heavens and all that is in the earth. No warrant you have for this. Do you say against **Allah** what you know not? (Darussalam, 2000)

Chapter Ibrahim　　　　　　　　　　　　　　　Chapter 14 Verse 8

And Musa said: "If you disbelieve, you and all on earth together, then verily, **Allah** is **Rich**, Owner of all praise." (Darussalam, 2000)

Chapter Al-Hajj　　　　　　　　　　　　　　　Chapter 22 Verse 64

To Him belongs all that is in the heavens and all that is on the earth. And verily **Allah** He is **Rich**, Worthy of all praise. (Darussalam, 2000)

Chapter An-Naml	Chapter 27 Verses 38-40

38. He Said: "O chiefs! Which of you can bring me her throne before they come to me surrendering themselves in obedience?"
39. An Ifrit (strong one) from the jinn said: "I will bring it to you before you rise from your place. And verily, I am indeed strong and trustworthy for such work."
40. One with whom was knowledge of the Scripture said: "I will bring it to you within the twinkling of an eye!" Then when he saw it placed before him, he said: "This is by the Grace of my **Lord** to test me whether I am grateful or ungrateful! And whoever is grateful, truly, his gratitude is for his own self; and whoever is ungrateful. Certainly, my **Lord** is **Rich**, Bountiful. (Darussalam, 2000)

Chapter Al-Ankabut	Chapter 29 Verses 5-6

5. Whoever hopes for the Meeting with **Allah**, then **Allah**'s Term is surely coming, and He is the All-Hearer, the All-Knower.
6. And whosoever strives, he strives only for himself. Verily, **Allah stands not in need of any of the 'Alamin** (worlds). (Darussalam, 2000)

Chapter Luqman	Chapter 31 Verse 12

And indeed, we bestowed upon Luqman Al-Hikmah (wisdom) saying: "Give thanks to **Allah**." And whoever gives thanks, he gives thanks for his own self. And whoever is unthankful, then verily, **Allah** is **All-Rich**, Worthy of all praise. (Darussalam, 2000)

Chapter Luqman	Chapter 31 Verse 26

To **Allah** belongs whatsoever is in the heavens and the earth. Verily, **Allah**, He is **Al-Ghani (Rich)**, Worthy of all praise. (Darussalam, 2000)

Chapter Fatir	Chapter 35 Verse 15

O Mankind! it is you who stand in need of **Allah**. But **Allah** is **Rich**, Worthy of all praise. (Darussalam, 2000)

Chapter Az-Zumar	Chapter 39 Verse 7

If you disbelieve, then verily, **Allah is not in need of you**; He likes not disbelief for His slaves. And if you are grateful, He is pleased therewith for you. No bearer of burdens shall bear the burden of another. Then to you **Lord** is your return, and He will inform you what you used to do. Verily, He is the All-Knower of that which is in breasts. (Darussalam, 2000)

Chapter Muhammad   Chapter 47 Verse 38

Behold! You are those who are called to spend in the Cause of **Allah**, yet among you are some who are niggardly. And whoever is niggardly, it is only at the expense of his own self. But **Allah** is **Rich**, and you are poor. And if you turn away, He will exchange you for some other people and they will not be your likes. (Darussalam, 2000)

Chapter Al-Hadid   Chapter 57 Verse 24

Those who are misers and enjoin upon people miserliness. And whosoever turns away, then **Allah** is **Rich**, Worthy of all praise. (Darussalam, 2000)

Chapter Al-Mumtahanah   Chapter 60 Verses 5-6

5. "Our **Lord**! Make us not a trial for the disbelievers, and forgive us, our **Lord**! Verily, You, only You, are the All-Mighty, the All-Wise."
6. Certainly. There has been in them an excellent example for you to follow - for those who look forward to (the Meeting with) **Allah** and the last day. And whosoever turns away, then verily, **Allah** is **Rich**, Worthy of all praise. (Darussalam, 2000)

Chapter At-Taghabun   Chapter 64 Verse 6

That was because there came to them their Messengers with clear proofs, but they said: "Shall mere men guide us?" So they disbelieved and turned away but **Allah** was not in need (of them). And **Allah** is **Rich**, Worthy of all praise. (Darussalam, 2000)

An Nur   The Light

Chapter An-Nur   Chapter 24 Verse 35

Allah is the **Light** of the heavens and the earth. The parable of His Light is as a niche and within it a lamp: the lamp is in a glass, the glass as it were a brilliant star, lit from a blessed tree, an olive, neither of the east nor of the west, whose oil would almost flow forth, though no fire touched it. Light upon Light! **Allah** guides to His Light whom He wills. And **Allah** sets forth parables for mankind, and **Allah** is All-Knower of everything. (Darussalam, 2000)

Subsection 5

SUBSECTION 5

- *Al-Alim*   *The All-Knowing*
- *Al-Khabir*   *The All-Aware*
- *Al-Hakim*   *The Most Wise*
- *Al-Basir*   *The All-Seeing*
- *As-Sami*   *The All-Hearing*

Al-Alim   The All-Knowing

Chapter Al-Baqarah   Chapter 2 Verse 29
He it is who created for you all that is on earth. Then He rose over (Istawa) towards the heaven and made them seven heavens and He is the **All-Knower** of everything. (Darussalam, 1999)

Chapter Al-Baqarah   Chapter 2 Verses 31-32
31. And He taught Adam all the names, then He showed them to the angels and said, "Tell me the names of these if you are truthful."
32. They said: "Glory is to You; we have no knowledge except what You have taught us. Verily, it is You, the **All-Knower**, the All-Wise." (Darussalam, 1999)

Chapter Al-Baqarah   Chapter 2 Verses 94-95
94. Say: "If the home of the Hereafter with **Allah** is indeed for you specially and not for others, of mankind, then long for death if you are truthful.
95. But they will never long for it because of what their hands have sent before them. And **Allah** is **All-Aware** of the Zalimun (wrong-doers). (Darussalam, 1999)

Chapter Al-Baqarah   Chapter 2 Verse 115
And to **Allah** belong the east and the west, so wherever you turn there is the Face of **Allah**. Surely, **Allah** is All-Sufficient for His creature' needs, **All-Knowing**. (Darussalam, 1999)

Chapter Al-Baqarah   Chapter 2 Verse 127
And when Ibrahim and Ismail were raising the foundations of the House, "Our **Lord**! Accept from us. Verily, You are the All-Hearer, the **All-Knower**." (Darussalam, 1999)

Chapter Al-Baqarah   Chapter 2 Verse 137
So, if they believe in the like of that which you believe then they are rightly guided; but if they turn away, then they are only in opposition. So **Allah** will suffice for you against them. And He is the All-Hearer, the **All-Knower**. (Darussalam, 1999)

Chapter Al-Baqarah   Chapter 2 Verse 158
Verily, As-Safa and Al-Marwah (two mountains in Makkah) are of the symbols of **Allah**. So it is not a sin on him who performs Hajj or Umrah

(pilgrimage) of the House to perform the going between them. And whoever does good voluntarily, then **Allah** is All-Recogniser, **All-Knower**. (Darussalam, 1999)

Chapter Al-Baqarah   Chapter 2 Verses 180-181
180. It is prescribed for you, when death approaches any of you, if he leaves wealth, that he makes a bequest and next of kin, according to reasonable manners. A duty upon Al-Muttaqun (the pious).
181. Then whoever changes the bequest after hearing it, the sin shall be on those who make the change. Truly, **Allah** is All-Hearer, **All-Knower**. (Darussalam, 1999)

Chapter Al-Baqarah   Chapter 2 Verse 215
They ask you what they should spend, say: "Whatever you spend of good must be for parents and kindred and orphans and Al-Masakin (the poor) and the wayfarers, and whatever you do of good deeds, **Allah knows it well**." (Darussalam, 1999)

Chapter Al-Baqarah   Chapter 2 Verse 224
And make not **Allah**'s (Name) an excuse in your oaths against your doing good and acting piously, and making peace among mankind. And **Allah** is All-Hearer, **All-Knower**. (Darussalam, 1999)

Chapter Al-Baqarah   Chapter 2 Verses 226-227
226. These who take an oath not to have sexual relations with their wives must wait for four months, then if they return, verily, **Allah** is Oft-Forgiving, Most Merciful.
227. And if they decide upon divorce, then **Allah** is All-Hearer, **All-Knower**. (Darussalam, 1999)

Chapter Al-Baqarah   Chapter 2 Verse 231
And when you have divorced women and they have fulfilled the term of their prescribed period, either take them back on reasonable basis or set them free on reasonable basis. But do not take them back to hurt them, and whoever does that, then he has wronged himself. And treat not the Verses of **Allah** as a jest, but remember **Allah**'s Favours on you, and that which He has sent down to you of the book and Al-Hikmah (wisdom) whereby He instructs you. And fear **Allah**, and know that **Allah** is **All-Aware of everything**. (Darussalam, 1999)

Chapter Al-Baqarah　　　　　　　　　　　　　　Chapter 2 Verse 244
And fight in the way of **Allah** and know that **Allah** is All-Hearer, **All-Knower**. (Darussalam, 1999)

Chapter Al-Baqarah　　　　　　　　　　　　　　Chapter 2 Verse 246
246. Have you not thought about the group of the Children of Israel after Musa? When they said to a prophet of theirs, "Appoint for us a king and we will fight in **Allah**'s way." He said, "Would you then refrain from fighting, if fighting was prescribed for you?" They said, "Why should we not fight in **Allah**'s way while we have been driven out of our homes and our children?" But when fighting was ordered for them, they turned away, all except a few of them. And **Allah** is **All-Aware** of the Zalimun (wrong-doers).
247. And their prophet said to them, "Indeed **Allah** has appointed Talut as a king over you." They said, "How can he be a king over us when we are fitter than him for the kingdom, and he has not been given enough wealth." He said: "Verily, **Allah** has chosen him above you and has increased him abundantly in knowledge and stature. And **Allah** grants His kingdom to whom He wills. And **Allah** is All-Sufficient for His creatures' needs, **All-Knower**." (Darussalam, 1999)

Chapter Al-Baqarah　　　　　　　　　　　　　　Chapter 2 Verse 256
There is no compulsion in religion. Verily, the Right Path has become distinct from the wrong path. Whoever disbelievers in Taghut (false deities) and believes in **Allah**, then he has grasped the most trustworthy handhold that will never break. And **Allah** is All-Hearer, **All-Knower**. (Darussalam, 1999)

Chapter Al-Baqarah　　　　　　　　　　　　　　Chapter 2 Verse 261
The likeness of those who spend their wealth in the way of **Allah**, is as the likeness of a grain, it grows seven ears, and each ear has a hundred grains. **Allah** gives manifold increase to whom He wills. And **Allah** is All-Sufficient for His creatures' needs, **All-Knower**. (Darussalam, 1999)

Chapter Al-Baqarah　　　　　　　　　　　　　　Chapter 2 Verse 268
Shaitan (Satan) threatens you with poverty and orders you to commit Fahsha (indecency); whereas **Allah** promises you Forgiveness from Himself and bounty, and **Allah** is All-Sufficient for His creatures' needs, **All-Knower**. (Darussalam, 1999)

Chapter Al-Baqarah　　　　　　　　　　　　　　Chapter 2 Verse 273
(Charity is) for Fuqara (the poor), who in **Allah**'s cause are restricted, and cannot move about in the land. The one who knows them not, thinks that they

are rich because of their modesty. You may know them by their mark, they do not beg of people at all. And whatever you spend in good, surely, **Allah knows it well**. (Darussalam, 1999)

Chapter Al-Baqarah   Chapter 2 Verses 282-283

282. O you who believe! When you contract a debt for a fixed period, write it down. Let a scribe write it down in justice between you. Let not the scribe refuse to write as **Allah** has taught him, so let him write. Let him who incurs the liability dictate, and he must fear **Allah**, his **Lord**, and diminish not anything of what he owes. But if the debtor is of poor understanding, or weak, or is unable to dictate for himself, then let his guardian dictate in justice. And get two witnesses out of your own men. And if there are not two men, then a man and two women, such as you agree for witnesses, so that if one of them errs, the other can remind her. And the witnesses should not refuse when they are called. You should not become weary to write it, whether it be small or big, for its fixed term, that is more just with **Allah**; more solid as evidence, and more convenient to prevent doubts among yourselves, save when it is a present trade which you carry out on the spot among yourselves, then there is no sin on you if you do not write it down. But take witnesses whenever you make a commercial contract. Let neither scribe nor witness suffer any harm, but if you do, it would be wickedness in you. So be afraid of **Allah**; and **Allah** teaches you. And **Allah** is the **All-Knower** of each and everything.

283. And if you are on a journey and cannot find a scribe, then let there be a pledge taken, then if one of you entrusts the other, let the one who is entrusted discharge his trust, and let him be afraid of **Allah**, his **Lord**. And conceal not the evidence, for he who hides it, surely, his heart is sinful. And **Allah** is **All-Knower** of what you do. (Darussalam, 1999)

Chapter Al-Imran   Chapter 3 Verses 33~35

33. **Allah** chose Adam, Nuh, the family of Ibrahim and the family of Imran above the 'Alamin (worlds).

34. Offspring, one of the other, and **Allah** is All-Hearer, **All-Knower**.

35. When the wife of Imran said: "O my **Lord**! I have vowed to You what is in my womb to be dedicated for Your services, so accept this from me. Verily, You are the All-Hearer, the **All-Knowing**." (Darussalam, 1999)

Chapter Al-Imran   Chapter 3 Verses 62-63

62. Verily! This is the true narrative, and La ilaha illallah (none has the right to be worshipped but **Allah**). And indeed, **Allah** is the All-Mighty, the All-Wise.

63. And if they turn away, then surely, **Allah** is **All-Aware** of those who do mischief. (Darussalam, 1999)

Chapter Al-Imran   Chapter 3 Verse 73
And believe no one except the one who follows your religion." Say: "Verily, right guidance is the Guidance of **Allah**" and do not believe that anyone can receive like that which you have received, otherwise they would engage you in argument before your **Lord**." Say: "All the bounty is in the Hand of **Allah**; He grants to whom He wills. And **Allah** is All-Sufficient for His creatures' needs, **All-Knower**." (Darussalam, 1999)

Chapter Al-Imran   Chapter 3 Verse 92
By no means shall you attain Al-Birr (piety), unless you spend of that which you love; and whatever of good you love; and whatever of good you spend, **Allah** knows it well. (Darussalam, 1999)

Chapter Al-Imran   Chapter 3 Verse 99
Say: "O people of the scripture! Why do you stop those who have believed, from the path of **Allah**, seeking to make it seem crooked, while you are witnesses? And **Allah is not unaware of what you do.**" (Darussalam, 1999)

Chapter Al-Imran   Chapter 3 Verses 114-115
114. They believe in **Allah** and Last Day; they enjoin Al-Maruf (good) and forbid Al-Munkar (evil); and they hasten in good works; and they are among the righteous.
115. And whatever good they do; nothing will be rejected of them; for **Allah knows well** those who are Al-Muttaqun (the pious). (Darussalam, 1999)

Chapter Al-Imran   Chapter 3 Verses 119~121
119. Lo! you are the ones who love them but they love you not, and you believe in all the Scriptures. And when they meet you, they say, "We believe." But when they are alone, they bite the tips of their fingers at you in rage. Say: "Perish in your rage. Certainly, **Allah** knows what is in the breasts."
120. If a good befalls you, it grieves them, but if some evil overtakes you, they rejoice at it. But if you remain patient and become Al-Muttaqun (the pious), not the least harm will their cunning do to you. Surely, **Allah** surrounds all that they do.
121. And when you left your household in the morning to post the believers at their stations for the battle (of Uhad). And **Allah** is All-Hearer, **All-Knower**. (Darussalam, 1999)

Chapter Al-Imran   Chapter 3 Verse 154

Then after the distress, He sent down security for you. Slumber overtook a party of you, while another party was thinking about themselves and thought wrongly of **Allah** - the thought of ignorance. They said, "Have we any part in the affair?" Say: "Indeed the affair belongs wholly to **Allah**." They hide within themselves what they dare not reveal to you, saying: "If we had anything to do with the affair, none of us would have been killed here." Say: "Even if you had remained in your homes, those for whom death was decreed would certainly have gone forth to the place of their death," but that **Allah** might test what is in your breasts; and to purify that which was in your hearts, and **Allah** is **All-Knower** of what is in breasts. (Darussalam, 1999)

Chapter An-Nisa   Chapter 4 Verses 11-12

11. **Allah** commands you as regard your children's (inheritance): to the male, a portion equal to that of two females; if only daughters, two or more, their share is two-thirds of the inheritance; if only one, her share is a half. For parents, a sixth share of inheritance to each if the deceased left children; if no children, and the parents are the heirs, the mother has a third; if the deceased left brothers or (sisters), the mother has a sixth. After the payment of legacies, he may have bequeathed or debts. You know not which of them, whether your parents or your children, are nearest to you in benefit; (these fixed shares) are ordained by **Allah**. And **Allah** is ever **All-Knower**, All-Wise.
12. In that which your wives leave, your share is a half if they have no child; but if they leave a child, you get a fourth of that which they leave after payment of legacies that they may have bequeathed or debts. In that which you leave, their share is a fourth if you leave no child; but if you leave a child, they get an eighth of that which you leave after payment of legacies that you may have bequeathed or debts. If the man or woman whose inheritance is in question has left neither ascendants nor descendants, but has left a brother or a sister, each one of the two gets a sixth; but if more than two, they share in a third, after payment of legacies he may have bequeathed or debts, so that no loss is caused. This is a commandment from **Allah**; and **Allah** is ever **All-Knowing**, Most-Forbearing. (Darussalam, 1999)

Chapter An-Nisa   Chapter 4 Verse 17

Allah accepts only the repentance of those who do evil in ignorance and foolishness and repent soon afterwards; it is they whom **Allah** will forgive and **Allah** is ever **All-Knower**, All-Wise. (Darussalam, 1999)

Chapter An-Nisa											Chapter 4 Verses 23-24

23. Forbidden to you are: your mothers, your daughters, your sisters, your father's sisters, your mother's sisters, your brother's daughters, your sister's daughters, your foster mothers who gave you suck, your foster milk suckling sisters, your wives' mothers. Your stepdaughters under your guardianship, born of your wives to whom you have gone in – but there is no sin on you if you have not gone in them, - the wives of your sons who from your own loins, and two sisters in wedlock at the same time, except for what has already passed; verily, **Allah** is Oft-Forgiving, Most Merciful.

24. Also women already married, except those whom your right hands possess. Thus has **Allah** ordained for you. All others are lawful, provided you seek with Mahr (bridal money) from your property, desiring chastity, not committing illegal sexual intercourse, so with those of whom you have enjoyed sexual relations, give them their Mahr (bridal money) as prescribed, but if after a Mahr (bridal money) is prescribed, you agree mutually, there is no sin on you. Surely, **Allah** is Ever **All-Knowing**, All-Wise. (Darussalam, 1999)

Chapter An-Nisa											Chapter 4 Verse 26

Allah wishes to make clear to you, and to show you the ways of those before you, and accept your repentance, and **Allah** is **All-Knower**, All-Wise. (Darussalam, 1999)

Chapter An-Nisa											Chapter 4 Verse 32

And wish not for the things in which **Allah** has made some of you to excel others. For men there is reward for what they have earned, for women there is reward for what they have earned, and ask **Allah** of His Bounty. Surely, **Allah** is ever **All-Knower** of everything. (Darussalam, 1999)

Chapter An-Nisa											Chapter 4 Verses 34-35

34. Men are the protectors and maintainers of women, because **Allah** has made one of them to excel the other, and because they spend from their means. Therefore, the righteous women are devoutly obedient, and guard in the husband's absence what **Allah** orders them to guard. As to those women on whose part you see ill-conduct, admonish them, refuse to share their beds, beat them; but if they return to obedience, seek not against them means. Surely, **Allah** is Ever Most High, Most Great.

35. If you fear a beach between them twain, appoint arbitrators, one from his family and the other from hers; if they both wish for peace, **Allah** will cause their reconciliation. Indeed, **Allah** is Ever **All-Knower**, Well-Acquainted with all things. (Darussalam, 1999)

Chapter An-Nisa	Chapter 4 Verse 39

And what loss have they if they had believed in **Allah** and in the Last day, and they spend out of what **Allah** has given them for sustenance? And **Allah** is ever **All-Knower** of them. (Darussalam, 1999)

Chapter An-Nisa	Chapter 4 Verses 69-70

69. And whoso obey **Allah** and the Messenger, then they will be in the company of those on whom **Allah** has bestowed His Grace, of the Prophets, the Siddiqun (the truthful), the martyrs, and the righteous. And how excellent these companions are!
70. Such is the Bounty from **Allah**, and **Allah** is Sufficient as **All-Knower**. (Darussalam, 1999)

Chapter An-Nisa	Chapter 4 Verse 92

It is not for a believer to kill a believer except by mistake; and whosoever kills a believer by mistake, he must set free a believing slave and a compensation be given to the deceased's family unless they remit it. If the deceased belonged to a people at war with you and he was a believer, the freeing of a believing slave; and if he belonged to a people with whom you have a treaty of mutual alliance, compensation must be paid to his family, and a believing slave must be freed. And whoso finds this beyond his means; he must fast for two consecutive months in order to seek repentance from **Allah**. And **Allah** is ever **All-Knowing**, All-Wise. (Darussalam, 1999)

Chapter An-Nisa	Chapter 4 Verse 104

And don't be weak in the pursuit of the enemy; if you are suffering then surely, they are suffering as you are suffering, but you have hope from **Allah** that for which they hope not; and **Allah** is ever **All-Knowing**, All-Wise. (Darussalam, 1999)

Chapter An-Nisa	Chapter 4 Verses 110-111

110. And whoever does evil or wrongs himself but afterwards seeks **Allah**'s Forgiveness, he will find **Allah** Oft-Forgiving, Most Merciful.
111. And whoever earns sin, he earns it only against himself. And **Allah** is **Ever All-Knowing**, All-Wise. (Darussalam, 1999)

Chapter An-Nisa	Chapter 4 Verse 127

The ask your legal instruction concerning women, say: **Allah** instructs you about them, and about what is recited unto you in the book concerning the orphan girls whom you give not the prescribed portions and yet whom you desire to marry, and the children who are weak and oppressed, and that you stand firm for justice to orphans. And whatever good you do, **Allah** is ever **All-Aware** of it. (Darussalam, 1999)

Chapter An-Nisa   Chapter 4 Verses 147-148
147. Why should **Allah** punish you if you have thanked and have believed in Him. And **Allah** is ever All-Appreciative, **All-Knowing**.
148. **Allah** does not like that the evil should be uttered in public except by him who has been wronged. And **Allah** is ever All-Hearer, **All-Knower**. (Darussalam, 1999)

Chapter An-Nisa   Chapter 4 Verse 170
O mankind! Verily, there has come to you the Messenger with the truth from your **Lord**. So believe in him, it is better for you. But if you disbelieve, then certainly to **Allah** belongs all that is in the heavens and the earth. And **Allah** is ever **All-Knower**, All-Wise. (Darussalam, 1999)

Chapter An-Nisa   Chapter 4 Verse 176
They ask you for a legal verdict, say: "**Allah** directs about Al-Kalalah (who leaves behind no lineal). If it is a man that dies leaving a sister, but no child, she shall have half the inheritance. If a woman, who left no child, her brother takes her inheritance. If there are two sisters, they shall have two-thirds of the inheritance; if there are brothers and sisters, the male will have twice the share of the female. (Thus) does **Allah** make clear to you lest you go astray. And **Allah** is the **All-Knower** of everything." (Darussalam, 1999)

Chapter Al-Ma'idah   Chapter 5 Verse 7
And remember **Allah**'s Favour to you and His covenant with which He bound you when you said: "We hear and we obey." And fear **Allah**. Verily, **Allah** is **All-Knower** of that which is in breasts. (Darussalam, 1999)

Chapter Al-Ma'idah   Chapter 5 Verse 54
O you who believe! Whoever from among you turns back from his religion, **Allah** will bring a people whom He will love and they will love Him; humble towards the believers, stern towards the disbelievers, fighting in the way of **Allah**, and never fear of the blame of the blamers. That is the Grace of **Allah** which He bestows on whom He wills. And **Allah** is All-Sufficient for His creatures' needs, **All-Knower**. (Darussalam, 1999)

Chapter Al-Ma'idah   Chapter 5 Verse 76
Say: "How do you worship besides **Allah** something which has no power either to harm or benefit you? But it is **Allah** who is the All-Hearer, **All-Knower**." (Darussalam, 1999)

Chapter Al-Ma'idah   Chapter 5 Verse 97
Allah has made the Ka'bah, the Sacred house, an asylum of security and benefits for mankind, and also the Sacred Month and the animals of offerings and the garlanded, that you may know that **Allah** has knowledge of all that is in the heavens and all that is in the earth, and that **Allah** is the **All-Knower** of each and everything. (Darussalam, 1999)

Chapter Al-An'am   Chapter 6 Verse 13
And to Him belongs whatsoever exists in the night and the day, and He is the All-Hearing, the **All-Knowing**." (Darussalam, 1999)

Chapter Al-An'am   Chapter 6 Verse 82-83
82. It is those who believe and confuse not their Belief with Zulm, for them there is security and they are the guided.
83. And that was our Proof which we gave Ibrahim against his people. We raise whom We will in degrees. Certainly, your **Lord** is All-Wise, **All-Knowing**. (Darussalam, 1999)

Chapter Al-An'am   Chapter 6 Verse 96
(He is the) Cleaver of the daybreak. He has appointed the night for resting, and the sun and the moon for reckoning. Such is the measuring of the All-Mighty, the **All-Knowing**. (Darussalam, 1999)

Chapter Al-An'am   Chapter 6 Verse 101
He is the Originator of the heavens and the earth. How can He have children when He has no wife? He created all things and He is the **All-Knower** of everything. (Darussalam, 1999)

Chapter Al-An'am   Chapter 6 Verse 115
And the word of your **Lord** has been fulfilled in truth and in justice. None can change His Words. And He is the All-Hearer, the **All-Knower**. (Darussalam, 1999)

Chapter Al-An'am   Chapter 6 Verse 128
And on the Day when He will gather them together: "O you assembly of jinn! Many did you mislead of men," and their Auliya (friends and helpers, etc.)

amongst men will say: "Our **Lord**! We benefited one from the other, but now we have reached our appointed term which You did appoint for us." He will say: "The Fire be your dwelling place, you will dwell therein forever, except as **Allah** may will. Certainly, your **Lord** is All-Wise, **All-Knowing**." (Darussalam, 1999)

Chapter Al-An'am   Chapter 6 Verse 139
And they say: "What is in the bellies of such and such cattle is for our males alone, and forbidden to our females, but if it is born dead, then all have shares therein." He will punish them for their attribution. Verily, He is All-Wise, **All-Knower**. (Darussalam, 1999)

Chapter Al-A'raf   Chapter 7 Verse 200
And if an evil whisper comes to you from Shaitan (Satan), then seek refuge with **Allah**. Verily, He is All-Hearer, **All-Knower**. (Darussalam, 1999)

Chapter Al-Anfal   Chapter 8 Verses 16-17
16. And whoever turns his back to them on such a day – unless it be a stratagem of war, or to retreat to a troop, - he indeed has drawn upon himself wrath from **Allah**. And his abode is Hell, and worst indeed is that destination.
17. You killed them not, but **Allah** killed them. And you threw not when you did throw but **Allah** threw, that He might test the believers by a fair trial from Him. Verily, **Allah** is All-Hearer, **All-Knower.** (Darussalam, 1999)

Chapter Al-Anfal   Chapter 8 Verses 42-43
42. When you were on the near side of the valley, and they on the farther side, and the caravan on the ground lower than you. Even if you had made a mutual appointment to meet, you would certainly have failed in the appointment, but that **Allah** might accomplish a matter already ordained, so that those who were to be destroyed might be destroyed after clear evidence, and those who were to live might live after clear evidence. And surely, **Allah** is All-Hearer, **All-Knower**.
43. When **Allah** showed them to you as few in your dream; if He had shown them to you as many, you would surely, have been discouraged, and you would surely, have disputed in making a decision. But **Allah** saved (you). Certainly, He is the **All-Knower** of what is in the breasts. (Darussalam, 1999)

Chapter Al-Anfal   Chapter 8 Verse 53
That is so because **Allah** will never change a Grace which He has bestowed on a people until they change what is in their own selves. And verily, **Allah** is All-Hearer, **All-Knower**. (Darussalam, 1999)

Chapter Al-Anfal   Chapter 8 Verse 61
But if they incline to peace, you also incline to it, and trust in **Allah**. Verily, He is the All-Hearer, the **All-Knower**. (Darussalam, 1999)

Chapter Al-Anfal   Chapter 8 Verses 70-71
70. O Prophet! Say to the captives that are in your hands: "If **Allah** knows any good in your hearts, He will give you something better than what has been taken from you, and He will forgive you, and **Allah** is Oft-Forgiving, Most Merciful."
71. But if they intend to betray you, they indeed betrayed **Allah** before. So He gave (you) power over them. And **Allah** is **All-Knower**, All-Wise. (Darussalam, 1999)

Chapter Al-Anfal   Chapter 8 Verse 75
And these who believed afterwards, and emigrated and strove hard along with you, they are of you. But kindred by blood are nearer to one another in the decree ordained by **Allah**. Verily, **Allah** is the **All-Knower** of everything. (Darussalam, 1999)

Chapter At-Taubah   Chapter 9 Verses 14-15
14. Fight against them so that **Allah** will punish them by your hands and disgrace them and give you victory over them and heal the breasts of a believing people.
15. And remove the anger of their hearts. **Allah** accepts the repentance of whom He wills. **Allah** is **All-Knowing**, All-Wise. (Darussalam, 1999)

Chapter At-Taubah   Chapter 9 Verse 28
O you who believe! Verily, the Mushrikun (polytheists) are Najasun (impure), so let them not come near All-Masjid Al-Haram after this year; and if you fear poverty, **Allah** will enrich you if He wills, out of His Bounty. Surely, **Allah** is **All-Knowing**, All-Wise. (Darussalam, 1999)

Chapter At-Taubah   Chapter 9 Verse 44
Those who believe in **Allah** and the last day would not ask your leave to be exempted from fighting with their properties and their lives; and **Allah** is the **All-Knower** of Al-Muttaqun (the pious). (Darussalam, 1999)

| Chapter At-Taubah | Chapter 9 Verses 46-47 |

46. And if they had intended to march out, certainly, they would have made some preparation for it; but **Allah** was averse to their being sent forth, so He made them lag behind, and it was said: "Sit you among those who sit."
47. Had they marched out with you, they would have added to you nothing except disorder, and they would have hurried about in your midst and sowing sedition among you – and there are some among you who would have listened to them. And **Allah** is the **All-Knower** of the Zalimun (wrong-doers). (Darussalam, 1999)

| Chapter At-Taubah | Chapter 9 Verse 60 |

As-Sadaqat (alms) are only for the Fuqara (poor), and Al-Masakin (the poor) and those employed to collect; and to attract the hearts of those who have been inclined; and to free the captives; and for those in debt; and for **Allah**'s cause, and for the wayfarer; a duty imposed by **Allah**. And **Allah** is **All-Knower**, All-Wise. (Darussalam, 1999)

| Chapter At-Taubah | Chapter 9 Verses 97-98 |

97. The bedouins are the worst in disbelief and hypocrisy, and more likely to be in ignorance of the limits which **Allah** has revealed to His Messenger. And **Allah** is **All-Knower**, All-Wise.
98. And of the bedouins there are some who look upon what they spend as a fine and watch for calamities for you, on them be the calamity of evil. And **Allah** is All-Hearer, **All-Knower**. (Darussalam, 2000)

| Chapter At-Taubah | Chapter 9 Verses 102-103 |

102. And others who have acknowledged their sins, they have mixed a deed that was righteous with another that was evil. Perhaps **Allah** will turn unto them in forgiveness. Surely, **Allah** is Oft-Forgiving, Most Merciful.
103. Take Sadaqat (alms) from their wealth in order to purify them and sanctify them with it, and invoke **Allah** for them. Verily, your invocations are a source of security for them; and **Allah** is All-Hearer, **All-Knower**. (Darussalam, 2000)

| Chapter At-Taubah | Chapter 9 Verses 105-106 |

105. And say: "Do deeds! **Allah** will see your deeds, and His Messenger and the believers. And you will be brought back to the **All-Knower** of the unseen and the seen. Then He will inform you of what you used to do." (Darussalam, 2000)
106. And others await for **Allah**'s decree, whether He will punish them or will forgive them. And **Allah** is **All-Knowing**, All-Wise. (Darussalam, 2000)

Chapter At-Taubah Chapter 9 Verses 109-110

109. Is it then he who laid the foundation of his building on piety to **Allah** and His Good Pleasure better, or he who laid the foundation of his building on the brink of an undetermined precipice ready to crumble down, so that it crumbled to pieces with him into the fire of Hell. And **Allah** guides not the people who are the Zalimun (wrong-doers).

110. The building which they built will never cease to be a cause of hypocrisy and doubt in their hearts unless their hearts are cut to pieces. And **Allah** is **All-Knowing**, All-Wise. (Darussalam, 2000)

Chapter At-Taubah Chapter 9 Verse 115

And **Allah** will never lead a people astray after He has guided them until He makes clear to them as to what they should avoid. Verily, **Allah** is the **All-Knower** of everything. (Darussalam, 2000)

Chapter Yunus Chapter 10 Verses 35-36

35. Say: Is there of your partners one that guides to the truth? "Say: "It is **Allah** who guides to the truth. Is then He who guides to the truth more worthy to be followed, or he who finds not guidance unless he is guided? Then, what is the matter with you? How judge you?"

36. And most of them follow nothing but conjecture. Certainly, conjecture can be of no avail against the truth. Surely, **Allah** is **All-Aware** of what they do. (Darussalam, 2000)

Chapter Yunus Chapter 10 Verse 65

And let not their speech grieve you, for all power and honour belong to **Allah**. He is the All-Hearer, the **All-Knower**. (Darussalam, 2000)

Chapter Hud Chapter 11 Verse 5

No doubt! They did fold up their breast, that they may hide from Him. Surely, even when they cover themselves with their garments, He knows what they conceal and what they reveal. Verily, He is the **All-Knower** of the (innermost secrets) of the breasts. (Darussalam, 2000)

Chapter Yusuf Chapter 12 Verses 5-6

5. He said: "O my son! Relate not your vision to your brothers, lest they should arrange a plot against you. Verily, Shaitan (Satan) is to man an open enemy!

6. "Thus will your **Lord** choose you and teach you the interpretations of dreams and perfect His Favour on you and on the offspring of Yaqub, as He

perfected it on your father, Ibrahim and Ishaq aforetime! Verily, your **Lord** is **All-Knowing**, All-Wise." (Darussalam, 2000)

Chapter Yusuf	Chapter 12 Verse 19

And there came a caravan of travelers and they sent their water-drawer, and he let down his bucket. He said: "What a good news! Here is a boy." So, they hid him as merchandise. And **Allah** was the **All-Knower** of what they did. (Darussalam, 2000)

Chapter Yusuf	Chapter 12 Verses 33-34

33. He said: "O my **Lord**! Prison is dearer to me than that to which they invite me. Unless You turn away their plot from me, I will feel inclined towards them and be one of the ignorant."
34. So his **Lord** answered his invocation and turned away from him their plot. Verily, He is the All-Hearer, the **All-Knower**. (Darussalam, 2000)

Chapter Yusuf	Chapter 12 Verses 81~83

81. "Return to your father and say, 'O our father! Verily, your son has stolen, and we testify not except according to what we know, and we could not know the Unseen!
82. "And ask the town where we have been, and the caravan in which we returned, and indeed we are telling the truth."
83. He said: "Nay, but your own selves have beguiled you into something. So patience is most fitting. May be **Allah** will bring them all to me. Truly, He! Only He is **All-Knowing**, All-Wise." (Darussalam, 2000)

Chapter Yusuf	Chapter 12 Verses 99-100

99. Then, when they came in before Yusuf, he took his parents to himself and said: "Enter Egypt, if **Allah** wills in security.
100. And he (Yusuf) raised his parents to the throne and they fell down before him prostrate. And he said: "O my father! This is the interpretation of my dream aforetime! My **Lord** has made it come true! He was indeed good to me, when He took me out of the prison, and brought you out of the bedouin – life, after Shaitan (Satan) had sown enmity between me and my brothers. Certainly, my **Lord** is the Most Courteous and kind unto whom He wills. Truly, He! Only He is the **All-Knowing**, the All-Wise. (Darussalam, 2000)

Chapter Al-Hijr	Chapter 15 Verses 24-25

24. And indeed, We know the first generations of you who had passed away, and indeed, we know the present generations of you, and also those who will come afterwards.

25. And verily, your **Lord** will gather them together. Truly, He is All-Wise, **All-Knowing**. (Darussalam, 2000)

Chapter Al-Hijr   Chapter 15 Verses 85-86
85. And We created not the heavens and the earth and all that is between them except with truth, and the Hour is surely coming, so overlook, their faults with gracious forgiveness.
86. Verily, your **Lord** is the **All-Knowing** Creator. (Darussalam, 2000)

Chapter An-Nahl   Chapter 16 Verse 70
And **Allah** has created you and then He will cause you to die; and of you there are some who are sent back to senility, so that they know nothing after having known. Truly, **Allah** is **All-Knowing**, All-Powerful. (Darussalam, 2000)

Chapter Al-Anbiya   Chapter 21 Verses 1~4
1. Draws near for mankind their reckoning, while they turn away in heedlessness.
2. Comes not unto them an admonition from their **Lord** as a recent revelation but they listen to it while they play,
3. With their hearts occupied. Those who do wrong, conceal their private counsels, (saying): "Is this more than a human being like you? Will you submit to magic while you see it?"
4. He said: "My **Lord** knows word in the heavens and on earth. And He is the All-Hearer, the **All-Knower**." (Darussalam, 2000)

Chapter Al-Hajj   Chapter 22 Verse 52
Never did we send a Messenger or a Prophet before you but when he did recite the Revelation or narrated or spoke, Shaitan (Satan) threw in it. But **Allah** abolishes that which Shaitan (Satan) throws in. Then **Allah** establishes His Revelations. And **Allah** is **All-Knower**, All-Wise. (Darussalam, 2000)

Chapter Al-Hajj   Chapter 22 Verse 59
Truly, He will make them enter an entrance with which they shall be well-pleased, and verily, **Allah** indeed is **All-Knowing**, Most Forbearing. (Darussalam, 2000)

Chapter Al-Mu'minun   Chapter 23 Verse 51
O Messengers! Eat of the Tayyibat (all kinds of Halal foods) and do righteous deeds. Verily, I am **Well-Acquainted** with what you do. (Darussalam, 2000)

| Chapter An-Nur | Chapter 24 Verse 18 |

And **Allah** makes the Ayat (signs) plain to you, and **Allah** is **All-Knowing**, All-Wise. (Darussalam, 2000)

| Chapter An-Nur | Chapter 24 Verse 21 |

O you who believe! Follow not the footsteps of Shaitan (Satan). And whosoever follows the footsteps of Shaitan (Satan), then, verily, he commands Al-Fahsha (immorality), and Al-Munkar (evil). And had it not been for the Grace of **Allah** and His mercy on you, not one of you would ever have been pure from sins. But **Allah** purifies whom He wills, and **Allah** is All-Hearer, **All-Knower**. (Darussalam, 2000)

| Chapter An-Nur | Chapter 24 Verses 27-28 |

27. O you who believe! Enter not houses other than your own, until you have asked permission and greeted those in them; that is better for you, in order that you may remember.
28. And if you find no one therein, still, enter not until permission has been given. And if you are asked to go back, go back, for it is purer for you. And **Allah** is **All-Knower** of what you do. (Darussalam, 2000)

| Chapter An-Nur | Chapter 24 Verse 32 |

And marry those among you who are single and the Salihun (pious) of your slaves and maidservants. If they be poor, **Allah** will enrich them out of His Bounty. And **Allah** is All-Sufficient for His Creatures' needs, **All-Knowing**. (Darussalam, 2000)

| Chapter An-Nur | Chapter 24 Verse 35 |

Allah is the Light of the heavens and the earth. The parable of His Light is as a niche and within it a lamp: the lamp is in a glass, the glass as it were a brilliant star, lit from a blessed tree, an olive, neither of the east nor of the west, whose oil would almost flow forth, though no fire touched it. Light upon Light! **Allah** guides to His Light whom He wills. And **Allah** sets forth parables for mankind, and **Allah** is **All-Knower** of everything. (Darussalam, 2000)

| Chapter An-Nur | Chapter 24 Verse 41 |

See you not that **Allah**, He it is Whom glorify whosoever is in the heavens and the earth, and the birds with wings outspread? Of each one He knows indeed his Salat (prayer) and his glorification; and **Allah** is **All-Aware** of what they do. (Darussalam, 2000)

Chapter An-Nur   Chapter 24 Verses 58~60

58. O you who believe! Let your legal slaves and slave-girls, and those among you who have not come to the age of puberty ask your permission on three occasions; before Fajr (morning) Salat (prayer), and while you put off your clothes for the noonday, and after the 'Isha' (night) Salat (prayer). (These) three times are of privacy for you, other than these times there is no sin on you or on them to move about, attending to each other. Thus, **Allah** makes clear the Ayat (Verses) to you. And **Allah** is **All-Knowing**, All-Wise.

59. And when the children among you come to puberty, then let them ask for permission, as those senior to them. Thus, **Allah** makes clear His Ayat (Verses) for you. And **Allah** is **All-Knowing**, All-Wise.

60. And as for women past childbearing who do not except wedlock, it is no sin on them if they discard their clothing in such a way as not to show their adornment. But to refrain is better for them. And **Allah** is All-Hearer, **All-Knower**. (Darussalam, 2000)

Chapter An-Nur   Chapter 24 Verse 64

Certainly, to **Allah** belongs all that is in the heavens and the earth. Surely, He knows your condition and the Day when they will be brought back to Him, then He will inform them of what they did. And **Allah** is **All-Knower** of everything. (Darussalam, 2000)

Chapter Ash-Shu'ara   Chapter 26 Verses 217~220

217. And put you trust in the All-Mighty, the Most Merciful.
218. Who sees you when you stand up.
219. And your movements among those who fall prostrate.
220. Verily, He, only He is the All-Hearer, the **All-Knower**. (Darussalam, 2000)

Chapter An-Naml   Chapter 27 Verse 6

And verily, you are being taught the Quran from One, All-Wise, **All-Knowing**. (Darussalam, 2000)

Chapter An-Naml   Chapter 27 Verse 74

And verily, your **Lord knows** what their breasts conceal and what they reveal. (Darussalam, 2000)

Chapter An-Naml   Chapter 27 Verses 78-79

78. Verily, your **Lord** will decide between them by His judgment. And He is the All-Mighty, the **All-Knowing**.

79. So put your trust in **Allah**; surely, you are on manifest truth. (Darussalam, 2000)

Chapter Al-Qasas   Chapter 28 Verse 85
Verily, He Who has given you the Quran will surely, bring you back to Ma'ad (the place of return). Say: "My **Lord** is **Aware** of him who brings guidance, and of him who is in manifest error." (Darussalam, 2000)

Chapter Al-Ankabut   Chapter 29 Verse 5
Whoever hopes for the meeting with **Allah**, then **Allah**'s Term is surely coming, and He is the All-Hearer, the **All-Knower**. (Darussalam, 2000)

Chapter Al-Ankabut   Chapter 29 Verse 52
Say: "Sufficient is **Allah** for a witness between me and you. He **knows** what is in the heaven and on earth." And those who believe in batil (falsehood), and disbelieve in **Allah**, it is they who are the losers. (Darussalam, 2000)

Chapter Al-Ankabut   Chapter 29 Verse 60
And so many a moving creature carries not its own provision! **Allah** provides for it and for you. And He is the All-Hearer, the **All-Knower**. (Darussalam, 2000)

Chapter Al-Ankabut   Chapter 29 Verse 62
Allah enlarges the provision for whom He wills of His slaves, and straitens it for whom (He wills). Verily, **Allah** is the **All-Knower** of everything. (Darussalam, 2000)

Chapter Ar-Rum   Chapter 30 Verse 54
Allah is He who created you in weakness, then gave you strength after weakness, then after strength gave weakness and grey hair. He creates what He wills. And it is He who is the **All-Knowing**, the All-Powerful. (Darussalam, 2000)

Chapter Luqman   Chapter 31 Verse 23
And whoever disbelievers, let not his disbelief grieve you. To Us is their return, and We shall inform them what they have done. **Allah** is the **All-Knower** of what is in the breasts. (Darussalam, 2000)

Chapter Luqman   Chapter 31 Verse 34
Verily, **Allah**, with Him is knowledge of the hour, He sends down the rain, and knows that which is in the wombs. No person knows what he will earn

tomorrow, and no person knows in what land he will die. Verily, **Allah** is **All-Knower**, All-Aware. (Darussalam, 2000)

Chapter Al-Ahzab   Chapter 33 Verse 1
O Prophet! Keep your duty to **Allah**, and obey not the disbelievers and the hypocrites. Verily, Allah is **Ever Knower,** All-Wise. (Darussalam, 2000)

Chapter Al-Ahzab   Chapter 33 Verse 40
Muhammad is not the father of any of your men, but he is Messenger of **Allah** and the last of the Prophets. And **Allah** is ever **All-Aware** of everything. (Darussalam, 2000)

Chapter Al-Ahzab   Chapter 33 Verse 51
You (O Muhammad) can postpone whom you will of them (your wives), and you may receive whom you will. And whomsoever you desire of those whom you have set aside, it is no sin on you; that is better that they may be comforted and not grieved, and may all be pleased with what you give them. **Allah** knows what is in your hearts. And **Allah** is ever **All-Knowing**, Most Forbearing. (Darussalam, 2000)

Chapter Al-Ahzab   Chapter 33 Verse 54
Whether you reveal anything or conceal it, verily, **Allah** is ever **All-Knower** of everything. (Darussalam, 2000)

Chapter Saba   Chapter 34 Verse 26
Say: "Our **Lord** will assemble us all together, then He will judge between us with truth. And He is the Just Judge, the **All-Knower** of the true state of affairs." (Darussalam, 2000)

Chapter Fatir   Chapter 35 Verse 7-8
7. Those who disbelieve, theirs will be a severe torment; and those who believe and do righteous good deeds, theirs will be forgiveness and a great reward.
8. Is he, then, to whom the evil of his deeds is made fair-seeming, so that he considers it as good? Verily, **Allah** sends astray whom He wills, and guides whom He wills. So, destroy not yourself in sorrow for them. Truly, **Allah** is the **All-Knower** of what they do! (Darussalam, 2000)

Chapter Fatir   Chapter 35 Verse 38
Verily, **Allah** is the **All-Knower** of the unseen of the heavens and the earth. Verily, He is the **All-Knower** of that is in the breasts. (Darussalam, 2000)

Chapter Fatir   Chapter 35 Verse 44

Have they not traveled in the land, and seen what was the end of those before them - thought they were superior to them in power? **Allah** is not such that anything in the heavens or in the earth escapes Him. Verily, He is **All-Knowing**, All-Omnipotent. (Darussalam, 2000)

Chapter Ya-Sin   Chapter 36 Verse 38

And the sun runs on its fixed course for a term. That is the decree of the All-Mighty, the **All-Knowing**. (Darussalam, 2000)

Chapter Ya-Sin   Chapter 36 Verses 78-79

78. And he puts forth for Us a parable, and forgets his own creation. He says: "Who will give life to these bones after they are rotten and have become dust?"
79. Say: "He will give life to them who created them for the first time! And He is the **All-Knower** of every creation!" (Darussalam, 2000)

Chapter Ya-Sin   Chapter 36 Verse 81

Is not He who created the heavens and the earth, Able to create the like of them? Yes. Indeed! He is the **All-Knowing** Supreme Creator. (Darussalam, 2000)

Chapter Az-Zumar   Chapter 39 Verse 7

If you disbelieve, then verily, **Allah** is not in need of you; He likes not disbelief for His slaves. And if you are grateful, He is pleased therewith for you. No bearer of burdens shall bear the burden of another. Then to your **Lord** is your return, so He will inform you what you used to do. Verily, He is the **All-Knower** of that which is in breasts. (Darussalam, 2000)

Chapter Ghafir   Chapter 40 Verse 2

The revelation of the book is from **Allah**, the All-Mighty, the **All-Knower**. (Darussalam, 2000)

Chapter Fussilat   Chapter 41 Verses 11-12

11. Then He rose over (Istawa) towards the heaven when it was smoke, and said to it and to the earth: "Come both of you willingly or unwillingly." They both said: "We come willingly."
12. Then He completed and finished from their creation seven heavens in two Days and He made in each heaven its affair. And we adorned the nearest

heaven with lamps to be an adornment as well as to guard. Such is the Decree of Him the All-Mighty, the **All-Knower**. (Darussalam, 2000)

Chapter Fussilat   Chapter 41 Verse 36
And if an evil whisper from Shaitan (Satan) tries to turn you away, then seek refuge in **Allah**. Verily, He is the All-Hearer, The **All-Knower**. (Darussalam, 2000)

Chapter Ash-Shura   Chapter 42 Verse 12
To Him belong the keys of the heavens and the earth. He enlarges provision for whom He wills, and straitens. Verily, He is the **All-Knower** of everything. (Darussalam, 2000)

Chapter Ash-Shura   Chapter 42 Verse 24
Or say they: "He has invented a lie against **Allah**?" If **Allah** willed, He could have sealed up your heart. And **Allah** wipes out falsehood, and establishes the truth by His word. Verily, **He knows well** what are in the breasts. (Darussalam, 2000)

Chapter Ash-Shura   Chapter 42 Verses 49-50
49. To **Allah** belongs the kingdom of the heavens and the earth. He creates what He wills. He bestows female upon whom He wills, and bestows male upon whom He wills.
50. Or He bestows both males and females, and He renders barren whom He wills. Verily, He is the **All-Knower** and is Able to do all things. (Darussalam, 2000)

Chapter Az-Zukhruf   Chapter 43 Verse 9
And indeed, if you ask them: "Who has created the heavens and the earth? "They will surely say: "The All-Mighty, the **All-Knower** created them." (Darussalam, 2000)

Chapter Az-Zukhruf   Chapter 43 Verse 84
It is He who is the only Ilah (God) in the heaven and the only Ilah (God) on the earth. And He is the All-Wise, the **All-Knower**. (Darussalam, 2000)

Chapter Ad-Dukhan   Chapter 44 Verses 1~6
1. Ha-Mim
2. By the manifest book that makes thing clear.
3. We sent it down on a blessed night. Verily, We are ever warning.
4. Therein is decreed every matter of ordainments.

5. As a command from Us. Verily, We are ever sending.
6. (As) a mercy from your **Lord**. Verily, He is the All-Hearer, the **All-Knower**. (Darussalam, 2000)

Chapter Al-Fath   Chapter 48 Verse 4
He it is who sent down As-Sakinah (peace) into the hearts of the believers, that they may grow more in Faith along with their (present) Faith. And to **Allah** belong the hosts of the heavens and the earth, and **Allah** is ever **All-Knower**, All-Wise. (Darussalam, 2000)

Chapter Al-Fath   Chapter 48 Verse 26
When those who disbelieve had put in their hearts pride and haughtiness- the pride and haughtiness of the time of ignorance, - then **Allah** sent down His Sakinah (peace) upon His Messenger and upon the believers, and made them stick to the piety; and they were well entitled to it and worthy of it. And **Allah** is the **All-Knower** of everything. (Darussalam, 2000)

Chapter Al-Hujurat   Chapter 49 Verse 1
O you who believe! Make not (a decision) in advance before **Allah** and His Messenger, and fear **Allah**. Verily, **Allah** is All-Hearing, **All-Knowing**. (Darussalam, 2000)

Chapter Al-Hujurat   Chapter 49 Verses 7-8
7. And know that among you there is the Messenger of **Allah**. If he were to obey you in much of the matter, you would surely be in trouble. But **Allah** has endeared the Faith to you and has beautified it in your hearts, and has made disbelief, wickedness disobedience hateful to you. Such are they who are the rightly guided.
8. (This is) a Grace from Allah and His Favour. And Allah is **All-Knowing**, All-Wise. (Darussalam, 2000)

Chapter Al-Hujurat   Chapter 49 Verse 13
O mankind! We have created you from a male and a female, and made you into nations and tribes, that you may know one another. Verily, the most honourable of you with **Allah** is that who has At-Taqwa (piety). **Allah** is **All-Knowing**, All-Aware. (Darussalam, 2000)

Chapter Al-Hujurat   Chapter 49 Verse 16
Say: "Will you inform **Allah** of your religion while **Allah** knows all that is in the heavens and all that is in the earth, and **Allah** is **All-Aware** of everything. (Darussalam, 2000)

Chapter Adh-Dhariyat   Chapter 51 Verses 24~30

24. Has the story reached you, of the honoured guests of Ibrahim?
25. When they came in to him, and said, "Salam (peace)!" He answered; "Salam (peace)," and said: "You are a people unknown to me,"
26. Then he turned to his household, so brought out a roasted calf.
27. And placed it before them, (saying): "Will you not eat?"
28. Then he conceived a fear of them. They said: "Fear not." And they gave him glad tidings of a son having knowledge.
29. Then his wife came forward with a loud voice; she smote her face, and said: "A barren old woman!"
30. They said: "Even so says your **Lord**. Verily, He is the All-Wise, the **All-Knower**." (Darussalam, 2000)

Chapter Al-Hadid   Chapter 57 Verse 3

3. He is the First and the Last, the Most High and the Most Near. And He is the All-Knower of everything. (Darussalam, 2000)

Chapter Al-Hadid   Chapter 57 Verse 6

He merges night into day, and merges day into night, and **He has full knowledge** of whatsoever is in the breasts. (Darussalam, 2000)

Chapter Al-Mujadilah   Chapter 58 Verse 7

Have you not seen that **Allah** knows whatsoever is in the heavens and whatsoever is on the earth? There is no Najwa (secret counsel) of three but He is their fourth, - nor of five but He is their sixth, -nor of less than that or more but He is with them wheresoever they may be. And afterwards on the Day of Resurrection He will inform them of what they did. Verily, **Allah** is the **All-Knower** of everything. (Darussalam, 2000)

Chapter Al-Mumtahanah   Chapter 60 Verse 10

O you who believe! When believing women come to you as emigrants, examine them; **Allah** knows best as to their Faith, then if you ascertain that they are true believers, send them not back to the disbelievers. They are not lawful for the disbelievers nor are the disbelievers lawful for them. But give them (disbelievers) that which they have spent to them. And there will be no sin on you to marry them if you have paid their Mahr (bridal money) to them. Likewise hold not the disbelieving women as wives, and ask for that which you have spent and let them ask back for that which they have spent. That is the Judgement of **Allah**, He judges between you. And **Allah** is **All-Knowing**, All-Wise. (Darussalam, 2000)

Chapter Al-Jumu'ah   Chapter 62 Verses 6-7
6. Say: "O you Jews! If you pretend that you are friends of **Allah**, to the exclusion of other mankind, then long for death if you are truthful.
7. But they will never long for it, because of what their hands have sent before them! And **Allah knows well** the Zalimun (wrong-doers). (Darussalam, 2000)

Chapter At-Taghabun   Chapter 64 Verse 4
He knows what is in the heavens and on earth, and He knows what you conceal and what you reveal. And **Allah** is the **All-Knower** of what is in the breasts. (Darussalam, 2000)

Chapter At-Taghabun   Chapter 64 Verse 11
No calamity befalls, but by the leave of **Allah**, and whosoever believes in **Allah**, He guides his heart. And **Allah** is the **All-Knower** of everything. (Darussalam, 2000)

Chapter At-Tahrim   Chapter 66 Verses 2-3
2. Allah has already ordained for you the absolution from your oaths. And **Allah** is your Maula (your Lord, Master, Protector) and He is the **All-Knower**, the All-Wise.
3. And when the Prophet disclosed a matter in confidence to one of his wives, then she told it. And **Allah** made it known to him; He informed part thereof and left a part. Then when he told her thereof, she said: "Who told you this?" He said: "The **All-Knower**, the All-Aware has told me." (Darussalam, 2000)

Chapter Al-Mulk   Chapter 67 Verse 13
And whether you keep your talk secret or disclose it, verily, He is the **All-Knower** of what is in the breasts. (Darussalam, 2000)

Chapter Al-Insan   Chapter 76 Verses 29-30
29. Verily, this is an admonition, so whoever wills, let him take a Path to his **Lord**.
30. But you cannot will unless **Allah** wills. Verily, **Allah** is Ever **All-Knowing**, All-Wise. (Darussalam, 2000)

Chapter Al-A'la   Chapter 87 Verses 6-7
6. We shall make you to recite, so you shall not forget.
7. Except what **Allah** may will. He **knows** what is apparent and what is hidden. (Darussalam, 2000)

Al-Khabir   The All-Aware

Chapter Al-Baqarah   Chapter 2 Verse 234
And those of you who die and leave wives behind them, they shall wait for four months and ten days, then when they have fulfilled their term, there is no sin on you if they dispose of themselves in a just and honourable manner. And **Allah** is **Well-Acquainted** with what you do. (Darussalam, 1999)

Chapter Al-Baqarah   Chapter 2 Verse 271
If you disclose your Sadaqat (alms), it is well; but if you conceal them and give them to the poor, that is better for you. (**Allah**) will expiate you some of your sins. And **Allah** is **Well-Acquainted (well-Aware)** with what you do. (Darussalam, 1999)

Chapter Al-Imran   Chapter 3 Verse 153
(And remember) when you ran away without even casting a side-glance at anyone, and the Messenger was in your rear calling you back. There did **Allah** give you one distress after another by way of requital to teach you not to grieve for that which had escaped you, nor for that which had befallen you. And **Allah** is **Well-Aware** of all that you do. (Darussalam, 1999)

Chapter Al-Imran   Chapter 3 Verse 180
And let not those who covetously withhold of that which **Allah** has bestowed on them of His Bounty think that it is good for them. Nay, it will be worse for them; the things which they covetously withheld, shell be tied to their necks like a collar on the Day of Resurrection. And to **Allah** belongs the heritage of the heavens and the earth; and **Allah** is **Well-Acquainted (Well-Aware)** with all that you do. (Darussalam, 1999)

Chapter An-Nisa   Chapter 4 Verse 35
If you fear a breach between them twain (the man and his wife), appoint arbitrators, one from his family and the other from hers; if they both wish for peace, **Allah** will cause their reconciliation. Indeed, **Allah** is ever All-Knower, **Well-Acquainted (Well-Aware)** with all thing. (Darussalam, 1999)

Chapter An-Nisa   Chapter 4 Verse 94
O you who believe! When you go in the Cause of **Allah**, verify, and say not to anyone who greets you: "You are not a believer"; seeking the perishable

goods of the worldly life. There are much more profits and booties with **Allah**. Even as he is now, so were you yourselves before till **Allah** conferred on you His Favours, therefore, be cautious in discrimination. **Allah** is Ever **Well-Aware** of what you do. (Darussalam, 1999)

Chapter An-Nisa　　　　　　　　　　　　　　　　Chapter 4 Verse 128
And if a woman fears cruelty or desertion on her husband's part, there is no sin on them both if they make terms of peace between themselves; and making peace is better. And human inner-selves are swayed by greed. But if you do good and keep away from evil, verily, **Allah** is **Well-Acquainted** (Well-Aware) with what you do. (Darussalam, 1999)

Chapter An-Nisa　　　　　　　　　　　　　　　　Chapter 4 Verse 135
O you who believe! Stand out firmly for justice, as witnesses to **Allah**, even though it be against yourselves, or your parents, or your kin, be he rich or poor. **Allah** is a Better Protector to both. So, follow not lusts, lest you avoid justice; and if you distort your witness or refuse to give it, verily, **Allah** is Ever **Well-Acquainted** (Well-Aware) with what you do. (Darussalam, 1999)

Chapter Al-Ma'idah　　　　　　　　　　　　　　　Chapter 5 Verse 8
O you who believe! Stand out firmly for **Allah** as just witnesses; and let not the enmity and hatred of others make you avoid justice. Be just: that is nearer to piety; and fear **Allah.** Verily, **Allah** is **Well-Acquainted** (Well-Aware) with what you do. (Darussalam, 1999)

Chapter Al-An'am　　　　　　　　　　　　　　　　Chapter 6 Verse 18
And He is the Irresistible (Supreme), above His slaves, and He is the All-Wise, **Well-Acquainted with all things**. (Darussalam, 1999)

Chapter Al-An'am　　　　　　　　　　　　　　　　Chapter 6 Verse 73
It is He who has created the heavens and the earth in truth, and on the Day, He will say: "Be!" – and it is! His word is the Truth. His will be the dominion on the Day when the Trumpet will be blown. All-Knower of the unseen and the seen. He is the All-Wise, **Well-Aware**. (Darussalam, 1999)

Chapter Al-An'am　　　　　　　　　　　　　　　　Chapter 6 Verse 103
No vision can grasp Him, but He grasps all vision. He is **Al-Latif** (the Most Subtle and Courteous), **Well-Acquainted** with all things. (Darussalam, 1999)

Chapter At-Taubah   Chapter 9 Verse 16
Do you think that you shall be left alone while **Allah** has not yet tested those among you who have striven hard and fought and have not taken Walijah (helpers) besides **Allah** and His Messenger, and the believers. **Allah** is **Well-Acquainted** with what you do. (Darussalam, 1999)

Chapter Hud   Chapter 11 Verse 1
Alif-Lam-Ra, A Book, the Verses whereof are perfected, and then explained in detail from One (**Allah**), Who is All-Wise **Well-Acquainted**. (Darussalam, 2000)

Chapter Hud   Chapter 11 Verses 110-111
110. Indeed, We gave the Book to Musa (Moses), but differences arose therein, and had it not been for a Word that had gone forth before from your **Lord**, the case would have been judged between them, and indeed they are in grave doubt concerning it.
111. And verily, to each of them your **Lord** will repay their works in full. Surely, He is **All-Aware** of what they do. (Darussalam, 2000)

Chapter Al-Isra   Chapter 17 Verse 17
And how many generations have We destroyed after Nuh! And Sufficient is your **Lord** as an **All-Knower** and All-Seer of the sins of His slaves. (Darussalam, 2000)

Chapter Al-Isra   Chapter 17 Verse 30
Truly, your **Lord** enlarges the provision for whom He wills and straitens. Verily, He is Ever **All-Knower**, All-Seer of His slaves. (Darussalam, 2000)

Chapter Al-Isra   Chapter 17 Verse 96
Say: "Sufficient is **Allah** for a witness between me and you. Verily, He is Ever the **All-Knower**, the All-Seer of His slaves." (Darussalam, 2000)

Chapter Al-Hajj   Chapter 22 Verse 63
See you not that **Allah** sends down water from the sky, and then the earth becomes green? Verily, **Allah** is Most Kind and Courteous, **Well-Acquainted** with all things. (Darussalam, 2000)

Chapter Nur   Chapter 24 Verse 30
Tell the believing men to lower their gaze, and protect their private parts. That is purer for them. Verily, **Allah** is **All-Aware** of what they do. (Darussalam, 2000)

Chapter Nur   Chapter 24 Verse 53
They swear by **Allah** their strongest oaths, that if only you would order them, they would leave. Say: "Swear you not; obedience is known. Verily, **Allah knows well what you do.**" (Darussalam, 2000)

Chapter Al-Furqan   Chapter 25 Verses 58-59
58. And put your trust in the Ever living One Who dies not, and glorify His Praises, and Sufficient is He as the **All-Knower** of the sins of His slaves.
59. Who created the heavens and the earth and all that is between them in six Days. Then He rose over (Istawa) the Throne. The Most Gracious! Ask Him, as He is **Al-Khabir (All-Knower).** (Darussalam, 2000)

Chapter An-Naml   Chapter 27 Verse 88
And you will see the mountains and think them solid, but they shall pass away as the passing away of the clouds. The Work of **Allah**, Who perfected all things, verily! He is **Well-Acquainted** with what you do. (Darussalam, 2000)

Chapter Luqman   Chapter 31 Verse 16
"O my son! If it be equal to the weight of a grain of mustard seed, and though it be in a rock, or in the heavens or in the earth, **Allah** will bring it forth. Verily, **Allah** is Subtle, **Well-Aware.** (Darussalam, 2000)

Chapter Luqman   Chapter 31 Verse 29
See you not that **Allah** merges the night into the day and merges the day into the night, and has subjected the sun and the moon, each running its cause for a term appointed; and that **Allah** is **All-Aware** of what you do. (Darussalam, 2000)

Chapter Luqman   Chapter 31 Verse 34
Verily, **Allah**, with Him is the knowledge of the hour, He sends down the rain, and knows that which is in the wombs. No person knows what He will earn tomorrow, and no person knows in what land He will die. Verily, **Allah** is All-Knower, **All-Aware.** (Darussalam, 2000)

Chapter Al-Ahzab   Chapter 33 Verses 1-2
1. O Prophet! Keep your duty to **Allah**, and obey not the disbelievers and the hypocrites. Verily, **Allah** is Ever All-Knower, All-Wise.
2. And follow that which is revealed to you from your **Lord**. Verily, **Allah** is **Well-Acquainted** with what you do. (Darussalam, 2000)

<u>Chapter Al-Ahzab</u>   Chapter 33 Verse 34
And remember, that which is recited in your houses of the Verses of **Allah** and Al-Hikmah. Verily, **Allah** is Ever Most Courteous, **Well-Acquainted** with all things. (Darussalam, 2000)

<u>Chapter Saba</u>   Chapter 34 Verse 1
All the praises and thanks be to **Allah**, to Whom belongs all that is in the heavens and all that is in the earth. His is all the praises and thanks in the Hereafter, and He is the All-Wise, **All-Aware**. (Darussalam, 2000)

<u>Chapter Fatir</u>   Chapter 35 Verse 31
And what We have revealed to you, of the Book, it is the truth confirming that which was before it. Verily, **Allah** is indeed **All-Aware**, and All-Seer of His slaves. (Darussalam, 2000)

<u>Chapter Ash-Shura</u>   Chapter 42 Verse 27
And if **Allah** were to enlarge the provision for His slaves, they would surely rebel in the earth, but He sends down by measure as He wills. Verily, He is, in respect of His slaves, the **Well-Aware**, the All-Seer. (Darussalam, 2000)

<u>Chapter Al-Fath</u>   Chapter 48 Verse 11
Those of the bedouins who lagged behind will say to you: "Our possessions and our families occupied us, so ask forgiveness for us." They say with their tongues what is not in their hearts. Say: "Who then has any power at all on your behalf with **Allah**, if He intends you hurt or intends you benefit? Nay, but **Allah** is Ever **All-Aware** of what you do. (Darussalam, 2000)

<u>Chapter Al-Hujurat</u>   Chapter 49 Verse 13
O mankind! We have created you from a male and a female, and made you into nations and tribes, that you may know one another. Verily, the most honourable of you with **Allah** is that who has At-Taqwa (piety). **Allah** is All-Knowing, **All-Aware**. (Darussalam, 2000)

<u>Chapter Al-Hadid</u>   Chapter 57 Verse 10
And what is the matter with you that you spend not in the Cause of **Allah**? And to **Allah** belongs the heritage of the heavens and the earth. Not equal among you are those who spent and fought before the conquering. Such are higher in degree than those who spent and fought afterwards. But to all, **Allah** has promised the best. And **Allah** is **All-Aware** of what you do. (Darussalam, 2000)

Chapter Al-Mujadilah   Chapter 58 Verse 3

And those who make unlawful to them (their wives) by Az-Zihar and wish to free themselves from what they uttered, in that case (is) the freeing of a slave before they touch each other. That is an admonition to you. And **Allah** is **All-Aware** of what you do. (Darussalam, 2000)

Chapter Al-Mujadilah   Chapter 58 Verse 11

O you who believe! When you are told to make room in the assemblies, make room. **Allah** will give you room. And when you are told to rise up, rise up. **Allah** will exalt in degree those of you who believe, and those who have been granted knowledge. And **Allah** is **Well-Acquainted** with what you do. (Darussalam, 2000)

Chapter Al-Mujadilah   Chapter 58 Verse 13

Are you afraid of spending in charity before your private consultation? If then you do it not, and **Allah** has forgiven you, then perform As-Salat (prayer) and give Zakat (charity-alms) and obey **Allah**. And **Allah** is **All-Aware** of what you do. (Darussalam, 2000)

Chapter Al-Hashr   Chapter 59 Verse 18

O you who believe! Fear **Allah** and keep your duty to Him. And let every person look to what he has sent forth for tomorrow, and fear **Allah**. Verily, **Allah** is **All-Aware** of what you do. (Darussalam, 2000)

Chapter Al-Munafiqun   Chapter 63 Verse 11

And **Allah** grants respite to none when his appointed time (death) comes. And **Allah** is **All-Aware** of what you do. (Darussalam, 2000)

Chapter At-Taghabun   Chapter 64 Verses 7-8

7. The disbelievers pretend that they will never be resurrected. Say: "Yes! By my **Lord**, you will certainly be resurrected, then you will be informed of what you did, and that is easy for **Allah**.
8. Therefore, believe in **Allah** and His Messenger, and in the Light which We have sent down. And **Allah** is **All-Aware** of what you do. (Darussalam, 2000)

Chapter At-Tahrim   Chapter 66 Verse 3

3. And when the Prophet disclosed a matter in confidence to one of his wives (Hafsah), then she told it (to another i.e., 'Aishah). And **Allah** made it known to him; he informed part thereof and left a part. Then when he told her (Hafsah) thereof, she said: "Who told you this?" He said: "The All-Knower, the **All-Aware** (**Allah**) has told me." (Darussalam, 2000)

Chapter Al-Mulk   Chapter 67 Verse 14
Should not He Who has created know? And He is the Most Kind and Courteous, **All-Aware**. (Darussalam, 2000)

Chapter Al-Adiyat   Chapter 100 Verses 6~11
6. Verily! Man is ungrateful to his **Lord**;
7. And to that fact he bears witness;
8. And verily, he is violent in the love of wealth.
9. Knows he not that when the contents of the graves are poured forth.
10. And that which is in the breasts shall be made known?
11. Verily, that Day their **Lord** will be **Well-Acquainted** with them. (Darussalam, 2000)

Al-Hakim   The Most Wise

Chapter Al-Baqarah   Chapter 2 Verses 31-32
31. And He taught Adam all the names, then He showed them to the angels and said, "Tell Me the names of these if you are truthful."
32. They said: Glory is to You; we have no knowledge except what You have taught us. Verily, it is You, the All-Knower, the **All-Wise**." (Darussalam, 1999)

Chapter Al-Baqarah   Chapter 2 Verses 208-209
208. O you who believe! Enter perfectly in Islam and follow not the footsteps of Shaitan (Satan). Verily, he is to you a plain enemy.
209. Then if you slide back after the clear signs have come to you, then know that **Allah** is All-Mighty, **All-Wise**. (Darussalam, 1999)

Chapter Al-Baqarah   Chapter 2 Verses 219-220
219. They ask you concerning alcoholic drink and gambling. Say: "In them is a great sin, and (some) benefit for men, but the sin of them is greater than their benefit." And they ask you what they ought to spend. Say: "That which is beyond your needs." Thus, **Allah** makes clear to you His Laws in order that you may give thought.
220. In (to) this worldly life and in the hereafter. And they ask you concerning orphans. Say: "The best thing is to work honestly in their property, and if you mix your affairs with theirs, then they are your brothers. And **Allah** knows him who means mischief from him who means good. And if **Allah** had

wished, He could have put you into difficulties. Truly, **Allah** is All-Mighty, **All-Wise**." (Darussalam, 1999)

Chapter Al-Baqarah   Chapter 2 Verse 228
And divorced women shall wait for three menstrual periods, and it is not lawful for them to conceal what **Allah** has created in their wombs, if they believe in **Allah** and the Last Day. And their husbands have the better right to take them back in that period, if they wish for reconciliation. And they have rights similar over them to what is reasonable, but men have a degree over them. And **Allah** is All-Mighty, **All-Wise**. (Darussalam, 1999)

Chapter Al-Baqarah   Chapter 2 Verse 240
And those of you who die and leave behind wives should bequeath for their wives a year's maintenance and residence without turning them out, but if they leave, there is no sin on you for that which they do of themselves, provided it is honourable. And **Allah** is All-Mighty, **All-Wise**. (Darussalam, 1999)

Chapter Al-Baqarah   Chapter 2 Verse 260
And when Ibrahim said, "My **Lord**! Show me how You give life to the dead." He said: "Do you not believe?" He said: "Yes, but to be stronger in Faith." He said: "Take four birds, then cause them to incline towards you, and then put a portion of them on every hill, and call them, they will come to you in haste. And know that **Allah** is All-Mighty, **All-Wise**." (Darussalam, 1999)

Chapter Al-Imran   Chapter 3 Verse 6
He it is Who shapes you in the wombs as He wills, La ilaha illa Huwa (none has the right to be worshipped but He), the All-Mighty, the **All-Wise**. (Darussalam, 1999)

Chapter Al-Imran   Chapter 3 Verse 18
Allah bears witness that La ilaha illa Huwa (none has the right to be worshipped but He), and the angels, and those having knowledge; (He always) maintains His creation in justice, La ilaha illa Huwa (none has the right to be worshipped but He), the All-Mighty, the **All-Wise**. (Darussalam, 1999)

Chapter Al-Imran   Chapter 3 Verse 62
Verily! This is the true narrative, and La ilaha illallah (none has the right to be worshipped but **Allah**). And indeed, **Allah** is the All-Mighty, the **All-Wise**. (Darussalam, 1999)

Chapter Al-Imran Chapter 3 Verses 125-126

125. "Yes, if you hold on to patience and piety, and the enemy comes rushing at you; your **Lord** will help you with five thousand angels having marks."
126. **Allah** made it not but as a message of good news for you and as an assurance to your hearts. And there is no victory except from **Allah**, the All-Mighty, the **All-Wise**. (Darussalam, 1999)

Chapter An-Nisa Chapter 4 Verse 11

Allah commands you as regard your children's: to the male, a portion equal to that of two females; if only daughters, two or more, their share is two-thirds of the inheritance; if only one, her share is a half. For parents, a sixth share of inheritance to each if the deceased left children; if no children, and the parents are the heirs, the mother has a third; if the deceased left brothers or (sisters), the mother has a sixth. After the payment of legacies, he may have bequeathed or debts. You know not which of them, whether your parents or your children, are nearest to you in benefit; (these fixed shares) are ordained by **Allah**. And **Allah** is ever All-Knower, **All-Wise**. (Darussalam, 1999)

Chapter An-Nisa Chapter 4 Verse 17

Allah accepts only the repentance of those who do evil in ignorance and foolishness and repent soon afterwards; it is they whom **Allah** will forgive and **Allah** is ever All-Knower, **All-Wise**. (Darussalam, 1999)

Chapter An-Nisa Chapter 4 Verses 23-24

23. Forbidden to you are: your mothers, your daughters, your sisters, your father's sisters, your mother's sisters, your brother's daughters, your sister's daughters, your foster mothers who gave you suck, your foster milk suckling sisters, your wives' mothers, your stepdaughters under your guardianship, born of your wives to whom you have gone in – but there is no sin on you if you have not gone in them, - the wives of your sons who from your own loins, and two sisters in wedlock at the same time, except for what has already passed; verily, **Allah** is Oft-Forgiving, Most Merciful.
24. Also women already married, except those whom your right hands possess. Thus has **Allah** ordained for you. All others are lawful, provided you seek with Mahr (bridal money) from your property, desiring chastity, not committing illegal sexual intercourse, so with those of whom you have enjoyed sexual relations, give their Mahr (bridal money) as prescribed, but if after a Mahr (bridal money) is prescribed, you agree mutually (to give more),

there is no sin on you. Surely, **Allah** is Ever All-Knowing, **All-Wise**. (Darussalam, 1999)

Chapter An-Nisa   Chapter 4 Verse 26
Allah wishes to make clear to you, and to show you the ways of those before you, and accept your repentance, and **Allah** is All-Knower, **All-Wise**. (Darussalam, 1999)

Chapter An-Nisa   Chapter 4 Verse 56
Surely, those who disbelieved in Our Ayat (Verses), We shall burn them in Fire. As often as their skins are roasted through, We shall change them for other skins that they may taste the punishment. Truly, **Allah** is Ever Most Powerful, **All-Wise**. (Darussalam, 1999)

Chapter An-Nisa   Chapter 4 Verse 92
It is not for a believer to kill a believer except by mistake; and whosoever kills a believer by mistake, he must set free a believing slave and a compensation be given to the deceased's family unless they remit it. If the deceased belonged to a people at war with you and he was a believer, the freeing of a believing slave; and if he belonged to a people with whom you have a treaty of mutual alliance, compensation must be paid to his family, and a believing slave must be freed. And whoso finds this beyond his means; he must fast for two consecutive months in order to seek repentance from **Allah**. And **Allah** is Ever All-Knowing, **All-Wise**. (Darussalam, 1999)

Chapter An-Nisa   Chapter 4 Verse 104
And don't be weak in the pursuit of the enemy; if you are suffering then surely, they are suffering as you are suffering, but you have a hope from **Allah** that for which they hope not; and **Allah** is Ever All-Knowing, **All-Wise**. (Darussalam, 1999)

Chapter An-Nisa   Chapter 4 Verses 110-111
110. And whoever does evil or wrongs himself but afterwards seeks **Allah**'s Forgiveness, he will find **Allah** Oft-Forgiving, Most Merciful.
111. And whoever earns sin, he earns it only against himself. And **Allah** is Ever All-Knowing, **All-Wise**. (Darussalam, 1999)

Chapter An-Nisa   Chapter 4 Verses 129-130
129. You will never be able to do perfect justice between wives even if it is your ardent desire, so do not incline too much to one of them so as to leave the other hanging. And if you do justice, and do all that is right and fear **Allah**

by keeping away from all that is wrong, then **Allah** is Ever Oft-Forgiving, Most Merciful.

130. But if they separate, **Allah** will provide abundance for every one of them from His Bounty. And **Allah** is Ever All-Sufficient for His creatures' need, **All-Wise**. (Darussalam, 1999)

Chapter An-Nisa   Chapter 4 Verses 157-158

157. And because of their saying, "We killed Messiah Isa, son of Maryam, the Messenger of **Allah**", but they killed him not, nor crucified him, but it appeared so to them, and those who differ therein are full of doubts. They have no knowledge; they follow nothing but conjecture. For surely; they killed him not;

158. But **Allah** raised him up unto Himself. And **Allah** is Ever All-Powerful (All-Mighty), **All-Wise**. (Darussalam, 1999)

Chapter An-Nisa   Chapter 4 Verses 164-165

164. And Messengers We have mentioned to you before, and Messengers We have not mentioned to you, - and to Musa **Allah** spoke directly.

165. Messengers as bearers of good news as well as of warning in order that mankind should have no plea against **Allah** after the Messengers. And **Allah** is Ever All-Powerful, **All-Wise**. (Darussalam, 1999)

Chapter An-Nisa   Chapter 4 Verse 170

O mankind! Verily, there has come to you the Messenger with the truth from your **Lord**. So, believe in him, it is better for you. But if you disbelieve, then certainly to **Allah** belongs all that is in the heavens and the earth. And **Allah** is ever All-Knower, **All-Wise**. (Darussalam, 1999)

Chapter Al-Ma'idah   Chapter 5 Verse 38

And the male thief and the female thief, cut off their hands as a recompense for that which they committed, a punishment by way of example from **Allah**, And **Allah** is All-Powerful, **All-Wise**. (Darussalam, 1999)

Chapter Al-Ma'idah   Chapter 5 Verses 116-118

116. And when **Allah** will say: "O 'Isa, son of Maryam! Did you say unto men: 'Worship me and my mother as two gods besides **Allah**?'" He will say: "Glory be to You! It was not for me to say what I had no right. Had I said such a thing, You would surely have known it. You know what is in my inner-self though I do not know what is in Yours, truly, You, only You, are the All-Knower of all that is hidden.

117. "Never did I say to them aught except what You did command me to say: 'Worship **Allah**, my **Lord** and your **Lord**.' And I was a witness over them while I dwelt amongst them, but when You took me up, You were the Watcher over them, and You are a Witness to all things.
118. "If You punish them, they are Your slaves, and if You forgive them, verily You, only You are the All-Mighty, the **All-Wise**." (Darussalam, 1999)

Chapter Al-An'am   Chapter 6 Verses 17-18
17. And if Allah touches you with harm, none can remove it but He, and if He touches you with good, then He is Able to do all things.
18. And He is the Irresistible (Supreme), above His slaves, and He is the **All-Wise**, Well-Acquainted with all things. (Darussalam, 1999)

Chapter Al-An'am   Chapter 6 Verse 73
It is He who has created the heavens and the earth in truth, and on the Day, He will say: "Be!" – and it is! His word is the truth. His will be the dominion on the Day when the Trumpet will be blown. All-Knower of the unseen and the seen. He is the **All-Wise**, Well-Aware. (Darussalam, 1999)

Chapter Al-An'am   Chapter 6 Verses 82-83
82. It is those who believe and confuse not their Belief with Zulm (wrong-doing), for them there is security and they are the guided.
83. And that was our Proof which We gave Ibrahim against his people. We raise whom We will in degrees. Certainly, your **Lord** is **All-Wise**, All-Knowing. (Darussalam, 1999)

Chapter Al-An'am   Chapter 6 Verse 128
And on the Day when He will gather them together: "O you assembly of jinn! Many did you mislead of men," and their Auliya (friends and helpers, etc.) amongst men will say: "Our **Lord**! We benefited one from the other, but now we have reached our appointed term which You did appoint for us." He will say: "The fire be your dwelling place, you will dwell therein forever, except as **Allah** may will. Certainly, your **Lord** is **All-Wise**, All-Knowing." (Darussalam, 1999)

Chapter Al-An'am   Chapter 6 Verse 139
And they say: "What is in the bellies of such and such cattle is for our males alone, and forbidden to our females, but if it is born dead, then all have shares therein." He will punish them for their attribution. Verily, He is **All-Wise**, All-Knower. (Darussalam, 1999)

Chapter Al-Anfal   Chapter 8 Verses 9-10
9. When you sought help of your **Lord** and He answered you: "I will help you with a thousand of the angels each behind the other in succession."
10. **Allah** made it only as glad tidings, and that your hearts be at rest therewith. And there is no victory except from **Allah.** Verily, **Allah** is All-Mighty, **All-Wise**. (Darussalam, 1999)

Chapter Al-Anfal   Chapter 8 Verse 49
When the hypocrites and those in whose hearts was a disease said: "These people are deceived by their religion." But whoever puts his trust in **Allah**, then surely, **Allah** is All-Mighty, **All-Wise**. (Darussalam, 1999)

Chapter Al-Anfal   Chapter 8 Verse 63
And He has united their hearts. If you had spent all that is in the earth, you could not have united their hearts, but **Allah** has united them. Certainly, He is All-Mighty, **All-Wise**. (Darussalam, 1999)

Chapter Al-Anfal   Chapter 8 Verse 67
It is not for a Prophet that he should have prisoners of war until he had made a great slaughter in the land. You desire the good of this world, but **Allah** desires the Hereafter. And **Allah** is All-Mighty, **All-Wise**. (Darussalam, 1999)

Chapter Al-Anfal   Chapter 8 Verses 70-71
70. O Prophet! Say to the captives that are in your hands: "If **Allah** knows any good in your hearts, He will give you something better than what has been taken from you, and He will forgive you, and **Allah** is Oft-Forgiving, Most Merciful."
71. But if they intend to betray you, they indeed betrayed **Allah** before. So He gave power over them. And **Allah** is All-Knower, **All-Wise**. (Darussalam, 1999)

Chapter At-Taubah   Chapter 9 Verses 14-15
14. Fight against them so that **Allah** will punish them by your hands and disgrace them and give you victory over them and heal the breasts of a believing people.
15. And remove the anger of their hearts. **Allah** accepts the repentance of whom He wills. **Allah** is All-Knowing, **All-Wise**. (Darussalam, 1999)

Chapter At-Taubah   Chapter 9 Verse 28
O you who believe! Verily, the Mushrikun (polytheists) are Najasun (impure), so let them not come near Al-Masjid Al-Haram (at Makkah) after this year; and if you fear poverty, **Allah** will enrich you if He wills, out of His Bounty. Surely, **Allah** is All-Knowing, **All-Wise**. (Darussalam, 1999)

Chapter At-Taubah   Chapter 9 Verse 40
If you help him not, for **Allah** did indeed help him when the disbelievers drove him out, the second of the two; when they were in the cave, he said to his companion: "Be not sad, surely, **Allah** is with us." Then **Allah** sent down his Sakinah (peace) upon him, and strengthened him with forces which you saw not, and made the word of those who disbelieved the lowermost, while the Word of **Allah** that become the uppermost; and **Allah** is All-Mighty, **All-Wise**. (Darussalam, 1999)

Chapter At-Taubah   Chapter 9 Verse 60
As-Sadaqat (alms) are only for the Fuqara (poor), and Al-Masakin (the poor) and those employed to collect; and to attract the hearts of those who have been inclined; and to free the captives; and for those in debt; and for **Allah**'s Cause, and for the wayfarer; a duty imposed by **Allah**. And **Allah** is All-Knower, **All-Wise**. (Darussalam, 1999)

Chapter At-Taubah   Chapter 9 Verse 71
The believers, men and women, are Auliya (friends and helpers, etc.) of one another; they enjoin Al-Maruf (good), and forbid from Al-Munkar (evil); they perform As-Salat (prayer), and give the Zakat (charity-alms) and obey **Allah** and His Messenger, **Allah** will have His Mercy on them. Surely, **Allah** is All-Mighty, **All-Wise**. (Darussalam, 1999)

Chapter At-Taubah   Chapter 9 Verse 97
The bedouins are the worst in disbelief and hypocrisy, and more likely to be in ignorance of the limits which **Allah** has revealed to His Messenger. And **Allah** is All-Knower, **All-Wise**. (Darussalam, 2000)

Chapter At-Taubah   Chapter 9 Verses 105-106
105. And say: "Do deeds! **Allah** will see your deeds, and His Messenger and the believers. And you will be brought back to the All-Knower of the unseen and the seen. Then He will inform you of what you used to do."
106. And others are made to await for **Allah**'s Decree, whether He will punish them or will forgive them. And **Allah** is All-Knowing, **All-Wise**. (Darussalam, 2000)

Chapter At-Taubah   Chapter 9 Verses 109-110

109. Is it then he who laid the foundation of his building on piety to **Allah** and His Good Pleasure better, or he who laid the foundation of his building on the brink of an undetermined precipice ready to crumble down, so that it crumbled to pieces with him into the fire of Hell. And **Allah** guides not the people who are the Zalimun (wrong-doers).
110. The building which they built will never cease to be a cause of hypocrisy and doubt in their hearts unless their hearts are cut to pieces. And **Allah** is All-Knowing, **All-Wise**. (Darussalam, 2000)

Chapter Hud   Chapter 11 Verse 1
Alif-Lam-Ra, A Book, the verses whereof are perfected, and then explained in detail from One, Who is **All-Wise**, Well-Acquainted. (Darussalam, 2000)

Chapter Yusuf   Chapter 12 Verses 5-6
5. He said: "O my son! Relate not your vision to your brothers, lest they should arrange a plot against you. Verily, Shaitan (Satan) is to man an open enemy!
6. "Thus will your **Lord** choose you and teach you the interpretations of dreams and perfect His Favour on you and on the offspring of Yaqub, as He perfected it on your fathers, Ibrahim and Ishaq aforetime! Verily, your **Lord** is All-Knowing, **All-Wise**." (Darussalam, 2000)

Chapter Yusuf   Chapter 12 Verses 81~83
81. "Return to your father and say, 'O our father! Verily, your son has stolen, and we testify not except according to what we know, and we could not know the Unseen!
82. "And ask the town where we have been, and the caravan in which we returned, and indeed we are telling the truth."
83. He said: "Nay, but your own selves have beguiled you into something. So patience is most fitting. May be **Allah** will bring them all to me. Truly, He! Only He is **All-Knowing**, All-Wise." (Darussalam, 2000)

Chapter Yusuf   Chapter 12 Verses 99-100
99. Then, when they came in before Yusuf, he took his parents to himself and said: "Enter Egypt, if **Allah** wills, in security.
100. And he (Yusuf) raised his parents to the throne and they fell down before him prostrate. And he said: "O my father! This is the interpretation of my dream aforetime! My **Lord** has made it come true! He was indeed good to me, when He took me out of the prison, and brought you out of the Bedouin

– life, after Shaitan (Satan) had sown enmity between me and my brothers. Certainly, my **Lord** is the Most Courteous and Kind unto whom He wills. Truly, He! Only He is the All-Knowing, the **All-Wise**. (Darussalam, 2000)

Chapter Ibrahim   Chapter 14 Verse 4
And We sent not a Messenger except with the language of his people, in order that he might make clear for them. Then **Allah** misleads whom He wills and guides whom He wills. And He is the All-Mighty, the **All-Wise**. (Darussalam, 2000)

Chapter Al-Hijr   Chapter 15 Verses 24-25
24. And indeed, We know the first generations of you who had passed away, and indeed, We know the present generations of you, and also those who will come afterwards.
25. And verily, your **Lord** will gather them together. Truly, He is **All-Wise**, All-Knowing. (Darussalam, 2000)

Chapter An-Nahl   Chapter 16 Verse 60
For those who believe not in the **H**ereafter is an evil description, and for **Allah** is the highest description. And He is the All-Mighty, The **All-Wise**. (Darussalam, 2000)

Chapter Al-Hajj   Chapter 22 Verse 52
Never did We send a Messenger or a Prophet before you but when he did recite the Revelation or narrated or spoke, Shaitan (Satan) threw in it. But **Allah** abolishes that which Shaitan (Satan) throws in. Then **Allah** establishes His Revelations. And **Allah** is All-Knower, **All-Wise**. (Darussalam, 2000)

Chapter An-Nur   Chapter 24 Verses 6~10
6. And for those who accuse their wives, but have no witnesses except themselves, let the testimony of one of them be four testimonies by **Allah** that he is one of those who speak the truth.
7. And the fifth the invoking of the Curse of **Allah** on him if he be of those who tell a lie.
8. But it shall avert the punishment from her, if she bears witness four times by **Allah**, that he is telling a lie.
9. And the fifth should be that the Wrath of **Allah** be upon her if he speaks the truth.
10. And had it not been for the Grace of **Allah** and His Mercy on you! And that **Allah** is the One Who forgives and accepts repentance, the **All-Wise**. (Darussalam, 2000)

Chapter An-Nur   Chapter 24 Verse 18
18. And Allah makes the Ayat (verses) plain to you, and Allah is All-Knowing, All-Wise. (Darussalam, 2000)

Chapter An-Nur   Chapter 24 Verses 58-59
58. O you who believe! Let your legal slaves and slave-girls, and those among you who have not come to the age of puberty ask your permission on three occasions; before Fajr (morning) Salat (prayer), and while you put off your clothes for the noonday, and after the 'Isha' (night) Salat (prayer). (These) three times are of privacy for you, other than these times there is no sin on you or on them to move about, attending to each other. Thus **Allah** makes clear the Ayat (Verses) to you. And **Allah** is All-Knowing, **All-Wise.**
59. And when the children among you come to puberty, then let them ask for permission, as those senior to them. Thus **Allah** makes clear His Ayat (Verses) for you. And **Allah** is All-Knowing, **All-Wise**. (Darussalam, 2000)

Chapter An-Naml   Chapter 27 Verse 6
And verily, you are being taught the Quran from One, **All-Wise**, All-Knowing. (Darussalam, 2000)

Chapter An-Naml   Chapter 27 Verse 9
O Musa! Verily, it is I, **Allah**, the All Mighty, the **All-Wise**. (Darussalam, 2000)

Chapter Al-Ankabut   Chapter 29 Verse 26
So Lut believed in him. He said: "I will emigrate for the sake of my **Lord**. Verily, He is the All-Mighty, the **All-Wise**." (Darussalam, 2000)

Chapter Al-Ankabut   Chapter 29 Verses 41~43
41. The likeness of those who take Auliya (friends and helpers, etc.) other than **Allah** is the likeness of a spider who builds a house; but verily, the frailest of house is the spider's house if they but knew.
42. Verily, **Allah** knows what things they invoke instead of Him. He is the All-Mighty, the **All-Wise**.
43. And these similitudes We put forward for mankind; but none will understand them except those who have knowledge. (Darussalam, 2000)

Chapter Ar-Rum   Chapter 30 Verses 26-27
26. To Him belongs whatever is in the heavens and the earth. All are obedient to Him.

27. And He it is Who originates the creation, then He will repeat it; and this is easier for Him. His is the highest deception in the heavens and in the earth. And He is the All-Mighty, the **All-Wise**. (Darussalam, 2000)

Chapter Luqman Chapter 31 Verses 8-9
8. Verily, those who believe and do righteous good deeds, for them are Gardens of Delight.
9. To bide therein, it is a Promise of **Allah** in truth. And He is the All-Mighty, the **All-Wise**. (Darussalam, 2000)

Chapter Luqman Chapter 31 Verse 27
27. And if all the trees on the earth were pens and the sea, with seven seas behind it to add to its (supply), yet the Words of **Allah** would not be exhausted. Verily, **Allah** is All-Mighty, **All-Wise**. (Darussalam, 2000)

Chapter Al-Ahzab Chapter 33 Verse 1
O Prophet! Keep your duty to **Allah**, and obey not the disbelievers and the hypocrites. Verily, **Allah** is Ever All-Knower, **All-Wise**. (Darussalam, 2000)

Chapter Saba Chapter 34 Verse 1
All the praises and thanks be to **Allah**, to Whom belongs all that is in the heavens and all that is in the earth. His is all the praises and thanks in the Hereafter, and He is the **All-Wise**, the All-Aware. (Darussalam, 2000)

Chapter Saba Chapter 34 Verse 27
Say: "Show me those whom you have joined with Him as partners. Nay! But He is **Allah**, the All-Mighty, the **All-Wise**. (Darussalam, 2000)

Chapter Fatir Chapter 35 Verse 2
Whatever of mercy, **Allah** may grant to mankind, none can withhold it; and whatever He may withhold, none can grant it thereafter. And He is the All-Mighty, the **All-Wise**. (Darussalam, 2000)

Chapter Az-Zumar Chapter 39 Verse 1
The revelation of this book is from **Allah**, the All-Mighty, the **All-Wise**. (Darussalam, 2000)

Chapter Ghafir Chapter 40 Verses 7~9
7. Those who bear the Throne and those around it glorify the praises of their **Lord**, and believe in Him, and ask forgiveness for those who believe: "Our **Lord**! You comprehend all things in mercy and knowledge, so forgive those

who repent and follow Your way, and save them from the torment of the blazing fire!

8. Our **Lord**! And make them enter the 'Adn Paradise which you have promised them – and to the righteous among their fathers, their wives, and their offspring! Verily, You are the All-Mighty, the **All-Wise**.

9. "And save them from the sins, and whomsoever You save from the sins that Day, him verily, You have taken into mercy." And that is the Supreme Success. (Darussalam, 2000)

Chapter Fussilat   Chapter 41 Verses 41-42
41. Verily, those who disbelieved in the Reminder when it came to them. And verily, it is an honourable well-fortified respected book.
42. Falsehood cannot come to it from before it or behind it, sent down by the **All-Wise**, Worthy of all praise. (Darussalam, 2000)

Chapter Ash-Shura   Chapter 42 Verses 1~3
1. Ha-Mim
2. Ain-Sin-Qaf
3. Likewise **Allah**, the All-Mighty, the **All-Wise** sends Revelation to you as those before you. (Darussalam, 2000)

Chapter Ash-Shura   Chapter 42 Verse 51
It is not given to any human being that **Allah** should speak to him unless by Revelation, or from behind a veil, or He sends a Messenger to reveal what He wills by His leave. Verily, He is Most High, **Most Wise**. (Darussalam, 2000)

Chapter Az-Zukhruf   Chapter 43 Verse 84
It is He who is the only Ilah (God) in the heaven and the only Ilah (God) on the earth. And He is the **All-Wise**, the All-Knower. (Darussalam, 2000)

Chapter Al-Jathiyah   Chapter 45 Verses 1-2
1. Ha-Mim
2. The revelation of the Book is from **Allah**, the All-Mighty, the **All-Wise**. (Darussalam, 2000)

Chapter Al-Jathiyah   Chapter 45 Verses 36-37
36. So all praises and thanks be to **Allah**, the **Lord** of the heavens and the **Lord** of the earth, and the **Lord** of the 'Alamin (worlds).
37. And His is the Majesty in the heavens and the earth, He is the All-Mighty, the **All-Wise**. (Darussalam, 2000)

Chapter Al-Ahqaf   Chapter 46 Verses 1-2
1. Ha-Mim
2. The revelations of the book is from **Allah**, the All-Mighty, the **All-Wise**. (Darussalam, 2000)

Chapter Al-Fath   Chapter 48 Verse 4
He it is Who sent down As-Sakinah (peace) into the hearts of the believers, that they may grow more in Faith along with their (present) Faith. And to **Allah** belong the hosts of the heavens and the earth, and **Allah** is Ever All-Knower, **All-Wise**. (Darussalam, 2000)

Chapter Al-Fath   Chapter 48 Verse 7
And to **Allah** belong the hosts of the heavens and the earth. And **Allah** is Ever All-Mighty, the **All-Wise**. (Darussalam, 2000)

Chapter Al-Fath   Chapter 48 Verses 18-19
18. Indeed, **Allah** was pleased with the believers when they gave the Bai'ah (pledge) to you under the tree, He knew what was in their hearts, and He sent down As-Sakinah (peace) upon them, and He rewarded them with a near victory.
19. And abundant spoils that they will capture. And **Allah** is Ever All-Mighty, the **All-Wise**. (Darussalam, 2000)

Chapter Al-Hujurat   Chapter 49 Verses 7-8
7. And know that among you there is the Messenger of **Allah**. If he were to obey you in much of the matter, you would surely be in trouble. But **Allah** has endeared the Faith to you and has beautiful it in your hearts, and has made disbelief, wickedness and disobedience hateful to you. Such are they who are the rightly guided.
8. (This is) a Grace from **Allah** and His favour. And **Allah** is All-Knowing, **All-Wise**. (Darussalam, 2000)

Chapter Adh-Dhariyat   Chapter 51 Verses 24~30
24. Has the story reached you, of the honoured guests of Ibrahim?
25. When they came in to him, and said, "Salam (peace)!" He answered; "Salam (peace)," and said: "You are a people unknown to me,"
26. Then he turned to his household and brought out a roasted calf.
27. And placed it before them, (saying): "Will you not eat?"
28. Then he conceived a fear of them. They said: "Fear not." And they gave him glad tidings of a son, having knowledge.

29. Then his wife came forward with a loud voice; she smote her face, and said: "A barren old woman!"
30. They said: "Even so says your **Lord**. Verily, He is the **All-Wise**, the All-Knower." (Darussalam, 2000)

Chapter Al-Hadid   Chapter 57 Verse 1
Whatsoever is in the heavens and the earth glorifies **Allah** and He is the All-Mighty, **All-Wise**. (Darussalam, 2000)

Chapter Al-Hashr   Chapter 59 Verse 1
Whatsoever is in the heavens and whatsoever is on the earth glorifies **Allah**. And He is the All-Mighty, **All-Wise**. (Darussalam, 2000)

Chapter Al-Hashr   Chapter 59 Verse 24
He is **Allah**, the Creator, the Inventor of all things, the Bestower of forms. To Him belong the Best Names. All that is in the heavens and the earth glorify Him. And He is the All-Mighty, the **All-Wise**. (Darussalam, 2000)

Chapter Al-Mumtahanah   Chapter 60 Verse 5
"O **Lord**! Make us not a trail for the disbelievers, and forgive us, Our **Lord**! Verily, You, only You, are the All-Mighty, the **All-Wise**." (Darussalam, 2000)

Chapter Al-Mumtahanah   Chapter 60 Verse 10
O you who believe! When believing women come to you as emigrants, examine them, **Allah** knows best as to their Faith, then if you ascertain that they are true believers, send them not back to the disbelievers. They are not lawful for the disbelievers nor are the disbelievers lawful for them. But give them (disbelievers) that which they have spent to them. And there will be no sin on you to marry them if you have paid their Mahr (bridal money) to them. Likewise hold not the disbelieving women as wives, and ask for that which you have spent and let them ask back for that which they have spent. That is the Judgement of **Allah**. He judges between you. And **Allah** is All-Knowing, **All-Wise**. (Darussalam, 2000)

Chapter As-Saff   Chapter 61 Verse 1
Whatsoever is in the heavens and whatsoever is on the earth glorifies **Allah**. And He is the All-Mighty, **All-Wise**. (Darussalam, 2000)

Chapter Al-Jumu`ah Chapter 62 Verses 1~3
1. Whatsoever is in the heavens and whatsoever is on the earth glorifies **Allah**, the King, the Holy, the All-Mighty, the **All-Wise**.
2. He it is Who sent among the unlettered ones a Messenger from among themselves, reciting to them His verses, purifying them, and teaching them the Book and Al-Hikmah (wisdom). And verily, they had been before in manifest error;
3. And others among them who have not yet joined them. And He is the All-Mighty, the **All-Wise**. (Darussalam, 2000)

Chapter At-Taghabun Chapter 64 Verses 17-18
17. If you lend to **Allah** a goodly loan, He will double it for you, and will forgive you. And **Allah** is Most Ready to appreciate and to reward, Most Forbearing.
18. All-Knower of the unseen and seen, the All-Mighty, the **All-Wise**. (Darussalam, 2000)

Chapter At-Tahrim Chapter 66 Verses 1-2
1. O Prophet! Why do you forbid that which **Allah** has allowed to you, seeking to please your wives? And **Allah** is Oft-Forgiving, Most Merciful.
2. **Allah** has already ordained for you the absolution from your oaths. And **Allah** is your Maula (Protector) and He is the All-Knower, the **All-Wise**. (Darussalam, 2000)

Chapter Al-Insan Chapter 76 Verses 29-30
29. Verily! This is an admonition, so whosoever wills, let him take a Path to his **Lord**.
30. But you cannot will, unless **Allah** wills. Verily, **Allah** is Ever All-Knowing, **All-Wise**. (Darussalam, 2000)

Al-Basir   The All-Seeing

Chapter Al-Baqarah Chapter 2 Verses 94~96
94. Say: "If the home of the Hereafter with **Allah** is indeed for you specially and not for others, of mankind, then long for death if you are truthful.
95. But they will never long for it because of what their hands have sent before them. And **Allah** is All-Aware of the Zalimun (wrong-doers).
96. And verily, you will find them the greediest of mankind for life and then those who ascribe partners to **Allah**. Every one of them wishes that he could

be given a life of a thousand years. But the grant of such life will not save him even a little from punishment. And **Allah** is **All-Seer** of what they do. (Darussalam, 1999)

Chapter Al-Baqarah   Chapter 2 Verse 110
And perform As-Salat (prayer), and give Zakat (charity-alms), and whatever of good you send fourth for yourselves before you, you shall find it with **Allah**. Certainly, **Allah** is **All-Seer** of what you do. (Darussalam, 1999)

Chapter Al-Baqarah   Chapter 2 Verse 233
The mothers shall give suck to their children for two whole years, for those who desire to complete the term of suckling, but the father of the child shall bear the cost of the mother's food and clothing on a reasonable basis. No person shall have a burden laid on him greater than he can bear. No mother shall be treated unfairly on account of her child, nor father on account of his child, and on the heir is incumbent the like of that. If they both decide on weaning, by mutual consent, and after due consultation, there is no sin on them. And if you decide on a foster suckling- mother for your children, there is no sin on you, provided you pay what you agreed on reasonable basis. And fear **Allah** and know that **Allah** is **All-Seer** of what you do. (Darussalam, 1999)

Chapter Al-Baqarah   Chapter 2 Verse 237
And if you divorce them (women) before you have touched them, and you have appointed unto them the Mahr (bridal money), then pay half of that, unless they (the women) agree to forego it, or he, in whose hands is the marriage tie, agrees to forego and give her full-appointed Mahr (bridal money). And to forego and give is nearer to At-Taqwa (piety). And do not forget liberality between yourselves. Truly, **Allah** is **All-Seer** of what you do. (Darussalam, 1999)

Chapter Al-Baqarah   Chapter 2 Verse 265
And the likeness of those who spend their wealth seeking **Allah**'s Pleasure while they in their own selves are sure and certain that **Allah** will reward them, is the likeness of a garden on a hill; heavy rain falls on it and it doubles its yield of harvest. And if it does not receive heavy rain, light rain suffices it. And **Allah** is **All-Seer** of what you do. (Darussalam, 1999)

Chapter Al-Imran   Chapter 3 Verses 14-15
14. Beautified for men is the love of things they covet; women, children, much of gold and silver, branded horses, cattle and well-tilled land. This is

the pleasure of the present worlds' life; but **Allah** has the excellent return with Him.
15. Say: "Shall I inform you of things far better than those? For Al-Muttaqun (the pious) there are Gardens with their **Lord**, underneath which rivers flow. Therein (is there) eternal (home) and Azwajun Mutahharatun (purified mates or wives). And **Allah** will be pleased with them. And **Allah** is **All-Seer** of the slaves." (Darussalam, 1999)

Chapter Al-Imran   Chapter 3 Verse 20
So, if they dispute with you say: "I have submitted myself to **Allah**, and those who follow me." And say to those who were given the Scripture and to those who are illiterates: "Do you submit yourselves?" If they do, they are rightly guided; but if they turn away, your duty is only to convey the Message; and **Allah** is **All-Seer** of (His) Slaves. (Darussalam, 1999)

Chapter Al-Imran   Chapter 3 Verse 156
O you who believe! Be not like those who disbelieve and who say to their brethren when they travel through the earth or go out to fight: "If they had stayed with us, they would not have died or been killed," so that **Allah** may make it a cause of regret in their hearts. It is **Allah** that gives life and causes death. And **Allah** is **All-Seer** of what you do. (Darussalam, 1999)

Chapter Al-Imran   Chapter 3 Verses 162-163
162. Is then one who follows the good Pleasure of **Allah** like the one who draws on himself the Wrath of **Allah**? – his abode is Hell, and worst, indeed is that destination!
163. They are in varying grades with **Allah**, and **Allah** is **All-Seer** of what they do. (Darussalam, 1999)

Chapter An-Nisa   Chapter 4 Verse 58
Verily, **Allah** commands that you should render back the trusts to those, to whom they are due; and when you judge between men, you judge with justice. Verily, how excellent is the teaching which He gives you! Truly, **Allah** is ever All-Hearer, **All-Seer**. (Darussalam, 1999)

Chapter An-Nisa   Chapter 4 Verse 134
Whoever desires a reward in this life of the world, then with **Allah** is the reward of this worldly life and of the Hereafter. And **Allah** is Ever All-Hearer, **All-Seer**. (Darussalam, 1999)

Chapter Al--Ma'idah   Chapter 5 Verse 71

They thought there will be no fitnah (trial), so they became blind and deaf; after that **Allah** turned to them; yet again many of them became blind and deaf. And **Allah** is the **All-Seer** of what they do. (Darussalam, 1999)

Chapter An-Anfal   Chapter 8 Verse 39

And fight them until there is no more fitnah (mischief), and religion will all be for **Allah** alone. But if they cease, then certainly, **Allah** is **All-Seer** of what they do. (Darussalam, 1999)

Chapter An-Anfal   Chapter 8 Verse 72

Verily, those who believed, and emigrated and strove hard and fought with their property and their lives in the Cause of **Allah** as well as those who gave asylum and help, - these are allies to one another. And as to those who believed but did not emigrate, you owe no duty of protection to them until they emigrate, but if they seek your help in religion, it is your duty to help them except against a people with whom you have treaty of mutual alliance; and **Allah** is the **All-Seer** of what you do. (Darussalam, 1999)

Chapter Hud   Chapter 11 Verse 112

So, stand you firm and straight as you are commanded and those who turn in repentance with you, and transgress not. Verily, He is **All-Seer** of what you do. (Darussalam, 2000)

Chapter Al-Isra   Chapter 17 Verse 1

Glorified be He who took His slave for a journey by night from Al-Masjid Al-Haram (Makkah) to Al-Masjid Al-Aqsa, the neighborhood whereof We have blessed, in order that We might show him of Our Ayat (signs). Verily, He is the All-Hearer, the **All-Seer**. (Darussalam, 2000)

Chapter Al-Isra   Chapter 17 Verse 17

And how many generations have We destroyed after Nuh! And Sufficient is your **Lord** as an All-Knower and **All-Seer** of the sins of His slaves. (Darussalam, 2000)

Chapter Al-Isra   Chapter 17 Verse 30

Truly, your **Lord** enlarges the provision for whom He wills and straitens. Verily, He is Ever All-Knower; **All-Seer** of His slaves. (Darussalam, 2000)

Chapter Al-Isra   Chapter 17 Verse 96

Say: "Sufficient is **Allah** for a witness between me and you. Verily, He is Ever the All-Knower, the **All-Seer** of His slaves." (Darussalam, 2000)

Chapter Ta-Ha   Chapter 20 Verses 29~35

29. "And appoint for me a helper from my family,
30. "Harun, my brother.
31. "Increase my strength with him,
32. "And let him share my task,
33. "That we may glorify You much,
34. "And remember, You much,
35. "Verily, You are Ever a **Well-Seer** of us." (Darussalam, 2000)

Chapter Al-Hajj   Chapter 22 Verse 61

That is because **Allah** merges the night into the day, and He merges the day into the night. And verily, **Allah** is All-Hearer, **All-Seer**. (Darussalam, 2000)

Chapter Al-Hajj   Chapter 22 Verse 75

Allah chooses Messengers from angels and from men. Verily, **Allah** is All-Hearer, **All-Seer**. (Darussalam, 2000)

Chapter Al-Furqan   Chapter 25 Verse 20

And we never sent before you any of the Messengers but verily, they ate food and walked in the markets. And We have made some of you as a trial for others; will you have patience? And your **Lord** is Ever **All-Seer**. (Darussalam, 2000)

Chapter Luqman   Chapter 31 Verse 28

The creation of you all and the resurrection of you all are only as single person. Verily, **Allah** is All-Hearer, **All-Seer**. (Darussalam, 2000)

Chapter Al-Ahzab   Chapter 33 Verse 9

O you who believe! Remember **Allah**'s Favour to you, when there came against you hosts, and We sent against them a wind and forces that you saw not. And **Allah** is ever **All-Seer** of what you do. (Darussalam, 2000)

Chapter Saba   Chapter 34 Verses 10-11

10. And indeed We bestowed grace on Dawud from us: "O you mountains, Glorify with him! And you birds! And We made the iron soft for him."

11. Saying: "Make you perfect coats of mail, and balance well the rings of chain Armor, and work you (men) righteousness. Truly, I am **All-Seer** of what you do. (Darussalam, 2000)

Chapter Fatir   Chapter 35 Verse 31
And what we have revealed to you, of the Book, it is the truth confirming that which was before it. Verily, **Allah** is indeed All-Aware, and **All-Seer** of His slaves. (Darussalam, 2000)

Chapter Fatir   Chapter 35 Verse 45
And if **Allah** were to punish men for that which they earned, He would not leave a moving creature on the surface of the earth; but He gives them respite to an appointed term, and when their term comes, then verily, **Allah** is Ever **All-Seer** of His slaves. (Darussalam, 2000)

Chapter Ghafir   Chapter 40 Verse 20
And **Allah** judges with truth, while those to whom they invoke besides Him, cannot judge anything. Certainly, **Allah**! He is the All-Hearer, the **All-Seer**. (Darussalam, 2000)

Chapter Ghafir   Chapter 40 Verses 42~44
42. "You invite me to disbelieve in **Allah**, and to join partners in worship with Him; of which I have no knowledge, and I invite you to the All-Mighty, the Oft-Forgiving!
43. "No doubt you call me to one who cannot grant my request in this world or in the Hereafter. And our return will be to **Allah**, and Al-Musrifun (polytheists)! they shall be the dwellers of the Fire!
44. "And you will remember what I am telling you, and my affair I leave it to **Allah**. Verily, **Allah** is the **All-Seer** of (His) slaves." (Darussalam, 2000)

Chapter Ghafir   Chapter 40 Verse 56
Verily, those who dispute about the Ayat (verses) of **Allah**, without any authority having come to them, there is nothing else in their breasts except pride. They will never have it. So seek refuge in **Allah**. Verily, it is He Who is the All-Hearer, the **All-Seer**. (Darussalam, 2000)

Chapter Fussilat   Chapter 41 Verse 40
Verily, those who turn away from our Ayat (verses) are not hidden from Us. Is he who is cast into the fire better or he who comes secure on the Day of Resurrection? Do what you will. Verily, He is **All-Seer** of what you do. (Darussalam, 2000)

Chapter Ash-Shura   Chapter 42 Verse 11
The Creator of the heavens and the earth. He has made for you mates from yourselves, and for the cattle mates. By this means He creates you. There is nothing like Him, and He is the All-Hearer, the **All-Seer**. (Darussalam, 2000)

Chapter Ash-Shura   Chapter 42 Verse 27
And if **Allah** were to enlarge the provision for His slaves, they would surely rebel in the earth, but He sends down by measure as He wills. Verily, He is, in respect of His slaves, the Well-Aware, the **All-Seer**. (Darussalam, 2000)

Chapter Al-Fath   Chapter 48 Verse 24
And He it is who has withheld their hands from you and your hands from them in the midst of Makkah, after He had made you victors over them. And **Allah** is Ever the **All-Seer** of what you do. (Darussalam, 2000)

Chapter Al-Hujurat   Chapter 49 Verse 18
Verily, **Allah** knows the Unseen of the heavens and the earth. And **Allah** is the **All-Seer** of what you do. (Darussalam, 2000)

Chapter Al-Hadid   Chapter 57 Verse 4
He it is Who created the heavens and the earth in six Days and then Istawa (rose over) the Throne. He knows what goes into the earth and what comes forth from it, what descends from the heaven and what ascends thereto. And He is with you wheresoever you may be. And **Allah** is the **All-Seer** of what you do. (Darussalam, 2000)

Chapter Al-Mujadilah   Chapter 58 Verse 1
Indeed, **Allah** has heard the statement of her that disputes with you concerning her husband, and complains to **Allah**. And **Allah** hears the argument between you both. Verily, **Allah** is All-Hearer, **All-Seer**. (Darussalam, 2000)

Chapter Al-Mumtahanah   Chapter 60 Verse 3
Neither your relatives nor your children will benefit you on the Day of Resurrection. He will judge between you. And **Allah** is the **All-Seer** or what you do. (Darussalam, 2000)

Chapter At-Taghabun   Chapter 64 Verse 2
He it is Who created you, then some of you are disbelievers and some of you are believers, and **Allah** is **All-Seer** of what you do. (Darussalam, 2000)

Chapter Al--Mulk Chapter 67 Verse 19
Do they not see the birds above them, spreading out their wings and folding them in? None upholds them except the Most Gracious. Verily, He is the **All-Seer** or everything. (Darussalam, 2000)

Chapter Al-Inshiqaq Chapter 84 Verses 10~15
10. But whosoever is given his record behind his back,
11. He will invoke distribution
12. And he shall enter a blazing fire, and made to taste its burning.
13. Verily, he was among his people in joy!
14. Verily, he thought that he would never come back!
15. Yes! Verily, his **Lord** has been ever **beholding** him! (Darussalam, 2000)

As-Sami   The All-Hearing

Chapter Al-Baqarah Chapter 2 Verse 127
And when Ibrahim and Ismail were raising the foundations of the House, "Our **Lord**! Accept from us. Verily, You are the **All-Hearer**, the All-Knower." (Darussalam, 1999)

Chapter Al-Baqarah Chapter 2 Verse 137
So, if they believe in the like of that which you believe then they are rightly guided; but if they turn away, then they are only in opposition. So, **Allah** will suffice for you against them. And He is the **All-Hearer**, the All-Knower. (Darussalam, 1999)

Chapter Al-Baqarah Chapter 2 Verses 180-181
180. It is prescribed for you, when death approaches any of you, if he leaves wealth, that he makes a bequest to parents and next of kin, according to reasonable manners. (This is) a duty upon All-Muttaqun (pious).
181. Then whoever changes the bequest after hearing it, the sin shall be on those who make the change. Truly, **Allah** is **All-Hearer**, All-Knower. (Darussalam, 1999)

Chapter Al-Baqarah Chapter 2 Verse 224
And make not **Allah**'s (Name) an excuse in your oaths against your doing good and acting piously, and making peace among mankind. And **Allah** is **All-Hearer**, All-Knower. (Darussalam, 1999)

Chapter Al-Baqarah Chapter 2 Verses 226-227

226. Those who take an oath not to have sexual relation with their wives must wait for four months, then if they return, verily, **Allah** is Oft-Forgiving, Most Merciful.
227. And if they decide upon divorce, then **Allah** is **All-Hearer**, All-Knower. (Darussalam, 1999)

Chapter Al-Baqarah Chapter 2 Verse 244

And fight in the way of **Allah** and know that **Allah** is **All-Hearer**, All-Knower. (Darussalam, 1999)

Chapter Al-Baqarah Chapter 2 Verse 256

There is no compulsion in religion. Verily, the Right Path has become distinct from the wrong path. Whoever disbelievers in Taghut (false deities) and believes in **Allah**, then he has grasped the most trustworthy handhold that will never break. And **Allah** is **All-Hearer**, All-Knower. (Darussalam, 1999)

Chapter Al-Imran Chapter 3 Verses 33~38

33. **Allah** chose Adam, Nuh, the family of Ibrahim and the family of Imran above the 'Alamin (worlds).
34. Offspring, one of the other, and **Allah** is **All-Hearer**, All-Knower.
35. When the wife of Imran said: "O my **Lord**! I have vowed to You what is in my womb to be dedicated for Your services, so accept this from me. Verily, You are the **All-Hearer**, the All-Knowing.
36. Then when she gave birth to her, she said: "O my **Lord**! I have given birth to a female child," - and **Allah** knew better what she brought forth, - "And the male is not like the female, and I have named her Maryam, and I seek refuge with You for her and for her offspring from Shaitan (Satan), the outcast."
37. So her **Lord** accepted her with goodly acceptance. He made her grow in a good manner and put her under the care of Zakariya. Every time he entered Al-Mihrab (praying place) to her, he found her supplied with sustenance. He said: "O Maryam! From where have you got this? She said, "This is from **Allah**." Verily, **Allah** provides sustenance to whom He wills, without limit.
38. At that time Zakariya invoked his **Lord**, Saying: "O my **Lord**! Grant me from You, a good offspring. You are indeed the **All-Hearer** of invocation."
(Darussalam, 1999)

Chapter Al-Imran   Chapter 3 Verse 121
And when you left your household in the morning to post the believers at their stations for the battle (of Uhud). And **Allah** is **All-Hearer**, All-Knower. (Darussalam, 1999)

Chapter An-Nisa   Chapter 4 Verse 58
Verily, **Allah** commands that you should render back the trusts to those, to whom they are due; and that when you judge between men, you judge with justice. Verily, how excellent is the teaching which He gives you! Truly, **Allah** is ever **All-Hearer**, All-Seer. (Darussalam, 1999)

Chapter An-Nisa   Chapter 4 Verse 134
Whoever desires a reward in this life of the world, then with **Allah** is the reward of this worldly life and of the Hereafter. And **Allah** is ever **All-Hearer**, All-Seer. (Darussalam, 1999)

Chapter An-Nisa   Chapter 4 Verse 148
Allah does not like that the evil should be uttered in public except by him who has been wronged. And **Allah** is ever **All-Hearer**, All-Knower. (Darussalam, 1999)

Chapter Al-Ma'idah   Chapter 5 Verse 76
Say: "How do you worship besides **Allah** something which has no power either to harm or benefit you? But it is **Allah** Who is the **All-Hearer**, All-Knower. (Darussalam, 1999)

Chapter Al-An'am   Chapter 6 Verse 13
And to Him belongs whatsoever exists in the night and the day, and He is the **All-Hearing**, the All-Knowing. (Darussalam, 1999)

Chapter Al-An'am   Chapter 6 Verse 115
And the Word of your Lord has been fulfilled in truth and in justice. None can change His words. And He is the **All-Hearer**, the All-Knower. (Darussalam, 1999)

Chapter Al-A`raf   Chapter 7 Verse 200
And if evil whisper comes to you from Shaitan (Satan), then seek refuge with **Allah**. Verily, He is **All-Hearer**, the All-Knower. (Darussalam, 1999)

Chapter Al-Anfal   Chapter 8 Verse 17
You killed them not, but **Allah** killed them. And you threw not when you did throw, but **Allah** threw, that He might test the believers by a fair trial from Him. Verily, **Allah** is **All-Hearer**, the All-Knower. (Darussalam, 1999)

Chapter Al-Anfal   Chapter 8 Verse 42
When you were on the near side of the valley, and they on the farther side, and the caravan on the ground lower than you. Even if you had made a mutual appointment to meet, you would certainly have failed in the appointment, but that **Allah** might accomplish a matter already ordained, so that those who were to be destroyed might be destroyed after a clear evidence, and those who were to live might live after a clear evidence. And surely, **Allah** is **All-Hearer**, All-Knower. (Darussalam, 1999)

Chapter Al-Anfal   Chapter 8 Verse 53
That is so because **Allah** will never change a grace, which He has bestowed on a people until they change what is in their own selves. And verily, **Allah** is **All-Hearer**, All-Knower. (Darussalam, 1999)

Chapter Al-Anfal   Chapter 8 Verse 61
But if they incline to peace, you also incline to it, and trust in **Allah**. Verily, He is the **All-Hearer**, All-Knower. (Darussalam, 1999)

Chapter At-Taubah   Chapter 9 Verse 98
And of the bedouins there are some who look upon what they spend as a fine and watch for calamities for you, on them be the calamity of evil. And **Allah** is **All-Hearer**, All-Knower. (Darussalam, 2000)

Chapter At-Taubah   Chapter 9 Verse 103
Take Sadaqat (alms) from their wealth in order to purify them and sanctify them with it, and invoke **Allah** for them. Verily, your invocations are a source of security for them; and **Allah** is **All-Hearer**, All-Knower. (Darussalam, 2000)

Chapter Yunus   Chapter 10 Verse 65
And let not their speech grieve you, for all power and honour belong to **Allah**. He is the **All-Hearer**, All-Knower. (Darussalam, 2000)

Chapter Yusuf   Chapter 12 Verses 33-34

33. He said: "O my **Lord**! Prison is dearer to me than that to which they invite me. Unless You turn away their plot from me, I will feel inclined towards them and be one of the ignorant."
34. So his **Lord** answered his invocation and turned away from him their plot. Verily, He is the **All-Hearer**, All-Knower. (Darussalam, 2000)

Chapter Ibrahim   Chapter 14 Verse 39

"All the praises and thanks be to **Allah**, Who has given me in old age Ismail and Ishaq. Verily, my **Lord** is indeed the **All-Hearer** of invocations. (Darussalam, 2000)

Chapter Al-Isra   Chapter 17 Verse 1

Glorified be He who took His slave for a journey by night from Al-Masjid Al-Haram (Makkah) to Al-Masjid Al-Aqsa, the neighborhood whereof We have blessed, in order that We might show him of Our Ayat (signs). Verily, He is the **All-Hearer**, the **All-Seer**. (Darussalam, 2000)

Chapter Al--Anbiya   Chapter 21 Verses 1~4

1. Draws near for mankind their reckoning, while they turn away in heedlessness.
2. Comes not unto them an admonition from their **Lord** as a recent revelation but they listen to it while they play,
3. With their hearts occupied. Those who do wrong, conceal their private counsels, (saying): "Is this more than a human being like you? Will you submit to magic while you see it?"
4. He said: "My **Lord** knows word in the heavens and on earth. And He is the **All-Hearer**, the All-Knower." (Darussalam, 2000)

Chapter Al-Hajj   Chapter 22 Verse 61

That is because **Allah** merges the night into the day, and He merges the day into the night. And verily, **Allah** is **All-Hearer**, All-Seer. (Darussalam, 2000)

Chapter Al-Hajj   Chapter 22 Verse 75

Allah chooses Messengers from angels and from men. Verily, **Allah** is **All-Hearer**, All-Seer. (Darussalam, 2000)

Chapter An-Nur   Chapter 24 Verse 21

O you who believe! Follow not the footsteps of Shaitan (Satan). And whosoever follows the footsteps of Shaitan (Satan), then, verily, he commands Al-Fahsha (immorality), and Al-Munkar (evil). And had it not been for the Grace of **Allah** and His Mercy on you, not one of you would ever have been pure from sins. But **Allah** purifies whom He wills, and **Allah** is **All-Hearer**, All-Knower. (Darussalam, 2000)

Chapter An-Nur   Chapter 24 Verse 60
And as for women past childbearing who do not except wedlock, it is no sin on them if they discard their clothing in such a way as not to show their adornment. But to retrain is better for them. And **Allah** is **All-Hearer**, All-Knower. (Darussalam, 2000)

Chapter Ash-Shu'ara   Chapter 26 Verse 220
Verily, He, only He, is the **All-Hearer**, All-Knower. (Darussalam, 2000)

Chapter Al-Ankabut   Chapter 29 Verse 5
Whoever hopes for the meeting with **Allah**, then **Allah**'s Term is surely coming, and He is the **All-Hearer**, All-Knower. (Darussalam, 2000)

Chapter Al-Ankabut   Chapter 29 Verse 60
And so many a moving creature carries not its own provision! **Allah** provides for it and for you. And He is the **All-Hearer**, All-Knower. (Darussalam, 2000)

Chapter Luqman   Chapter 31 Verse 28
The creation of you all and the resurrection of you all are only as a single person. Verily, **Allah** is **All-Hearer**, All-Seer. (Darussalam, 2000)

Chapter Saba   Chapter 34 Verse 50
Say: "If I go astray, I shall stray only to my own loss. But if I remain guided, it is because of the Revelation of my **Lord** to me. Truly, He is **All-Hearer**, Ever Near. (Darussalam, 2000)

Chapter Ghafir   Chapter 40 Verse 20
And **Allah** judges with truth, while those to whom they invoke besides Him, cannot judge anything. Certainly, **Allah**! He is the **All-Hearer**, the All-Seer. (Darussalam, 2000)

Chapter Ghafir   Chapter 40 Verse 56
Verily, those who dispute about the Ayat (Verses) of **Allah**, without any authority having come to them, there is nothing else in their breasts except pride. They will never have it. So, seek refuge in **Allah**. Verily, it is He Who is the **All-Hearer**, the All-Seer. (Darussalam, 2000)

Chapter Fussilat — Chapter 41 Verse 36

And if an evil whisper from Shaitan (Satan) tries to turn you away, then seek refuge in **Allah**. Verily, He is the **All-Hearer**, the All-Knower. (Darussalam, 2000)

Chapter Ash-Shura — Chapter 42 Verse 11

The Creator of the heavens and the earth. He has made for you mates from yourselves, and for the cattle mates. By this means He creates you. There is nothing like Him, and He is the **All-Hearer**, the All-Seer. (Darussalam, 2000)

Chapter Ad-Dukhan — Chapter 44 Verse 1~6

1. Ha-Mim
2. By the manifest book that makes things clear.
3. We sent it down on a blessed night. Verily, we are ever warning.
4. Therein is decreed every matter of ordainments.
5. As a command from Us. Verily, We are ever sending.
6. (As) a Mercy from your **Lord**. Verily, He is **All-Hearer**, the All-Knower. (Darussalam, 2000)

Chapter Al-Hujurat — Chapter 49 Verse 1

O you who believe! Make not (a decision) in advance before **Allah** and His messenger, and fear **Allah**. Verily, **Allah** is **All-Hearing**, All-Knowing. (Darussalam, 2000)

Chapter Al-Mujadilah — Chapter 58 Verse 1

Indeed, **Allah** has heard the statement of her that dispute with you concerning her husband and complains to **Allah**. And **Allah** hears the argument between you both. Verily, **Allah** is **All-Hearer**, All-Seer. (Darussalam, 2000)

Subsection 6

SUBSECTION 6

- *Al-Khaliq*   **The Creator**
- *Al-Bari*   **The Maker**
- *Al-Musawwir*   **The Bestower of Forms**
- *Al-Badi*   **The Originator**

Al-Khaliq   The Creator

Chapter Al-An'am   Chapter 6 Verses 101-102
101. He is the Originator of the heavens and the earth. How can He have children when He has no wife? He created all things and He is the All-Knower of everything.
102. Such is **Allah**, your **Lord**! La ilaha illa Huwa (none has the right to be worshipped but He), the **Creator** of all thing. So, worship Him, and He is the Wakil (Trustee, Guardian) over all things. (Darussalam, 1999)

Chapter Ar-Ra`d   Chapter 13 Verse 16
Say: "Who is the **Lord** of the heavens and the earth? Say: "**Allah**." Have you then taken Auliya (friends and helpers, etc.) other than Him, such as have no power either for benefit or for harm to themselves?" Say: "Is the blind equal to the one who sees? Or darkness equal to light? Or do they assign to **Allah** partners who created the like of His creation, so that the creation seemed alike to them?" Say: "**Allah** is the **Creator** of all things: and He is the One, the Irresistible." (Darussalam, 2000)

Chapter An-Nur   Chapter 24 Verse 45
Allah has created every moving creature from water. Of them there are some that creep on their bellies, and some that walk on two legs, and some that walk on four. **Allah creates what He wills**. Verily, **Allah** is Able to do all things. (Darussalam, 2000)

Chapter Ya-sin   Chapter 36 Verse 81
Is not He who created the heavens and the earth, Able to create the like of them? Yes, indeed! He is the All-Knowing, **Supreme Creator**. (Darussalam, 2000)

Chapter Az-Zumar   Chapter 39 Verse 62
Allah is the **Creator** of all things, and He is the Wakil (Trustee, Guardian) over all things. (Darussalam, 2000)

Chapter Ghafir   Chapter 40 Verses 61-62
61. **Allah**, it is He Who has made the night for you that you may rest therein and the day for you to see. Truly, **Allah** is full of Bounty to mankind; yet, most of mankind give no thanks.

62. That is **Allah**, your **Lord**, the **Creator** of all things, La ilaha illa Huwa (none has the right to be worshipped but He). How then are you turning away? (Darussalam, 2000)

Chapter Fussilat   Chapter 41 Verse 21
And they will say to their skins, "Why do you testify against us?" They will say: "**Allah** has caused us to speak as He causes all things to speak," and **He created you** the first time, and to Him you are made to return. (Darussalam, 2000)

Chapter Fussilat   Ayat Sajada   Chapter 41 Verses 37-38
37. And from among His signs are the night and the day, and the sun and the moon. Prostrate yourselves not to the sun nor to the moon, but prostrate yourselves to **Allah Who created them** if you worship Him.
38. But if they are too proud, then there are those who are with your **Lord** glorify Him night and day, and never are they tired. (Darussalam, 2000)

Chapter Al-Waqi`ah   Chapter 56 Verses 57~59
57. We created you, then why do you believe not?
58. Then tell Me the semen that you emit.
59. Is it you who create it, or are We the Creator? (Darussalam, 2000)

Chapter Al-Hashr   Chapter 59 Verse 24
He is **Allah**, the **Creator**, the Inventor of all things, the Bestower of forms. To Him belong the Best Names. All that is in the heavens and the earth glorify Him. And He is the All-Mighty, the All-Wise. (Darussalam, 2000)

Al-Bari   The Maker

Chapter Al-Hashr   Chapter 59 Verse 24
He is **Allah**, the Creator, the **Inventor of all things**, the Bestower of forms. To Him belong the Best Names. All that is in the heavens and the earth glorify Him. And He is the All-Mighty, the All-Wise. (Darussalam, 2000)

Al-Musawwir   The Bestower of Forms

Chapter Ta-Ha   Chapter 20 Verses 49-50
49. Fir'aun said: "Who then, O Musa is the **Lord** of you two?"
50. Said: "Our **Lord** is **He Who gave to each thing its form and nature**, then guided it aright. (Darussalam, 2000)

Chapter Al-Hashr   Chapter 59 Verse 24
He is **Allah**, the Creator, the Inventor of all things, the **Bestower of forms**. To Him belong the Best names. All that is in the heavens and the earth glorify Him. And He is the All-Mighty, the All-Wise. (Darussalam, 2000)

Al-Badi   The Originator

Chapter Al-Baqarah   Chapter 2 Verse 117
The **Originator** of the heavens and the earth. When He decrees a matter, He only says to it: "Be! - and it is. (Darussalam, 1999)

Chapter Al-An'am   Chapter 6 Verse 101
He is the **Originator** of the heavens and the earth. How can He have children when He has no wife? He created all things and He is the All-Knower of everything. (Darussalam, 1999)

Subsection 7

SUBSECTION 7

- *Al-Awwal* **The First One**
- *Al-Akhir* **The Last**
- *Al-Zahir* **The Manifest**
- *Al-Batin* **The Hidden**

Al-Awwal   The First One

Chapter Al-Hadid   Chapter 57 Verse 3
He is **the First** and the Last, the Most High and the Most Near. And He is the All-Knower of everything. (Darussalam, 2000)

Al-Akhir   The Last

Chapter Al-Hadid   Chapter 57 Verse 3
He is the First and **the Last**, the Most High and the Most Near. And He is the All-Knower of everything. (Darussalam, 2000)

Al-Zahir   The Manifest

Chapter Al-Hadid   Chapter 57 Verse 3
He is the First and the Last, **the Most High** and the Most Near. And He is the All-Knower of everything. (Darussalam, 2000)

Al-Batin   The Hidden

Chapter Al-Hadid   Chapter 57 Verse 3
He is the First and the Last, the Most High and **the Most Near**. And He is the All-Knower of everything. (Darussalam, 2000)

Subsection 8

SUBSECTION 8

- *Al-Quddus*   *The Most Holy*
- *Al-Salam*   *The Source of Peace*
- *Al-Mu'min*   *The Giver of Security*
- *Al-Muhaymin*   *The Protector*
- *Al-Hafiz*   *The Guardian*
- *Al-Fattah*   *The Opener*
- *Al-Wasi*   *The All-Sufficient*
- *Al-Hadi*   *The One Who Guides*
- *Al-Waliyy*   *The Protecting Friend*

Al-Quddus   The Most Holy

Chapter Al-Hashr   Chapter 59 Verse 23
He is **Allah**, besides whom La ilaha illa Huwa (none has the right to be worshipped but He), the King, the **Holy**, the One Free from all defects, the Giver of Security, the Watcher over His creatures, the All-Mighty, the Compeller, the Supreme. Glory be to **Allah**! above all that they associate as partners with Him. (Darussalam, 2000)

Chapter Al-Jumu'ah   Chapter 62 Verse 1
Whatsoever is in the heavens and whatsoever is on the earth glorifies **Allah**, the King, the **Holy**, the All-Mighty, the All-Wise. (Darussalam, 2000)

Al-Salam   The Source of Peace

Chapter Al-Hashr   Chapter 59 Verse 23
He is **Allah**, besides whom La ilaha illa Huwa (none has the right to be worshipped but He), the King, the Holy, the **One Free from all defects**, the Giver of Security, the Watcher over His creatures, the All-Mighty, the Compeller, the Supreme. Glory be to **Allah**! above all that they associate as partners with Him. (Darussalam, 2000)

Al-Mu'min   The Giver of Security

Chapter Al-Hashr   Chapter 59 Verse 23
He is **Allah**, besides whom La ilaha illa Huwa (none has the right to be worshipped but He), the King, the Holy, the One Free from all defects, **the Giver of Security**, the Watcher over His creatures, the All-Mighty, the Compeller, the Supreme. Glory be to **Allah**! above all that they associate as partners with Him. (Darussalam, 2000)

Al-Muhaymin   The Protector, The Watcher over His creatures

Chapter Al-Hashr   Chapter 59 Verse 23
He is **Allah**, besides whom La ilaha illa Huwa (none has the right to be worshipped but He), the King, the Holy, the One Free from all defects, the Giver of Security, the **Watcher over His creatures**, the All-Mighty, the Compeller, the Supreme. Glory be to **Allah**! above all that they associate as partners with Him. (Darussalam, 2000)

Al-Hafiz   The Guardian

Chapter Hud   Chapter 11 Verse 57
"So if you turn away, still I have conveyed the Message with which I was sent to you. My **Lord** will make another people succeed you, and you will not harm Him in the least. Surely, My **Lord** is **Guardian over all things**." (Darussalam, 2000)

Chapter Saba   Chapter 34 Verses 20-21
20. And indeed Iblis (Satan) did prove true his thought about them, and they followed him, all except a group of true believers.
21. And he had no authority over them, - except that We might test him who believes in the Hereafter, from him who is in doubt about it. And your **Lord** is a **Hafiz (Watchful)** over everything. (Darussalam, 2000)

Chapter Ash-Shura   Chapter 42 Verse 6
And as for those who take as Auliya (friends and helpers, etc.) others besides Him- **Allah** is **Hafiz (Protector)** over them, and you are not a Wakil (Disposer of affairs) over them. (Darussalam, 2000)

Al-Fattah   The Opener, Judge

Chapter Al-A'raf   Chapter 7 Verse 89
"We should have invented a lie against **Allah** if we returned to your religion, after **Allah** has rescued us from it. And it is not for us to return to it unless **Allah**, our **Lord**, should will. Our **Lord** comprehends all things in His Knowledge. In **Allah** (Alone) we put our trust. Our **Lord**! Judge between us

and our people in truth, for You are the **Best of those who give judgment.** (Darussalam, 1999)

Chapter Saba   Chapter 34 Verse 26
Say: "Our **Lord** will assemble us all together, then He will judge between us with truth. And He is the **Just Judge**, the All-Knower of the true state of affairs." (Darussalam, 2000)

Al-Wasi   The All-Sufficient, The Boundless

Chapter Al-Baqarah   Chapter 2 Verse 115
And to **Allah** belong the east and the west, so wherever you turn there is the Face of **Allah**. Surely, **Allah is All-Sufficient for His creatures needs**, All-Knowing. (Darussalam, 1999)

Chapter Al-Baqarah   Chapter 2 Verse 247
And their Prophet said to them, "Indeed **Allah** has appointed Talut as a king over you." They said, "How can he be a king over us when we are fitter than him for the kingdom, and he has not been given enough wealth." He said: "Verily, **Allah** has chosen him above you and has increased him abundantly in knowledge and stature. And **Allah** grants His kingdom to whom He wills. And **Allah** is **All-Sufficient for His creatures' needs**, All-Knower." (Darussalam, 1999)

Chapter Al-Baqarah   Chapter 2 Verse 261
The likeness of those who spend their wealth in the way of **Allah**, is as the likeness of a grain; it grows, seven ears, and each ear has a hundred grains. **Allah** gives manifold increase to whom He wills. And **Allah** is **All-Sufficient for His creatures needs**, All-Knower. (Darussalam, 1999)

Chapter Al-Baqarah   Chapter 2 Verse 268
Shaitan (Satan) threatens you with poverty and orders you to commit Fahsha (indecency); whereas **Allah** promises you forgiveness from Himself and Bounty, and **Allah** is **All-Sufficient for His creatures' needs**, All-Knower. (Darussalam, 1999)

Chapter Al-Imran   Chapter 3 Verse 73

And believe no one except the one who follows your religion. Say: "Verily, right guidance is the Guidance of **Allah**" and do not believe that anyone can receive like that which you have received, otherwise they would engage you in argument before your **Lord**." Say: "All the Bounty is in the Hand of **Allah**; He grants to whom He wills. And **Allah is All-Sufficient for His creatures needs**, All-Knower. (Darussalam, 1999)

Chapter An-Nisa   Chapter 4 Verses 129-130

129. You will never be able to do perfect justice between wives even if it is your ardent desire, so do not incline too much to one of them so as to leave the other hanging. And if you do justice, and do all that is right and fear **Allah** by keeping away from all that is wrong, then **Allah** is Ever Oft-Forgiving, Most Merciful.
130. But if they separate, **Allah** will provide abundance for every one of them from His Bounty. And **Allah is Ever All-Sufficient for His creatures' need**, All-Wise. (Darussalam, 1999)

Chapter Al-Ma'idah   Chapter 5 Verse 54

O you who believe! Whoever from among you turns back from his religion, **Allah** will bring a people whom He will love and they will love Him; humble towards the believers, stern towards the disbelievers, fighting in the way of **Allah**, and never fear of the blame of the blamers. That is the Grace of **Allah** which He bestows on whom He wills. And **Allah is All-Sufficient for His creatures' needs**, All-Knower. (Darussalam, 1999)

Chapter An-Nur   Chapter 24 Verse 32

And marry those among you who are single and the salihun (pious) of your slaves and maid-servants. If they be poor, **Allah** will enrich them out of His Bounty. And **Allah is All-Sufficient for His creatures needs**, All-Knowing. (Darussalam, 2000)

Chapter An-Najm   Chapter 53 Verse 32

Those who avoid great sins and Al-Fawahish (illegal sexual intercourse, etc.) except the small faults, - verily, your **Lord** is of **Vast forgiveness**. He knows you well when He created you from the earth, and when you were fetuses in your mothers' wombs. So, ascribe not purity to yourselves. He knows best him who fears **Allah** and keeps his duty to Him. (Darussalam, 2000)

Al-Hadi   The One Who Guides

<u>Chapter Al-Imran</u>   Chapter 3 Verse 73
And believe no one except the one who follows your religion." Verily, right guidance is the **Guidance of Allah**" and do not believe that anyone can receive like that which you have received, otherwise they would engage you in argument before your **Lord**." Say: "All the Bounty is in the hand of **Allah**; He grants to whom He wills. And **Allah** is All-Sufficient for His creatures needs, All-Knower." (Darussalam, 1999)

<u>Chapter Al-Isra</u>   Chapter 17 Verse 97
And he whom **Allah guides**, he is led aright; but he whom he sends astray, for such you will find no Auliya (friends and helpers, etc.) besides Him, and We shall gather them together on the Day of Resurrection on their faces, blind, dumb and deaf; their abode will be Hell; whenever it abates, we shall increase for them the fierceness of the fire. (Darussalam, 2000)

<u>Chapter Al-Hajj</u>   Chapter 22 Verse 54
And that those who have been given knowledge may know that it is the truth from your **Lord**, so that they may believe therein, and their hearts may submit to it with humility. And verily, **Allah is the Guide of those who believe**, to the Straight Path. (Darussalam, 2000)

<u>Chapter Al-Furqan</u>   Chapter 25 Verse 31
Thus have We made for every Prophet an enemy among the Mujrimun (criminals). But sufficient is your **Lord** as a **Guide** and Helper. (Darussalam, 2000)

<u>Chapter Al-Qasas</u>   Chapter 28 Verses 49-50
49. Say: "Then bring a Book from **Allah**, which is a better guide than these two, that I may follow it, if you are truthful."
50. But if they answer you not, then know that they only follow their own lusts. And who is more astray than one who follows his own lusts, without guidance from **Allah**? Verily, **Allah guides not the people who are Zalimun (wrong-doers).** (Darussalam, 2000)

<u>Chapter Al-Qasas</u>   Chapter 28 Verse 56
Verily, you guide not whom you like, but **Allah guides whom He wills**. And He knows best those who are the guided. (Darussalam, 2000)

Al-Waliyy   The Protecting Friend

Chapter Al-Baqarah　　　　　　　　　　　　　　Chapter 2 Verse 107
Know you not that it is **Allah** to whom belongs the dominion of the heavens and the earth? And besides **Allah** you have neither any **Wali (protector)** nor any helper. (Darussalam, 1999)

Chapter Al-Baqarah　　　　　　　　　　　　　　Chapter 2 Verse 120
Never will the Jews nor the Christians be pleased with you till you follow their religion. Say: "Verily, the Guidance of **Allah** that is the Guidance. And if you were to follow their desires after what you have received of Knowledge, then you would have against **Allah** neither any **Wali (Protector)** nor any helper. (Darussalam, 1999)

Chapter Al-Baqarah　　　　　　　　　　　　　　Chapter 2 Verse 257
Allah is the Wali (Protector) of those who believe. He brings them out from darkness into light. But as for those who disbelieve, their Auliya (friends and helpers, etc.) are Taghut (false deities), they bring them out from light into darkness. Those are the dwellers of the Fire, and they will abide therein forever. (Darussalam, 1999)

Chapter Al-Imran　　　　　　　　　　　　　　　Chapter 3 Verse 68
Verily, among mankind who have the best claim to Ibrahim are those who followed him, and this Prophet and those who have believed. And **Allah is the Wali (Protector)** of the believers. (Darussalam, 1999)

Chapter Al-Imran　　　　　　　　　　　　　Chapter 3 Verses 121-122
121. And when you left your household in the morning to post the believers at their stations for the battle (of Uhud). And **Allah** is All-Hearer, All-Knower.
122. When two parties from among you were about to lose heart, but **Allah** was their **Wali (Protector)** And in **Allah** should the believers put their trust. (Darussalam, 1999)

Chapter An-Nisa　　　　　　　　　　　　　　　Chapter 4 Verse 45
Allah has full knowledge of your enemies, and **Allah** is Sufficient as a **Wali (Protector)**, and **Allah** is Sufficient as a Helper. (Darussalam, 1999)

Chapter An-Nisa	Chapter 4 Verse 123
It will not be in accordance with your desires, nor those of the Scripture, whosoever works evil, will have the recompense thereof, and he will not find **any protector** or helper besides **Allah**. (Darussalam, 1999)

Chapter An-Nisa	Chapter 4 Verse 173
So as for those who believed and did deeds of righteousness, He will give them their rewards- and more out of His Bounty. But as for those who refused His worship and were proud, He will punish them with a painful torment. And they will not find for themselves besides **Allah any protector** or helper. (Darussalam, 1999)

Chapter Al-Ma'idah	Chapter 5 Verse 55
Verily, your **Wali (Protector)** is none other than **Allah**, His messenger, and the believers, - those who perform As-Salat (prayer), and give Zakat (charity-alms), and they are Rakiun (bow down). (Darussalam, 1999)

Chapter Al-An'am	Chapter 6 Verse 14
Say: "Shall I take as a **Wali (Protector)** any other than **Allah**, the Creator of the heavens and the earth? And it is He who feeds but is not fed." Say: "Verily, I am commanded to be the first of those who submit themselves to **Allah**." And be not you of the Mushrikun (polytheists). (Darussalam, 1999)

Chapter Al-An'am	Chapter 6 Verses 126-127
126. And this is the path of your **Lord** leading straight. We have detailed our Revelations for a people who take heed.
127. For them will be the home of peace with their **Lord**. And He will be their **Wali (Protector)** because of what they used to do. (Darussalam, 1999)

Chapter Al-A'raf	Chapter 7 Verse 155
And Musa (Moses) chose out of his people seventy men for Our appointed time and place of meeting, and when they were seized with a violent earthquake, he said: "O my **Lord**, if it had been Your Will, You could have destroyed them and me before; would You destroy us for the deeds of the foolish ones among us? It is only Your Trial by which You lead astray whom You will, and keep guided whom You will. You are our **Wali (Protector)**, so forgive us and have Mercy on us, for You are the Best of those who forgive. (Darussalam, 1999)

Chapter Al-A'raf   Chapter 7 Verse 196
Verily, my **Wali (Protector) is Allah** Who has revealed the book, and He protects the righteous. (Darussalam, 1999)

Chapter At-Taubah   Chapter 9 Verse 116
Verily, **Allah**! Unto him belongs the dominion of the heavens and the earth, He gives life and He causes death. And besides **Allah** you have neither any **Wali (Protector)** nor any helper. (Darussalam, 2000)

Chapter Hud   Chapter 11 Verse 20
By no means will they escape on earth, nor have they **protectors** besides **Allah**! Their torment will be doubled! They could not bear to hear and they used not to see. (Darussalam, 2000)

Chapter Hud   Chapter 11 Verse 113
And incline not toward those who do wrong, lest the fire should touch you, and you have no **protectors** other than **Allah**, nor you would then be helped. (Darussalam, 2000)

Chapter Yusuf   Chapter 12 Verse 101
"My **Lord**! You indeed bestowed on me of the sovereignty, and taught me something of the interpretation of dreams- the Creator of the heavens and the earth! You are my **Wali (Protector)** in this world and in the Hereafter. Cause me to die as a Muslim, and join me with the righteous." (Darussalam, 2000)

Chapter Ar-Ra'd   Chapter 13 Verse 37
And thus have We sent it down to be a judgement of authority in Arabic. Were you to follow their (vain) desires after the knowledge which has come to you, then you will not have any **Wali (protector)** or Waq (defender) against **Allah**. (Darussalam, 2000)

Chapter Al-Kahf   Chapter 18 Verse 25-26
25. And they stayed in their Cave three hundred years, adding nine.
26. Say: "**Allah** knows best how long they stayed. With Him is the Unseen of the heavens and the earth. How clearly, He sees, and hears! They have no **Wali (Protector)** other than Him, and He makes none to share in His Decision and His Rule." (Darussalam, 2000)

Chapter Al-Ankabut   Chapter 29 Verse 22
And you cannot escape in the earth or in the heaven. And besides **Allah** you have neither any **Wali (Protector)** nor any helper. (Darussalam, 2000)

Chapter As-Sajdah Chapter 32 Verse 4
Allah it is He Who has created the heavens and the earth, and all that is between them in six Days. Then He rose over (Istawa) the Throne. You, have none, besides Him, as a **Wali (Protector)** or an intercessor. Will you not then remember? (Darussalam, 2000)

Chapter Al-Ahzab Chapter 33 Verse 17
Say: "Who is he who can protect you from **Allah** if He intends to harm you, or intends mercy on you?" and they will not find, besides **Allah**, for themselves any **Wali (Protector)** or any helper. (Darussalam, 2000)

Chapter Saba Chapter 34 Verses 40-41
40. And the Day when He will gather them all together, then He will say to the angels; "Was it you that these people used to worship?"
41. They will say: "Glorified be you! You are our **Wali (Protector)** instead of them. Nay, but they used to worship the jinn; most of them were believers in them." (Darussalam, 2000)

Chapter Ash-Shura Chapter 42 Verse 9
Or have they taken Auliya (friends and helpers, etc.) besides Him? But **Allah** – He Alone is the **Wali (Protector)**. And it is He Who gives life to the dead, and He is Able to do all things. (Darussalam, 2000)

Chapter Ash-Shura Chapter 42 Verse 28
And He it is Who sends down the rain after they have despaired and spreads His Mercy. And He is the **Wali (Protector)**, Worthy of all praise. (Darussalam, 2000)

Chapter Ash-Shura Chapter 42 Verse 31
And you cannot escape from **Allah** in the earth, and besides **Allah** you have neither any **Wali (guardian or a protector)** nor any helper. (Darussalam, 2000)

Chapter Al-Jathiyah Chapter 45 Verse 19
Verily, they can avail you nothing against **Allah**. Verily, the Zalimun (wrong-doers) are Auliya (friends and helpers, etc.) of one another, but **Allah** is the **Wali (Protector)** of the Muttaqun (pious). (Darussalam, 2000)

Subsection 9

SUBSECTION 9

- *Al-A'la* — **The Most High**
- *Al-Aziz* — **The All-Mighty**
- *Al-Qawi* — **The Most Strong**
- *Al-Qadir* — **The All-Capable**
- *Al-Matin* — **The Firm, The Most Strong**
- *Ar-Raqib* — **The Watchful**
- *Al-Hasib* — **The Reckoner**
- *Al-Jaami* — **The Gatherer**
- *Ash-Shahid* — **The Witness**
- *Al-Wakil* — **The Trustee**, The Best Disposer of affairs
- *Al-Hakam* — **The Judge**
- *Al-Jabbar* — **The Compeller**
- *Al-Mutakabir* — **The Supremely Great**
- *Al-Muqtadir* — **The Powerful Determiner**

Al-A'la   The Most High

Chapter Al-Baqarah   Chapter 2 Verse 255
Allah! La ilaha illa Huwa (none has the right to be worshipped but He), Al-Hayyul-Qayyum (the Ever Living, the One Who Sustains and Protects all that exists). Neither slumber nor sleep overtakes Him. To Him belongs whatever is in the heavens and whatever is on the earth. Who is he that can intercede with Him except with His permission? He knows what happens to them in this world, and what will happen to them in the Hereafter. And they will never compass anything of His knowledge except that which He wills. His Kursi (Chair) extends over the heavens and the earth, and He feels no fatigue in guarding and preserving them. And He is the **Most High**, the Most Great. (Darussalam, 1999)

Chapter An-Nisa   Chapter 4 Verse 34
Men are the protectors and maintainers of women, **Allah** has made one of them to excel the other, and because they spend from their means. Therefore, the righteous women are devoutly obedient, and guard in the husband's absence what **Allah** orders them to guard. As to those women on whose part you see ill-conduct, admonish them, refuse to share their beds, beat them; but if they return to obedience, seek not against them means. Surely, **Allah** is Ever **Most High**, Most Great. (Darussalam, 1999)

Chapter Al-Hajj   Chapter 22 Verses 61-62
61. That is because **Allah** merges the night into the day, and He merges the day into the night. And verily, **Allah** is All-Hearer, All-Seer.
62. That is because **Allah** He is the truth, and what they invoke besides Him, it is Batil (falsehood), And verily, **Allah** He is the **Most High**, the Most Great. (Darussalam, 2000)

Chapter Luqman   Chapter 31 Verses 29-30
29. See you not that **Allah** merges the night into the day and merges the day into the night, and has subjected the sun and the moon, each running its cause for a term appointed; and that **Allah** is All-Aware of what you do.
30. That is because **Allah**, He is the Truth, and that which they invoke besides Him is Al-Batil (falsehood); and that **Allah**, He is the **Most High**, the Most Great. (Darussalam, 2000)

| Chapter Saba | Chapter 34 Verses 22-23 |

22. Say: "Call upon those whom you assert besides **Allah**, they possess not even an atom's weight either in the heavens or on the earth, nor have they any share in either, nor there is for Him any support from among them.

23. Intercession with Him profits not except for him whom He permits. So much so that when fear is banished from their hearts, they say: "What is it that your **Lord** has said?" They say: "The Truth and He is the **Most High**, the Most Great." (Darussalam, 2000)

| Chapter Ghafir | Chapter 40 Verses 11-12 |

11. They will say: "Our **Lord**! You have made us to die twice, and you have given us life twice! Now we confess our sins, then is there any way to get out?"

12. This is because, when **Allah** Alone was invoked, you disbelieved, but when partners were joined to Him, you believed! So, the judgment is only with **Allah**, the **Most High**, the Most Great!" (Darussalam, 2000)

| Chapter Ash-Shura | Chapter 42 Verse 4 |

To Him belongs all that is in the heavens and all that is in the earth, and He is the **Most High**, the Most Great. (Darussalam, 2000)

| Chapter Ash-Shura | Chapter 42 Verse 51 |

It is not given to any human being that **Allah** should speak to him unless by Revelation, or from behind a veil, or He sends a Messenger to reveal what He wills by His Leave. Verily, He is **Most High**, Most Wise. (Darussalam, 2000)

| Chapter Al-A`la | Chapter 87 Verse 1 |

Glorify the name of your **Lord**, the **Most High**, (Darussalam, 2000)

Al-Aziz The All-Mighty

| Chapter Al-Baqarah | Chapter 2 Verse 129 |

"Our **Lord**! Send amongst them a Messenger of their own who shall recite unto them Your Verses and instruct them in the book and Al-Hikmah, and purify them. Verily, You are the **All-Mighty**, the All-Wise." (Darussalam, 1999)

Chapter Al-Baqarah   Chapter 2 Verses 208-209
208. O you who believe! Enter perfectly in Islam and follow not the footsteps of Shaitan (Satan). Verily, he is to you a plain enemy.
209. Then if you slide back after the clear signs have come to you, then know that **Allah** is **All-Mighty**, All-Wise. (Darussalam, 1999)

Chapter Al-Baqarah   Chapter 2 Verse 220
In this worldly life and in the hereafter, and they ask you concerning orphans say: "The best thing is to work honestly in their property, and if you mix your affairs with theirs, then they are your brothers. And **Allah** knows him who means mischief from him who means good. And if **Allah** had wished, He could have put you into difficulties. Truly, **Allah** is **All-Mighty**, All-Wise." (Darussalam, 1999)

Chapter Al-Baqarah   Chapter 2 Verse 228
And divorced women shall wait for three menstrual periods, and it is not lawful for them to conceal what **Allah** has created in their wombs, if they believe in **Allah** and the last day. And their husbands have the better right to take them back in that period, if they wish for reconciliation. And they have rights similar over them to what is reasonable, but men have a degree over them. And **Allah** is **All-Mighty**, All-Wise. (Darussalam, 1999)

Chapter Al-Baqarah   Chapter 2 Verse 240
And those of you who die and leave behind wives should bequeath for their wives a year's maintenance and residence without turning them out, but if they leave, there is no sin on you for that which they do of themselves, provided it is honourable. And **Allah** is **All-Mighty**, All-Wise. (Darussalam, 1999)

Chapter Al-Baqarah   Chapter 2 Verse 260
And when Ibrahim said, "My **Lord**! Show me how You give life to the dead." He said: "Do you not believe?" He said: "Yes, but to be stronger in Faith." He said: "Take four birds, then cause them to incline towards you, and then put a portion of them on every hill, and call them, they will come to you in haste. And know that **Allah** is **All-Mighty**, All-Wise." (Darussalam, 1999)

Chapter Al-Imran   Chapter 3 Verses 3-4
3. It is He Who has sent down the book to you with truth, confirming what came before it. And He sent down the Taurat and the Injil,
4. Aforetime, as a guidance to mankind. And He sent down the criterion. Truly, those who disbelieve in the Ayat (Verse) of **Allah**, for them there is a

severe torment; and **Allah** is **All-Mighty**, All-Able of Retribution. (Darussalam, 1999)

Chapter Al-Imran   Chapter 3 Verse 6
He it is Who shapes you in the wombs as He wills, La ilaha illa Huwa (none has the right to be worshipped but He), the **All-Mighty**, the All-Wise. (Darussalam, 1999)

Chapter Al-Imran   Chapter 3 Verse 18
Allah bears witness that La ilaha illa Huwa (none has the right to be worshipped but He), and the angels, and those having knowledge;(He always) maintains His creation in justice, La ilaha illa Huwa (none has the right to be worshipped but He), the **All-Mighty**, the All-Wise. (Darussalam, 1999)

Chapter Al-Imran   Chapter 3 Verse 62
Verily! this is the true narrative, and La ilaha illallah (none has the right to be worshipped but **Allah**). And indeed, **Allah** is the **All-Mighty**, the All-Wise. (Darussalam, 1999)

Chapter Al-Imran   Chapter 3 Verses 125-126
125. "Yes, if you hold on to patience and piety, and the enemy comes rushing at you; your **Lord** will help you with five thousand angels having marks."
126. **Allah** made it not but as a message of good news for you and as an assurance to your hearts. And there is no victory except from **Allah**, the **All-Mighty**, the All-Wise. (Darussalam, 1999)

Chapter An-Nisa   Chapter 4 Verse 56
Surely, those who disbelieved in Our Ayat (Verses), We shall burn them in fire. As often as their skins are roasted through, We shall change them for other skins that they may taste the punishment. Truly, **Allah** is **Ever Most Powerful**, All-Wise. (Darussalam, 1999)

Chapter An-Nisa   Chapter 4 Verses 157-158
157. And because of their saying, "We killed Messiah Isa, son of Maryam, the Messenger of **Allah**", but they killed him not, nor crucified him, but it appeared so to them, and those who differ therein are full of doubts. They have no knowledge; they follow nothing but conjecture. For surely; they killed him not;
158. But **Allah** raised him up unto Himself. And **Allah** is **Ever All-Powerful** (**All-Mighty**), All-Wise. (Darussalam, 1999)

| Chapter An-Nisa | Chapter 4 Verses 164-165 |

164. And Messengers We have mentioned to you before, and Messengers We have not mentioned to you, - and to Musa **Allah** spoke directly.
165. Messengers as bearers of good news as well as of warning in order that mankind should have no plea against **Allah** after the Messengers. And **Allah** is **Ever All-Powerful**, All-Wise. (Darussalam, 1999)

| Chapter Al-Ma'idah | Chapter 5 Verse 38 |

And the male thief and the female thief, cut off their hands as a recompense for that which they committed, a punishment by way of example from **Allah**. And **Allah** is **All-Powerful**, All-Wise. (Darussalam, 1999)

| Chapter Al-Ma'idah | Chapter 5 Verse 95 |

O you who believe! Kill not the game while you are in a state of Ihram, and whosoever of you kills it intentionally, the penalty is an offering, brought to the Ka'bah, of an eatable animal equivalent to the one he killed, as adjudged by two just men among you; or, for expiation, he should feed Masakin (poor person), or its equivalent in Saum (fasting), that he may taste the heaviness of his deed. **Allah** has forgiven what is past, but whosoever commits it again, **Allah** will take retribution from him. And **Allah** is **All-Mighty**, All-Able of Retribution. (Darussalam, 1999)

| Chapter Al-Ma'idah | Chapter 5 Verses 116~118 |

116. And when **Allah** will say: "O 'Isa, son of Maryam! Did you say unto men: 'Worship me and my mother as two gods besides **Allah**?'" He will say: "Glory be to You! It was not for me to say what I had no right. Had I said such a thing, You would surely have known it. You know what is in my inner-self though I do not know what is in Yours, truly, You, only You, are the All-Knower of all that is hidden.
117. "Never did I say to them aught except what You did command me to say: 'Worship **Allah**, my **Lord** and your **Lord**.' And I was a witness over them while I dwelt amongst them, but when You took me up, You were the Watcher over them, and You are a Witness to all things.
118. "If You punish them, they are Your slaves, and if You forgive them, verily You, only You are the **All-Mighty**, the All-Wise." (Darussalam, 1999)

| Chapter Al-An`am | Chapter 6 Verses 95-96 |

95. Verily, it is **Allah** Who causes the seed grain and the fruit stone to split and sprout. He brings forth the living from the dead, and it is He Who brings forth the dead from the living. Such is **Allah**, then how are you deluded away from the truth?

96. (He is the) Cleaver of the daybreak. He has appointed the night for resting, and the sun and the moon for reckoning. Such is the measuring of the **All-Mighty**, the All-Knowing. (Darussalam, 1999)

Chapter Al-Anfal   Chapter 8 Verses 9-10
9. When you sought help of your **Lord** and He answered you: "I will help you with a thousand of the angels each behind the other in succession."
10. **Allah** made it only as glad tidings, and that your hearts be at rest there with. And there is no victory except from **Allah**. Verily, **Allah** is **All-Mighty**, All-Wise. (Darussalam, 1999)

Chapter Al-Anfal   Chapter 8 Verse 49
When the hypocrites and those in whose hearts was a disease said: "These people are deceived by their religion." But whoever puts his trust in **Allah**, then surely, **Allah** is **All-Mighty**, All-Wise. (Darussalam, 1999)

Chapter Al-Anfal   Chapter 8 Verse 63
And He has united their hearts. If you had spent all that is in the earth, you could not have united their hearts, but **Allah** has united them. Certainly, He is **All-Mighty**, All-Wise. (Darussalam, 1999)

Chapter Al-Anfal   Chapter 8 Verse 67
It is not for a Prophet that he should have prisoners of war until he had made a great slaughter in the land. You desire the good of this world, but **Allah** desires the Hereafter. And **Allah** is **All-Mighty**, All-Wise. (Darussalam, 1999)

Chapter At-Taubah   Chapter 9 Verse 40
If you help him not, for **Allah** did indeed help him when the disbelievers drove him out, the second of the two; when they were in the cave, he said to his companion: "Be not sad, surely, **Allah** is with us." Then **Allah** sent down his Sakinah (peace) upon him, and strengthened him with forces which you saw not, and made the word of those who disbelieved the lowermost, while the Word of **Allah** that become the uppermost; and **Allah** is **All-Mighty**, All-Wise. (Darussalam, 1999)

Chapter At-Taubah   Chapter 9 Verse 71
The believers, men and women, are Auliya (friends and helpers, etc.) of one another; they enjoin Al-Maruf (good), and forbid from Al-Munkar (evil); they perform As-Salat (prayer), and give the Zakat (charity-alms) and obey

Allah and His Messenger, **Allah** will have His Mercy on them. Surely, **Allah** is **All-Mighty**, All-Wise. (Darussalam, 1999)

Chapter Hud   Chapter 11 Verses 66~68
66. So when Our Commandment came, We saved Salih and those who believed with him by a mercy from Us, and from the disgrace of that Day. Verily, your **Lord**- He is the All-Strong, the **All-Mighty**.
67. And As-Saihah (torment) overtook the wrongdoers, so they lay, prostrate in their homes.
68. As if they had never lived there. No doubt! Verily, Thamud disbelieved in their **Lord**. So, away with Thamud! (Darussalam, 2000)

Chapter Ibrahim   Chapter 14 Verse 1
Alif-Lam-Ra (This is) a book which We have revealed unto you in order that you might lead mankind out of darkness into light by their **Lord**'s Leave to the path of the **All-Mighty**, the Owner of all praise. (Darussalam, 2000)

Chapter Ibrahim   Chapter 14 Verse 4
And We sent not a Messenger except with the language of his people, in order that he might make clear for them. Then **Allah** misleads whom He wills and guides whom He wills. And He is the **All-Mighty**, the All-Wise. (Darussalam, 2000)

Chapter Ibrahim   Chapter 14 Verse 47
So think not that **Allah** will fail to keep His Promise to His Messengers. Certainly, **Allah** is **All-Mighty**, All Able of Retribution. (Darussalam, 2000)

Chapter An-Nahl   Chapter 16 Verse 60
For those who believe not in the **Hereafter** is an evil description, and for **Allah** is the highest description. And He is the **All-Mighty**, the All-Wise. (Darussalam, 2000)

Chapter Al-Hajj   Chapter 22 Verse 40
Those who have been expelled from their homes unjustly only because they said; "Our **Lord** is **Allah**." For had it not been that **Allah** checks one set of people by means of another, monasteries, churches, synagogues, and mosques, wherein the name of **Allah** is mentioned much would surely, have been pulled down. Verily, **Allah** will help those who help His (Cause). Truly, **Allah** is All-Strong, **All-Mighty**. (Darussalam, 2000)

Chapter Al-Hajj — Chapter 22 Verse 74

They have not estimated **Allah** His Rightful Estimate. Verily, **Allah** is All-Strong, **All-Mighty**. (Darussalam, 2000)

Chapter Ash-Shu'ara — Chapter 26 Verses 7~9

7. Do they not observe the earth how much of every good kind We cause to grow therein?
8. Verily, in this is an Ayah (sign), yet most of them are not believers.
9. And verily, your **Lord**, He is truly, the **All-Mighty**, the Most Merciful. (Darussalam, 2000)

Chapter Ash-Shu'ara — Chapter 26 Verses 61~68

61. And when the two hosts saw each other, the companions of Musa said: "We are sure to be overtaken."
62. Said "Nay, verily, with me is my **Lord**. He will guide me."
63. Then We revealed to Musa: "Strike the sea with your stick." And it parted, and each separate part become like huge mountain.
64. Then We brought near the others to that place.
65. And We save Musa and all those with him.
66. Then We drowned the others.
67. Verily, in this is indeed a sign, yet most of them are not believers.
68. And verily, your **Lord**, He is truly, the **All-Mighty**, the Most Merciful. (Darussalam, 2000)

Chapter Ash-Shu'ara — Chapter 26 Verses 91~104

91. And the fire will be place in full view of the erring.
92. And it will be said to them: Where are those that you used to worship.
93. "Instead of **Allah**? Can they help you or help themselves?"
94. Then they will be thrown on their faces into the (fire), they and the Ghawun (erring).
95. And the whole hosts of Iblis (Satan) together.
96. They will say while contending therein,
97. By **Allah**, we were truly in manifest error,
98. When we held you as equals with the **Lord** of the 'Alamin (worlds);
99. And none has brought us into error except the Mujrimun (criminals).
100. Now we have no intercessors,
101. Nor a close friend.
102. If we only had a chance to return, we shall truly be among the believers!
103. Verily, in this is indeed a sign, yet most of them are not believers.
104. And verily, your **Lord**, He is truly, the **All-Mighty**, the Most Merciful. (Darussalam, 2000)

Chapter Ash-Shu'ara   Chapter 26 Verses 116~122

116. They said: "If you cease not, O Nuh you will surely, be among those stoned."
117. He said: "My **Lord**! Verily, my people have belied me.
118. Therefore judge You between me and them, and save me and those of the believers who are with me."
119. And We saved him and those with him in the laden ship.
120. Then We drowned the rest thereafter.
121. Verily, in this is indeed a sign, yet most of them are not believers.
122. And verily, your **Lord**, He is indeed the **All-Mighty**, the Most Merciful. (Darussalam, 2000)

Chapter Ash-Shu'ara   Chapter 26 Verses 136~140

136. They said: "It is the same to us whether you preach or be not of those who preach."
137. "This is no other than the false tales and religion of the ancients."
138. "And we are not going to be punished."
139. So they belied him, and We destroyed them. Verily, in this is indeed a sign, yet most of them are not believers.
140. And verily, your **Lord**, He is indeed the **All-Mighty**, the Most Merciful. (Darussalam, 2000)

Chapter Ash-Shu'ara   Chapter 26 Verses 155~159

155. He said: "Here is a she camel: it has a right to drink, and you have a right to drink on a day known.
156. "And touch her not with harm, lest the torment of a great day should seize you."
157. But they killed her, and then they became regretful.
158. So the torment overtook them. Verily, in this is indeed a sign, yet most of them are not believers.
159. And verily, your **Lord**, He is indeed the **All-Mighty**, the Most Merciful. (Darussalam, 2000)

Chapter Ash-Shu'ara   Chapter 26 Verses 167~175

167. They said: "If you cease not. O Lot! Verily, you will be one of those who are driven out!"
168. He said: "I am, indeed of those who disapprove with severe anger and fury your action."
169. "My **Lord**! Save me and my family from what they do."
170. So We saved him and his family, all.

171. Except an old woman among those who remained behind.
172. Then afterward We destroyed the others.
173. And We rained on them a rain. And how evil was the rain of those who had been warned!
174. Verily, in this is indeed a sign, yet most of them are not believers.
175. And verily, you **Lord**; He is indeed the **All-Mighty**, the Most Merciful. (Darussalam, 2000)

Chapter Ash-Shu'ara   Chapter 26 Verses 185~191

185. They said: "You are only one of those bewitched!"
186. "You are but a human being like us and verily, we think that you are one of the liars!"
187. "So cause a piece of the heaven to fall on us, if you are of the truthful!"
188. He said: "My **Lord** is the Best Knower of what you do."
189. But they belied him, so the torment of the Day of Shadow seized them. Indeed, that was the torment of a Great Day.
190. Verily, in this is indeed a sign, yet most of them are not believers.
191. And verily, your **Lord**, He is indeed the **All-Mighty**, The Most Merciful. (Darussalam, 2000)

Chapter Ash-Shu'ara   Chapter 26 Verses 213~217

213. So invoke not with **Allah** another ilah (god) lest you should be among those who receive punishment.
214. And warn your tribe of near kindred.
215. And be kind and humble to the believers who follow you.
216. Then if they disobey you, say: "I am innocent of what you do."
217. And put your trust in the **All-Mighty**, the Most Merciful. (Darussalam, 2000)

Chapter An-Naml   Chapter 27 Verses 7~9

7. (Remember) when Musa said to his household: "Verily, I have seen a fire; I will bring you from this some information, or I will bring you a burning brand, that you may warn yourselves."
8. But when he came to it, he was called: "Blessed is whosoever is in the fire, and whosoever is round about it! And glorified be **Allah**, the **Lord** of the 'Alamin (worlds).
9. O Musa! Verily, it is I, **Allah**, the **All-Mighty**, the All-Wise. (Darussalam, 2000)

Chapter An-Naml — Chapter 27 Verses 76~79

76. Verily, this Quran narrates to the Children of Israel most of that in which they differ.
77. And truly, it is a guide and a mercy for the believers.
78. Verily, your **Lord** will decide between them by His Judgment. And He is the **All-Mighty**, the All-Knowing.
79. So put your trust in **Allah**; surely, you are on manifest truth. (Darussalam, 2000)

Chapter Al-Ankabut — Chapter 29 Verses 25~26

25. And said: "You have taken idols instead of **Allah**. The love between you is only in the life of this world, but on the Day of Resurrection, you shall disown each other, and curse each other, and your abode will be the fire, and you shall have no helper."
26. So Lut believed in him, he said: "I will emigrate for the sake of my **Lord**. Verily, He is the **All-Mighty**, the All-Wise." (Darussalam, 2000)

Chapter Al-Ankabut — Chapter 29 Verses 41~43

41. The likeness of those who take Auliya (friends and helpers, etc.) other than **Allah** is the likeness of a spider who builds a house; but verily, the frailest of houses is the spider's house if they but knew.
42. Verily, **Allah** knows what things they invoke instead of Him. He is the **All-Mighty**, the All-Wise.
43. And these similitudes We put forward for mankind; but none will understand them except those who have knowledge. (Darussalam, 2000)

Chapter Ar-Rum — Chapter 30 Verses 1~5

1. Alif-Lam-Mim
2. The Romans have been defeated.
3. In the nearest land, and they, after their defeat, will be victorious.
4. Within three to nine years. The decision of the matter, before and after is only with **Allah**. And on that day, the believers will rejoice.
5. With the help of **Allah**. He helps whom He wills, and He is the **All-Mighty**, the Most Merciful. (Darussalam, 2000)

Chapter Ar-Rum — Chapter 30 Verses 26-27

26. To Him belongs whatever is in the heavens and the earth. All are obedient to Him.
27. And He it is Who originates the creation, then He will repeat it; and this is easier for Him. His is the highest deception in the heavens and in the earth. And He is the **All-Mighty**, the All-Wise. (Darussalam, 2000)

Chapter Luqman   Chapter 31 Verses 8-9
8. Verily, those who believe and do righteous good deeds, for them are Gardens of Delight.
9. To bide therein, it is a Promise of **Allah** in truth and He is the **All-Mighty**, the All-Wise. (Darussalam, 2000)

Chapter Luqman   Chapter 31 Verse 27
And if all the trees on the earth were pens and the sea, with seven seas behind it to add to its (supply), yet the words of **Allah** would not be exhausted. Verily, **Allah** is **All-Mighty**, All-Wise. (Darussalam, 2000)

Chapter As-Sajdah   Chapter 32 Verses 5-6
5. He manages and regulates affair from the heavens to the earth; then it will go up to Him in one Day, the space whereof is a thousand years of your reckoning.
6. That is He, the All-Knower of the unseen and the seen, the **All-Mighty**, the Most Merciful. (Darussalam, 2000)

Chapter Al-Ahzab   Chapter 33 Verse 25
And **Allah** drove back those who disbelieved in their rage; they gained no advantage. **Allah** sufficed for the believers in the fighting. And **Allah** is Ever All-Strong, **All-Mighty**. (Darussalam, 2000)

Chapter Saba   Chapter 34 Verse 6
And those who have been given knowledge see that what is revealed to you from your **Lord** is the truth, and that it guides to the path of the **Exalted in might**, Owner of all praise. (Darussalam, 2000)

Chapter Saba   Chapter 34 Verse 27
Say: "Show me those whom you have joined with Him as partners. Nay! But He is **Allah**, the **All-Mighty**, the All-Wise." (Darussalam, 2000)

Chapter Fatir   Chapter 35 Verse 2
Whatever of mercy, **Allah** may grant to mankind, none can withhold it; and whatever He may withhold, none can grant it thereafter, And He is the **All-Mighty**, the All-Wise. (Darussalam, 2000)

| Chapter Fatir | Chapter 35 Verses 27-28 |

27. See you not that **Allah** sends down water from the sky, and We produce therewith fruits of various colours, and among the mountains are streaks white and red, of varying colours and very black.

28. And likewise, men and Ad-Dawabb (moving creatures) and cattle are of various colours. It is only those who have knowledge among His slaves that fear **Allah**. Verily, **Allah** is **All-Mighty**, Oft-Forgiving. (Darussalam, 2000)

| Chapter Ya-sin | Chapter 36 Verses 1~5 |

1. Ya-sin
2. By the Quran, full of wisdom,
3. Truly, you are one of the Messengers,
4. On the Straight Path.
5. (This is Revelation) sent down by the **All-Mighty**, the Most Merciful. (Darussalam, 2000)

| Chapter Ya-sin | Chapter 36 Verses 37~38 |

37. And a sign for them is the night. We withdraw there from the day, and behold, they are in darkness.
38. And the sun runs on its fixed course for a term. That is the Decree of the **All-Mighty**, the All-Knowing. (Darussalam, 2000)

| Chapter Sad | Chapter 38 Verses 5~9 |

5. "Has he made the aliha (gods) into One Ilah (God). Verily, this is a curious thing"!
6. And the leaders among them went about (saying): "Go on, and remain constant to your alihah (gods)! Verily, this is a thing designed!
7. "We have not heard of this in the religion of these later days, this is nothing but an invention!
8. "Has the Reminder been sent down to him from among us?" Nay but they are in doubt about My Reminder! Nay, but they have not tasted Torment!
9. Or have they the treasures of the Mercy of your **Lord**, the **All-Mighty**, the Real Bestower. (Darussalam, 2000)

| Chapter Sad | Chapter 38 Verses 65~66 |

65. Say: "I am only a warner and there is no Ilah (God) except **Allah** the One, the Irresistible,
66. "The **Lord** of the heavens and the earth and all that is between them, the **All-Mighty**, the Oft-Forgiving." (Darussalam, 2000)

Chapter Az-Zumar　　　　　　　　　　　　　　Chapter 39 Verse 1

The revelation of this Book is from **Allah**, the **All-Mighty**, the All-Wise. (Darussalam, 2000)

Chapter Az-Zumar　　　　　　　　　　　　　Chapter 39 Verses 4-5

4. Had **Allah** willed to take a son, He could have chosen whom He willed out of those whom He created. But glory be to Him! He is **Allah**, the One, the Irresistible.
5. He has created the heavens and the earth with truth. He makes the night to go in the day and makes the day to go in the night. And He has subjected the sun and the moon, each running for an appointed term. Verily, He is the **All-Mighty**, the Oft-Forgiving. (Darussalam, 2000)

Chapter Az-Zumar　　　　　　　　　　　　　Chapter 39 Verse 37

And whomsoever **Allah** guides, for him there will be no misleader. Is not **Allah All-Mighty**, Possessor of Retribution. (Darussalam, 2000)

Chapter Ghafir　　　　　　　　　　　　　　Chapter 40 Verses 1~3

1. Ha Mim
2. The revelation of the Book is from **Allah**, the **All-Mighty**, the All-Knower.
3. The forgiver of sin, the Acceptor of repentance, the Severe in punishment, the Bestower, La ilah illa Huwa (none has the right to be worshipped but He), to Him is the final return. (Darussalam, 2000)

Chapter Ghafir　　　　　　　　　　　　　　Chapter 40 Verses 7~9

7. Those who bear the Throne and those around it glorify the praises of their **Lord**, and believe in Him, and ask forgiveness for those who believe: "Our **Lord**! You comprehend all things in mercy and knowledge, so forgive those who repent and follow Your way, and save them from the torment of the blazing fire!
8. Our **Lord**! And make them enter the 'Adn Paradise which you have promised them – and to the righteous among their fathers, their wives, and their offspring! Verily, You are the **All-Mighty**, the All-Wise.
9. "And save them from the sins, and whomsoever You save from the sins that Day, him verily, You have taken into mercy." And that is the Supreme Success. (Darussalam, 2000)

Chapter Ghafir　　　　　　　　　　　　　Chapter 40 Verses 41-42

41. "And O my people! How is it that I call you to salvation while you call me to the fire!

42. You invite me to disbelieve in **Allah**, and to join partners in worship with Him of which I have no knowledge; and I invite you to the **All-Mighty**, the Oft-Forgiving! (Darussalam, 2000)

Chapter Fussilat   Chapter 41 Verses 9~12
9. Say: "Do you verily disbelieve in Him Who created the earth in two Days? And you set up rivals with Him? That is the **Lord** of the 'Alamin (worlds).
10. He placed therein firm mountains from above it, and He blessed it, and measured therein its sustenance in four days equal for all those who ask.
11. Then He rose over (Istawa) towards the heaven when it was smoke, and said to it and to the earth. "Come both of you willingly or unwillingly." They both said: "We come willingly."
12. Then He completed and finished from their creation seven heavens in two Days and He made in each heaven its affair. And We adorned the nearest heaven with lamps to be an adornment as well as to guard. Such is the Decree of Him, the **All-Mighty**, the All-Knower. (Darussalam, 2000)

Chapter Ash-Shura   Chapter 42 Verses 1-4
1. Ha-Mim
2. Ain-Sin-Qaf
3. Likewise **Allah**, the **All-Mighty** the All-Wise sends Revelation to you as those before you.
4. To Him belongs all that is in the heavens and all that is in the earth, and He is the Most High, the Most Great. (Darussalam, 2000)

Chapter Ash-Shura   Chapter 42 Verse 19
Allah is very Gracious and Kind to His slaves. He gives provisions to whom He wills. And He is the All-Strong, the **All-Mighty**. (Darussalam, 2000)

Chapter Az-Zukhruf   Chapter 43 Verse 9
And indeed, if you ask them: "Who has created the heavens and the earth?" They will surely say: "The **All-Mighty**, the All-Knower created them." (Darussalam, 2000)

Chapter Ad-Dukhan   Chapter 44 Verses 40~42
40. Verily, the Day of Judgment is the time appointed for all of them.
41. The Day when a Maula (a near relative) cannot avail a Maula (a near relative) in aught, and no help can they receive.
42. Except him on whom **Allah** has mercy. Verily, He is the **All-Mighty**, the **Most Merciful**. (Darussalam, 2000)

Chapter Al-Jathiyah   Chapter 45 Verses 1-2
1. Ha-Mim
2. The revelation of the Book is from **Allah**, the **All-Mighty**, the All-Wise. (Darussalam, 2000)

Chapter Al-Jathiyah   Chapter 45 Verses 36-37
36. So all the praises and thanks be to **Allah**, the **Lord** of the heavens and the **Lord** of the earth, and the **Lord** of the 'Alamin (worlds).
37. And His is the Majesty in the heavens and the earth, and He is the **All-Mighty**, the All-Wise. (Darussalam, 2000)

Chapter Al-Ahqaf   Chapter 46 Verses 1-2
1. Ha-Mim
2. The revelation of the Book is from **Allah**, the **All-Mighty**, the All-Wise. (Darussalam, 2000)

Chapter Al-Fath   Chapter 48 Verse 7
And to **Allah** belong the hosts of the heavens and the earth. And **Allah** is Ever **All-Mighty**, All-Wise. (Darussalam, 2000)

Chapter Al-Fath   Chapter 48 Verses 18-19
18. Indeed, **Allah** was pleased with the believers when they gave the Bai'ah (pledge) to you under the tree, He knew what was in their hearts, and He send down As-Sakinah (peace) upon them, and He rewarded them with a near victory.
19. And abundant spoils that they will capture. And **Allah** is Ever **All-Mighty**, All-Wise. (Darussalam, 2000)

Chapter Al-Qamar   Chapter 54 Verses 41-42
41. And indeed, warnings came to the people of Fir'aun.
42. (They) belied all Our Signs, so We seized them with a seizure of the **All-Mighty**, All-Capable. (Darussalam, 2000)

Chapter Al-Hadid   Chapter 57 Verse 1
Whatsoever is in the heavens and the earth glorifies **Allah** and He is the **All-Mighty**, All-Wise. (Darussalam, 2000)

Chapter Al-Hadid   Chapter 57 Verse 25
25. Indeed We have sent Our Messengers with clear proofs, and revealed with them the scripture and the Balance that mankind may keep up justice. And We brought forth iron wherein is mighty power, as well as many benefits for

mankind, that **Allah** may test who it is that will help Him and His Messengers in the unseen. Verily, **Allah** is All-Strong, **All Mighty**. (Darussalam, 2000)

Chapter Al-Mujadilah   Chapter 58 Verse 21
Allah has decreed: "Verily, it is I and My Messengers who shall be the victorious." Verily, **Allah** is All-Powerful, **All-Mighty**. (Darussalam, 2000)

Chapter Al-Hashr   Chapter 59 Verse 1
Whatsoever is in the heavens and whatsoever is on the earth glorifies **Allah**. And He is the **All-Mighty**, the All-Wise. (Darussalam, 2000)

Chapter Al-Hashr   Chapter 59 Verses 23-24
23. He is **Allah**, besides whom La ilaha illa Huwa (none has the right to be worshipped but He), the King, the Holy, the One Free from all defects, the Giver of Security, the Watcher over His creatures, the **All-Mighty**, the Compeller, the Supreme. Glory be to **Allah**! above all that they associate as partners with Him.
24. He is **Allah**, the Creator, the Inventor of all things, Bestower of forms. To Him belong the best Names. All that is in the heavens and the earth glorify Him. And He is the **All-Mighty**, the All-Wise. (Darussalam, 2000)

Chapter Al-Mumtahanah   Chapter 60 Verses 4-5
4. Indeed there has been an excellent example for you in Ibrahim and those with him, when they said to their people: "Verily, we are free from you and whatever you worship besides **Allah**, we have rejected you, and there has started between us and you, hospitality and hatred forever until you believe in **Allah** alone"- except the saying of Ibrahim to his father: "Verily, I will ask forgiveness for you, but I have no power to do anything for you before **Allah**." "Our **Lord**! In You we put our trust, and to You we turn in repentance, and to You is (our) final Return.
5. "Our **Lord**! Make us not a trial for the disbelievers, forgive us, Our **Lord**! Verily, You, only You, are the **All-Mighty**, the All-Wise." (Darussalam, 2000)

Chapter As-Saff   Chapter 61 Verse 1
Whatsoever is in the heavens and whatsoever is on the earth glorifies **Allah**. And He is the **All-Mighty**, the All-Wise. (Darussalam, 2000)

Chapter Al-Jumu'ah   Chapter 62 Verses 1~3
1. Whatsoever is in the heavens and whatsoever is on the earth glorifies **Allah**, the King, the Holy, the **All-Mighty**, the All-Wise.

2. He it is who sent among the unlettered ones a Messenger from among themselves, reciting to them His verses, purifying them, and teaching them the Book and Al-Hikmah (wisdom). And verily, they had been before in manifest error;
3. And others among them who have not yet joined them. And He is the **All-Mighty**, the All-Wise. (Darussalam, 2000)

Chapter At-Taghabun   Chapter 64 Verses 17-18
17. If you lend to **Allah** a goodly loan, He will double it for you, and will forgive you, And **Allah** is Most Ready to appreciate and to reward, Most Forbearing,
18. All-Knower of the unseen and seen, the **All-Mighty**, the All-Wise. (Darussalam, 2000)

Chapter Al-Mulk   Chapter 67 Verses 1-2
1. Blessed be He in Whose hands is the dominion; and He is Able to do all things.
2. Who has created death and life that He may test you which of you is best in deed, And He is the **All-Mighty**, the Oft-Forgiving. (Darussalam, 2000)

Chapter Al-Buruj   Chapter 85 Verses 1~9
1. By the heaven holding the big stars.
2. And by the Promised Day.
3. And by the Witnessing Day, and by the Witnessed Day.
4. Cursed were the people of the Ditch.
5. Of fire fed with fuel.
6. When they sat by it.
7. And they witnessed what they were doing against the believers.
8. And they had no fault except that they believed in **Allah**, the **All-Mighty**, Worthy of all praise!
9. To Whom belongs the dominion of the heavens and the earth! And **Allah** is Witness over everything. (Darussalam, 2000)

Al-Qawi   The Most Strong

Chapter Al-Anfal   Chapter 8 Verse 52
Similar to the behavior of the people of Fir'aun and of those before them – they rejected the Ayat (verse) of **Allah**, so **Allah** punished them for their sins. Verily **Allah** is **All-Strong**, Severe in punishment. (Darussalam, 1999)

Chapter Hud   Chapter 11 Verse 66

So when Our Commandment came, We saved Salih and those who believed with him by a mercy from Us, and from the disgrace of that Day. Verily, your **Lord** - He is the **All-Strong**, the All-Mighty. (Darussalam, 2000)

Chapter Al-Hajj   Chapter 22 Verse 40

Those who have been expelled from their homes unjustly only because they said: "Our **Lord** is **Allah**." For had it not been that **Allah** checks one set of people by means of another, monasteries, churches, synagogues, and mosques, wherein the Name of **Allah** is mentioned much would surely, have been pulled down. Verily, **Allah** will help those who help His (Cause). Truly, **Allah** is **All-Strong**, All-Mighty. (Darussalam, 2000)

Chapter Al-Hajj   Chapter 22 Verse 74

They have not estimated **Allah** His Rightful Estimate. Verily, **Allah** is **All-Strong**, All-Mighty. (Darussalam, 2000)

Chapter Al-Ahzab   Chapter 33 Verse 25

And **Allah** drove back those who disbelieved in their rage: they gained no advantage. **Allah** sufficed for the believers in the fighting. And **Allah** is Ever **All-Strong**, All-Mighty. (Darussalam, 2000)

Chapter Ghafir   Chapter 40 Verses 21-22

21. Have they not traveled in the land and seen what was the end of those who were before them? They were superior to them in strength, and in the traces in the land. But **Allah** seized them with punishment for their sins. And none had they to protect them from **Allah**.
22. That was because there came to them their Messengers with clear evidences but they disbelieved. So, **Allah** seized them. Verily, He is **All-Strong**, Severe in punishment. (Darussalam, 2000)

Chapter Ash-Shura   Chapter 42 Verse 19

Allah is very Gracious and Kind to His slaves. He gives provisions to whom He wills. And He is the **All-Strong**, All-Mighty. (Darussalam, 2000)

Chapter Adh-Dhariyat   Chapter 51 Verse 58

Verily, **Allah** is All-Provider, Owner of Power, the **Most Strong**. (Darussalam, 2000)

Chapter Al-Hadid Chapter 57 Verse 25
Indeed We have sent Our Messengers with clear proofs, and revealed with them the Scripture and the Balance that mankind may keep up justice. And We brought forth iron wherein is mighty power, as well as many benefits for mankind, that **Allah** may test who it is that will help Him and His Messengers in the unseen. Verily, **Allah** is **All-Strong**, All-Mighty. (Darussalam, 2000)

Chapter Al-Mujadilah Chapter 58 Verse 21
Allah has decreed: "Verily, it is I and My Messengers who shall be the victorious: Verily, **Allah** is **All-Powerful**, All-Mighty. (Darussalam, 2000)

Al-Qadir The All-Capable

Chapter Al-An`am Chapter 6 Verse 37
And they said: "Why is not a sign sent down to him from his **Lord**?" Say: "**Allah is certainly Able** to send down a sign but most of them know not." (Darussalam, 1999)

Chapter Al- An`am Chapter 6 Verse 65
Say: "He **has power to send** torment on you from above or from under your feet, or to cover you with confusion in party strife, and make you to taste the violence of one another." See how variously We explain the Ayat (verse), so that they may understand. (Darussalam, 1999)

Chapter Al-Isra Chapter 17 Verse 99
See they not that **Allah**, Who created the heavens and the earth, is **Able to create the like of them**. And He has decreed for them an appointed term, whereof there is no doubt. But the Zalimun (wrong-doers) refuse but disbelief. (Darussalam, 2000)

Chapter Al-Mu'minun Chapter 23 Verse 18
And We sent down from the sky water in measure, and We gave it lodging in the earth, and verily, **We are Able to take it away**. (Darussalam, 2000)

Chapter Al-Mu'minun Chapter 23 Verses 93~95
93. Say: "My **Lord**! If you would show me that with which they are threatened.
94. "My **Lord**! Then, put me not amongst the people who are the Zalimun (wrong-doers)."

95. And indeed **We are Able to show you** that with which We have threatened them. (Darussalam, 2000)

Chapter Ya-Sin   Chapter 36 Verse 81
81. Is not He Who created the heavens and the earth, **Able to create the like of them**? Yes, indeed! He is the All-Knowing Supreme Creator. (Darussalam, 2000)

Chapter Al-Ma'arij   Chapter 70 Verses 40-41
40. So, I swear by the **Lord** of all the points of sunrise and sunset in the east and the west that **surely, We are Able.**
41. To replace them by better than them; and We are not to be outrun. (Darussalam, 2000)

Chapter Al-Qiyamah   Chapter 75 Verses 3-4
3. Does man think that We shall not assemble his bones?
4. Yes, **We are Able to put together** in perfect order the tips of his fingers. (Darussalam, 2000)

Chapter Al-Mursalat   Chapter 77 Verses 20~23
20. Did We not create you from a despised water?
21. Then We place it in a place of safety.
22. For a known period?
23. So We did measure; and **We are the best to measure**. (Darussalam, 2000)

Chapter At-Tariq   Chapter 86 Verses 5~8
5. So let man see from what he is created!
6. He is created from a water gushing forth,
7. Proceeding from between the backbone and the ribs.
8. Verily, **(Allah) is Able to bring** him back! (Darussalam, 2000)

Al-Matin   The Firm, The Most Strong

Chapter Adh-Dhariyat   Chapter 51 Verse 58
Verily, **Allah** is the All-Provider, Owner of Power, **the Most Strong.** (Darussalam, 2000)

Ar-Raqib   The Watchful

Chapter An-Nisa   Chapter 4 Verse 1

O mankind! Be dutiful to your **Lord**, Who created you from a single person, and from him He created his wife, and from them both He created many men and women; and fear **Allah** through Whom you demand and the wombs. Surely, **Allah** is Ever an **All-Watcher** over you. (Darussalam, 1999)

Chapter Al-Ma'idah   Chapter 5 Verses 116-117

116. And when **Allah** will say: "O Isa, son of Maryam! Did you say unto men: 'Worship me and my mother as two gods besides **Allah**? He will say: "Glory be to You! It was not for me to say what I had no right (to say). Had I said such a thing, You would surely have known it. You know what is in my inner-self though I do not know what is in Yours; truly, You, only You, are the All-Knower of all that is hidden.
117. Never did I say to them aught except what You did command me to say: "Worship **Allah**, my **Lord** and your **Lord**.' And I was a witness over them while I dwelt amongst them, but when You took me up, You were the **Watcher** over them; and You are a Witness to all things. (Darussalam, 1999)

Chapter Al-Ahzab   Chapter 33 Verses 51-52

51. You (O Muhammad) can postpone whom you will of them and you may receive whom you will. And whomsoever you desire of those whom you have set aside, it is no sin on you; that is better that they may be comforted and not grieved, and may all be pleased with what you give them. **Allah** knows what is in your hearts. And **Allah** is Ever All-Knowing, Most Forbearing.
52. It is not lawful for you women after this, nor to change them for other wives even though their beauty attracts you, except those whom your right hand possesses. And **Allah** is Ever a **Watcher** over all things. (Darussalam, 2000)

Al-Hasib   The Reckoner

Chapter An-Nisa   Chapter 4 Verse 6

And try orphans until they reach the age of marriage; if then you find sound judgment in them, release their property to them, but consume it not wastefully and hastily fearing that they should grow up, and whoever is rich, he should take no wages, but if he is poor, let him have for himself what is just and reasonable. And when you release their property to them, take witness in their presence; and **Allah** is **All-Sufficient in taking account**. (Darussalam, 1999)

Chapter An-Nisa   Chapter 4 Verse 86
When you are greeted with a greeting, greet in return with what is better than it, or return it equally. Certainly, **Allah** is **Ever-careful account taker of all things.** (Darussalam, 1999)

Chapter Al-Ahzab   Chapter 33 Verses 38-39
38. There is no blame on the Prophet in that which **Allah** has made legal for him. That has been **Allah**'s way with those who have passed away of old. And the Command of **Allah** is decree determined.
39. Those who convey the Message of **Allah** and fear Him, and fear none save **Allah**. And sufficient is **Allah** as a **Reckoner**. (Darussalam, 2000)

Al-Jaami   The Gatherer

Chapter Imran   Chapter 3 Verse 9
"Our **Lord**! Verily, it is You **Who will gather mankind together** on the Day about which there is no doubt. Verily, **Allah** never breaks His promise." (Darussalam, 1999)

Chapter An-Nisa   Chapter 4 Verse 140
And it has already been revealed to you in the Book that when you hear the verses of **Allah** being denied and mocked at, then sit not with them, until they engage in a talk other than that; certainly, in that case you would be like them. Surely, **Allah will collect** the hypocrites and disbelievers all together in Hell. (Darussalam, 1999)

Ash-Shahid   The Witness

Chapter Al-Imran   Chapter 3 Verse 98
Say: "O people of the Scripture! Why do you reject the Ayat (verses) of **Allah** while **Allah** is **Witness** to what you do?" (Darussalam, 1999)

Chapter An-Nisa   Chapter 4 Verse 33
And to everyone, We have appointed heirs of that left by parents and relatives. To those also with whom you have made a pledge, give them their

due portion. Truly, **Allah** is Ever a **Witness** over all things. (Darussalam, 1999)

Chapter An-Nisa — Chapter 4 Verse 79
Whatever of good reaches you, is from **Allah**, but whatever of evil befalls you, is from yourself. And We have sent you as a Messenger to mankind, and **Allah** is Sufficient as a **Witness**. (Darussalam, 1999)

Chapter An-Nisa — Chapter 4 Verse 166
But **Allah** bears witness to that which He has sent down unto you; He has sent it down with His knowledge, and the angels bear witness. And **Allah** is All-Sufficient as a **Witness**. (Darussalam, 1999)

Chapter Al-Ma'idah — Chapter 5 Verses 116-117
116. And when **Allah** will say: "O Isa, son of Maryam! Did you say unto men: 'Worship me and my mother as two gods besides **Allah**?" He will say: "Glory be to You! It was not for me to say what I had no right. Had I said such a thing, You would surely have known it. You know what is in my innerself though I do not know what is in Yours; truly, You, only You, are the All-Knower of all that is hidden.
117. Never did I say to them aught what You did command me to say: 'Worship **Allah**, my **Lord** and your **Lord**! And I was a witness over them while I dwelt amongst them, but when You took me up, You were the Watcher over them; and You are a **Witness** to all things. (Darussalam, 1999)

Chapter Al-An'am — Chapter 6 Verse 19
Say: "What thing is the most great in witness? "Say: "**Allah** is **Witness** between me and you; this Quran has been revealed to me that I may therewith warn you and whomsoever it may reach. Can you verily, bear witness that besides **Allah** there are other aliha (gods)?" Say: "I bear no witness!" Say: "But in truth He is the only One Ilah (God). And truly, I am innocent of what you join in worship with Him." (Darussalam, 1999)

Chapter Yunus — Chapter 10 Verses 45-46
45. And on the Day when He shall gather them together, as if they had not stayed but an hour of a day. They will recognize each other. Ruined indeed will be those who denied the meeting with **Allah** and were not guided. (Darussalam, 2000)
46. Whether We show you some of what We promise them, - or We cause you to die, - still unto Us is their return, and moreover **Allah** is **Witness** over what they used to do. (Darussalam, 2000)

Chapter Ar-Ra'd — Chapter 13 Verse 43
And those who disbelieved, say "You are not a Messenger." Say: "Sufficient as a **Witness** between me and you is **Allah** and those too who have knowledge of the Scripture." (Darussalam, 2000)

Chapter Al-Isra — Chapter 17 Verse 96
Say: "Sufficient is **Allah** for a **Witness** between me and you. Verily, He is Ever the All-Knower, the All-Seer of His Slaves." (Darussalam, 2000)

Chapter Al-Hajj — Chapter 22 Verse 17
Verily, those who believe, and those who are Jews, and the Sabians, and the Christians, and the Majus, and those who worship others besides **Allah**; truly, **Allah** will judge between them on the Day of Resurrection. Verily, **Allah** is over all things a **Witness**. (Darussalam, 2000)

Chapter Al-Ankabut — Chapter 29 Verse 52
Say: "Sufficient is **Allah** for a **Witness** between me and you. He knows what is in the heavens and on earth." And those who believe in Batil (falsehood) and disbelieve in **Allah**, it is they who are the losers. (Darussalam, 2000)

Chapter Al-Ahzab — Chapter 33 Verses 54-55
54. Whether you reveal anything or conceal it, verily, **Allah** is Ever All-Knower of everything.
55. It is no sin on them (if they appear unveiled) before their fathers, or their sons, or their brothers, or their brother's sons, or the sons of their sisters, or their own women, or their slaves. And keep your duty to **Allah**. Verily, **Allah is Ever All-Witness** over everything. (Darussalam, 2000)

Chapter Saba — Chapter 34 Verse 47
Say: "Whatever wage I might have asked of you is yours. My wage is from **Allah** only, and He is a **Witness** over all things." (Darussalam, 2000)

Chapter Fussilat — Chapter 41 Verse 53
We will show them Our Signs in the universe, and in their own selves, until it becomes manifest to them that this is the truth. Is it not sufficient in regard to your **Lord** that He is a **Witness** over all things? (Darussalam, 2000)

Chapter Al-Ahqaf — Chapter 46 Verse 8
Or say they: "He has fabricated it." Say: "If I have fabricated it, still you have no power to support me against **Allah**. He knows best of what you say among

yourselves concerning it! Sufficient is He as a **Witness** between me and you! And He is the Oft-Forgiving, the **Most Merciful**." (Darussalam, 2000)

Chapter Al-Fath   Chapter 48 Verse 28
He it is Who has sent His Messenger with guidance and the religion of truth, that He may make it superior to all religions. And All-Sufficient is **Allah** as a **Witness**. (Darussalam, 2000)

Chapter Al-Mujadilah   Chapter 58 Verse 6
On the Day when **Allah** will resurrect them all together and inform them of what they did. **Allah** has kept account of it, while they have forgotten it. And **Allah** is **Witness** over all things. (Darussalam, 2000)

Chapter Al-Buruj   Chapter 85 Verses 1~9
1. By the heaven holding the big stars.
2. And by the Promised Day.
3. And by the Witnessing Day, and by the Witnessed Day.
4. Cursed were the people of the Ditch.
5. Of fire fed with fuel.
6. When they sat by it.
7. And they witnessed what they were doing against the believers.
8. And they had no fault except that they believed in **Allah**, the All-Mighty, Worthy of all praise!
9. To Whom belongs the dominion of the heavens and the earth! And **Allah** is **Witness** over everything. (Darussalam, 2000)

Al-Wakil *The Trustee, The Best Disposer of affairs*

Chapter Al-Imran   Chapter 3 Verse 173
Those unto whom the people said, "Verily, the people have gathered against you, therefore, fear them." But it increased them in Faith, and they said: "**Allah** is sufficient for us, and He is **Best Disposer of affairs**." (Darussalam, 1999)

Chapter An-Nisa   Chapter 4 Verse 81
They Say: "We are obedient," but when they leave you, a section of them spends all night in planning other than what you say. But **Allah** records their nightly. So, turn aside from them, and put your trust in **Allah**. And **Allah is Ever All-Sufficient as a Disposer of affairs**. (Darussalam, 1999)

Chapter An-Nisa   Chapter 4 Verse 132
And to **Allah** belongs all that is in the heavens and all that is in the earth. And **Allah** is Ever **All-Sufficient as Disposer of affairs.** (Darussalam, 1999)

Chapter An-Nisa   Chapter 4 Verse 171
O people of scripture! Do not exceed the limits in your religion, nor say of **Allah** aught but the truth. The Messiah Isa, Son of Maryam, was a Messenger of **Allah** and His word, which He bestowed on Maryam and a spirit created by Him; so, believe in **Allah** and His Messengers, say not: "Three!" Cease! (It is) better for you. For **Allah** is One Ilah (God), glory is to Him above having a son. To Him belongs all that is in the heavens and all that is in the earth. And **Allah** is **All-Sufficient as a Disposer of affairs**. (Darussalam, 1999)

Chapter Al-Ma'idah   Chapter 5 Verse 11
O you who believe! Remember the Favour of **Allah** unto you when some people desired to stretch out their hands against you, but (Allah) held back their hands from you. So, fear **Allah**. And in **Allah** let the believers put their trust. (Darussalam, 1999)

Chapter Al-An'am   Chapter 6 Verse 102
Such is **Allah**, your **Lord**! La ilaha illa Huwa (none has the right to be worshipped but He), the Creator of all things. So worship Him, and He is **Wakil** (Trustee) over all things. (Darussalam, 1999)

Chapter Hud   Chapter 11 Verse 12
So perchance you may give up a part of what is revealed unto you, and that your breasts feel straitened for it because they say, "Why has not a treasure been sent down unto him, or an angel has come with him?' But you are only a warner. And **Allah** is a **Wakil** (Trustee) over all things. (Darussalam, 2000)

Chapter Yusuf   Chapter 12 Verse 66
He (Yaqub) said: "I will not send him with you until you swear a solemn oath to me in **Allah**'s Name, that you will bring him back to me unless you are yourselves surrounded." And when they had sworn their solemn Oath, he said: "**Allah is the Witness (Wakil-Trustee)** to what we have said." (Darussalam, 2000)

Chapter Al-Isra — Chapter 17 Verse 65
"Verily, My slaves - you have no authority over them. And All-Sufficient is your **Lord** as a **Guardian (Wakil)**." (Darussalam, 2000)

Chapter Al-Qasas — Chapter 28 Verses 27-28
27. He said: "I intend to wed one of these two daughters of mine to you, on condition that you serve me for eight years; but if you complete ten years, it will be from you, But I intend not to place you under a difficulty. If **Allah** wills, you will find me one of the righteous."
28. He said: "That (is settled) between me and you: Whichever of two terms I fulfill, there will be no injustice to me, and **Allah** is **Surety (Wakil)** over what we say." (Darussalam, 2000)

Chapter Al-Ahzab — Chapter 33 Verse 3
And put your trust in **Allah**, and Sufficient is **Allah** as a **Wakil** (Trustee). (Darussalam, 2000)

Chapter Al-Ahzab — Chapter 33 Verse 48
And obey not the disbelievers and the hypocrites, and harm them not, and put your trust in **Allah**, and sufficient is **Allah** as a **Wakil** (Trustee). (Darussalam, 2000)

Chapter Az-Zumar — Chapter 39 Verse 62
Allah is the Creator of all things, and He is the **Wakil** (Trustee) over all things. (Darussalam, 2000)

Chapter Al-Muzzammil — Chapter 73 Verse 9
The **Lord** of the east and the west; La ilaha illa Huwa (none has the right to be worshipped but He), so take Him Alone as **Wakil (Disposer of your affairs).** (Darussalam, 2000)

Al-Hakam   The Judge

Chapter Al-An'am — Chapter 6 Verse 114
"Shall I seek a **Judge** other than **Allah** while it is He Who has send down unto you the Book, explained in detail." Those unto whom We gave the Scripture know that it is revealed from your **Lord** in truth. So be not you of those who doubt. (Darussalam, 2000)

Al-Jabbar   The Compeller

Chapter Al-Hashr   Chapter 59 Verse 23
He is **Allah**, besides Whom La ilaha illa Huwa (none has the right to be worshipped but He), the King, the Holy, the One Free from all defects, the Giver of Security, the Watcher over His creatures, the All-Mighty, the **Compeller**, the Supreme. Glory be to **Allah**! above all that they associate as partners with Him. (Darussalam, 2000)

Al-Mutakabir   The Supremely Great

Chapter Al-Hashr   Chapter 59 Verse 23
He is **Allah**, besides Whom La ilaha illa Huwa (none has the right to be worshipped but He), the King, the Holy, the One Free from all defects, the Giver of security, the Watcher over His creatures, the All-Mighty, the Compeller, **the Supreme**. Glory be to **Allah**! Above all that they associate as partners with Him. (Darussalam, 2000)

Al-Muqtadir   The Powerful Determiner

Chapter Al-Kahf   Chapter 18 Verse 45
And put forward to them the example of the life of this world; it is like the water, which We send down from the sky, and the vegetation of the earth mingles with it, and becomes fresh and green. But it becomes dry and broken pieces, which the winds scatter. **And Allah is Able to do everything.** (Darussalam, 2000)

Chapter Al-Qamar   Chapter 54 Verses 41-42
41. And indeed, warnings come to the people of Fir'aun.
42. (They) belied all Our Signs, so We seized them with a Seizure of the All-Mighty, **All–Capable**. (Darussalam, 2000)

References

Study the meaning of the English translation of The Noble Quran Word for Word from Arabic to English.
Complied by Darussalam. Volume 1 (Chapter 1 to Chapter 9 verse 93)
Darussalam Publishers and Distributors, Riyadh, Houston, New York, Lahore, 1999.

Study the meaning of the English translation of The Noble Quran Word for Word from Arabic to English.
Complied by Darussalam. Volume 2 (Chapter 9 verse 94 to Chapter 29 verse 45)
Darussalam Publishers and Distributors, Riyadh, Houston, New York, Lahore, 2000.

Study the meaning of the English translation of The Noble Quran Word for Word from Arabic to English.
Complied by Darussalam. Volume 3 (Chapter 29 verse 46 to Chapter 114)
Darussalam Publishers and Distributors, Riyadh, Houston, New York, Lahore, 2000.

To become a Muslim, one needs to make the following declaration:

*Ash-hadu alla ilaha illa Allah,
wa ash-hadu anna Muhammadan rasulu Allah*

I bear witness that there is no ilah (god) worthy of worship except Allah, and I bear witness that Muhammad is the Messenger of Allah

Made in the USA
Middletown, DE
31 December 2021